RIVER POLLUTION AND SOLUTION

RIVER POLLUTION AND SOLUTION

Shashi Dwivedi

Laboratory of Environmental Chemistry & Complexes
Dept of Chemistry, Udai Pratap Autonomous P G College, Varanasi

Anil K Dwivedi

Pollution & Environmental Assay Research Laboratory (PEARL)
Dept of Botany, Deen Dayal Upadhyay Gorakhpur University, Gorakhpur

New Central Book Agency (P) Ltd

LONDON

HYDERABAD ERNAKULAM BHUBANESWAR

DELHI KOLKATA PUNE GUWAHATI

NCBA

REGD OFFICE
8/1 Chintamoni Das Lane, Kolkata 700 009, India
email: ncbapvtltd@eth.net

OVERSEAS
NCBA (UK) Ltd, 149 Park Avenue North, Northampton, NN3 2HY, UK
email: ncbauk@yahoo.com

EXPORT
NCBA Exports Pvt. Ltd, 212 Shahpur Jat, New Delhi 110 049
email: ncbaexp@ncbapvtltd.com

BRANCHES

212 Shahpur Jat
New Delhi 110 049
email: ncbadel@ncbapvtltd.com

Shop Nos. 3 & 4, Vinayak Towers
681/B Budhwar Peth, Appa Balwant Chowk
Pune 411 002
email: ncbapune@ncbapvtltd.com

Shop No. 15, Bharati Towers, Ground Floor
Forest Park, **Bhubaneswar** 751 001
email: ncbabub@ncbapvtltd.com

House No. 3-1-315, 1st Floor
Nimboliadda, Kachiguda, **Hyderabad** 500 027
email: ncbahydb@ncbapvtltd.com

GSS Shopping Complex, 1st Floor
Opposite College Post Office, Convent Road
Ernakulam 682 035
email: ncbaernk@ncbapvtltd.com

Radhamayee Complex (Second Floor)
Opp. SBI, Panbazar, Jaswanta Road
Guwahati 781 001
email: ncbaguwahati@ncbapvtltd.com

RIVER POLLUTION AND SOLUTION • **Shashi Dwivedi & Anil K Dwivedi**

First Published: 2010
Reprinted: 2013

PUBLISHER AND TYPESETTER
New Central Book Agency (P) Ltd
8/1 Chintamoni Das Lane, Kolkata 700 009

PRINTER
New Central Book Agency (P) Ltd
Web-Offset Division, Dhulagarh, Sankrail, Howrah

COVER DESIGNER
Soumen Paul

COVER PRINTER
Biswanath Studio, Kolkata

TECHNICAL EDITOR
Subas Maitra

PROJECT TEAM
Prabhat Jas, Swapan Sarkar

ISBN 978 81 7381 622 2

Price: ₹ 495.00

CONTENTS

PREFACE

The book *River Pollution and Solution* is the output of years of studies conducted under the guidance and able supervision of many eminent scientists from Banaras Hindu University, Varanasi; Allahabad University, Allahabad; DDU Gorakhpur University, Gorakhpur; Udai Pratap Autonomous P.G. College, Varanasi, and many more. The authors do not claim for cent percent originality for each and every statement, figure, table and graph of the book; however, all the practical findings are original. The book is a compilation of independent research works directly conducted in the field. The complete content of the book is divided into thirteen chapters, where each and every chapter has been supported by adequate and relevant references and also by the authentic data obtained from fieldwork.

Chapter 1 consists of details about the need for **Standards of Water Quality**. It consists of standards established by different recognised agencies in the world. In this chapter, standards of water for different uses such as drinking, irrigation, etc. have been explained in detail.

Chapter 2 consists of the details of **Components of Polluted Water and Their Impact** on plants, animals and humans. It also explains the source of different pollutants, their quality, quantity, and their source of emission. It also deals with the various phenotypic abnormalities produced by the living components in the process of consumption.

In Chapter 3, we take an introductory glance at **River Pollution**. In this chapter, the pollution status of different rivers across the globe has been discussed along with the scientists involved in the study. This chapter also consists of the latest references pertaining to studies in this field.

In Chapter 4 we look at the **Case Study of Varuna: A Tropical River** in India. River Varuna has been selected as the ideal river in a tropical city on the basis of various ecological factors. In this chapter various sources of pollution in this river have been discussed, meteorological variations have been analysed and all the values have been correlated.

In continuation to this case study Chapter 5 details the study of **Variation in Properties of Water** of the river Varuna. Detailed study of this river has been conducted for the analysis of selected physico-chemical parameters throughout the year. Four study sites have been selected for analysis of the water quality of this river and all these parameters have been shown through graphs showing comparative variations among the sites.

The **Aquatic Macrophytic Diversity** in the river Varuna have been dealt with in Chapter 6. In this chapter density and frequency of various macrophytes in the river have been studied. Their values have been shown clearly through graphs. Similarity and dissimilarity indices have been calculated for the sites on the basis of macrophytes.

In Chapter 7, we study the **Quality of Water Sediments** in river Varuna. In this chapter mechanical properties, physico-chemical properties, pH, total nitrogen, organic carbon, and a few other parameters of the water sediments have been studied and expressed through a number of tables and graphs.

Chapter 8 deals with **Traditional Waste Water Treatment**. This chapter details all the methodologies traditionally used for the treatment of waste water. It also explains the science and practical viability of the treatments. The chapter explains the findings with the help of a number of figures and flowcharts.

In Chapter 9, we progress to the study of **Advanced Waste Water Treatment.** In this chapter, the advanced methods which are either in use elsewhere in the world or proposed methods yet to be used or are still in the laboratory testing stage have been discussed. The methods are mostly physical or chemical.

Chapter 10 deals with ***Exsitu* Treatment of River Water**. This chapter explains the laboratory experiments conducted to control water pollution in rivers. Chemical and biological methods have been applied in laboratory and the different results obtained in this treatment have been compared. The efficiency of macrophytes for controlling the water pollution has been found to be better in comparison. The results have been explained with the help of a number of graphs. This chapter opens a vista for new researchers in this field.

In Chapter 11 we initiate a **General Discussion** of all the previous chapters. All the findings of the experiment or the collected data or the meteorological data have been compared, correlated and discussed.

Chapter 12 enumerates the **Methodologies** used throughout the study, i.e. methods of sampling, methods of analysis of physico-chemical properties of water, physico-chemical properties of water sediments, macrophytic analysis, or statistical analysis.

The **Summary, Conclusion and Recommendations** of this volume are given in Chapter 13. This chapter is the soul of the book. It consists of the final findings and recommendations which can be applied to control water pollution of tropical rivers passing through cities like the Varuna river in Varanasi, India.

A detailed bibliography has been incorporated which consists of about 500 latest and relevant references of works done round the globe including that in India. We hope this is much useful for the scientists involved in parallel studies.

Finally, appendices consisting of results of statistical analyses, results of treatment of water samples of different sites are in detail in tabular form. This effort should be helpful to fellow researchers and aspiring scholars.

Authors

1

STANDARDS OF WATER QUALITY

The quality of air, water and soil has never been static. It varies from place to place and also from time to time. It is largely regulated by the biotic and abiotic agencies which come across or interact directly or indirectly with air, water or soil. Inspite of such large variations, the quality of air, water and soil required by human is always constant, no matter where they are spaced geographically. In light of the above, standards for air, water and soil was needed globally.

Different health agencies have prescribed standards for different categories of water. Some agencies are U.S. Public Health Service Drinking Water Standards (USPHS, 1992), Indian Council of Medical Research (ICMR, 1962), World Health Organisation (1992), etc. Standards are essential because the quality of water directly affects human health. Water quality standards prescribed for inland water by different agencies has been given in Table 1.1.

The Standards are periodically revised to take advantage of the new treatment techniques and to make use of the new test methods. The tests are carried out to determine whether or not the water being used meets the established bacteriological, physical, chemical and radioactivity standards.

Water, as one of the basic substance of life, is called upon to serve many beneficial uses. These uses may require a high degree of purity (potable water), may have to provide a suitable habitat for aquatic life: or these uses may depend merely on the most basic physicochemical properties of water. Quality requirements for other beneficial uses, such as industrial process, irrigation, recreation and aesthetic enjoyment in most cases lie somewhere in-between.

Beneficial uses of water are associated with domestic water supply, industrial water supply, agricultural water supply (irrigation), stock and wildlife watering, propagation of fish and other aquatic and marine life, swimming, bathing, boating and aesthetic enjoyment, dispersion and assimilation of wastes.

It should be realised that the same water source is frequently applied to more than one beneficial use. Obviously this is possible only when the uses are compatible, such as domestic water supply and irrigation. Under such

Table 1.1: Water Quality Standards for Inland Waters

Parameter	USPHS	ISI	WHO	ICMR
Temperature°C	—	40.0	—	—
Transparency/cm	—	—	—	—
EC Sm^{-1}	0.03	0.075	—	—
pH	6.0-8.5	6.5-8.6	7.0-8.5	6.5-9.2
DO mg L^{-1}	>4.0	>5.0	—	—
BOD mg L^{-1}	—	<3.0	—	—
COD mg L^{-1}	—	<20.0	—	—
Chloride mg L^{-1}	250	250	200	250
Alkalinity L^{-1} $CaCO_3$	—	—	—	81-120
Nitrate mg L^{-1}	10.0	50.0	45.0	20.0
Phosphate mg L^{-1}	0.1	—	—	—
Sulphate mg L^{-1}	250	150	200	200
Total hardness mg L^{-1} $CaCO_3$	500	300	100	300
Total solids mg L^{-1}	500	—	500	—
Calcium mg L^{-1}	100	75	75	75
Magnesium mg L^{-1}	—	30	—	50
Potassium mg L^{-1}	—	—	—	20
Sodium mg L^{-1}	—	—	50	—

(– = Not available)

circumstances the use with the most demanding water quality requirements determines the acceptable quality of the water source.

❒ Aesthetic and Recreation

The criteria which will ensure water quality which is aesthetically adequate are best described qualitatively. Hence, unless due to uncontrollable natural causes, surface waters should be free from materials that will settle to form objectionable deposits: floating debris, scum, oil and other comparable matter; substances that produce objectionable colour, odour, taste or turbidity; materials that are toxic or that produce undesirable physiological responses in human beings, fish, other animal life and plants.

Recreational use of water requires conformity with all of the aesthetic criteria plus certain others, depending on the kind of recreational use anticipated. Generally the water should be of bacteria proof quality adequate to avoid transmission of pathogens in the event of inadvertent ingestion. For swimming, the NTAC (National Technical Advisory Committee) recommends that the fecal coliform content should not exceed a log mean of 200 per 100 milliliter sample.

Recreational uses of water associated with fish and wildlife presuppose a water quality adequate for their survival and propagation. Fish and shellfish taken from recreational waters should be fit to eat and should be wholesome. Thus, these waters must be protected from adulteration or noxious substances, from toxins which can be biologically magnified and become poisonous and also from pathogenic organisms of all kinds.

Water bodies, in order to be suitable for swimming, require a pH within the range of 6.5 to 8.3. Water outside the range of 5-9 can cause irritation in eyes and other delicate membranes and tissues. Water temperatures also should fall within a standard as a temperature above 85°F can retard adequate heat rejection by an active swimmer and, in some cases, induce physiological distress. Safety requirements demand adequate water clarity in 'learn-to-swim' and diving areas adding to the standard of water quality for such purposes.

❐ Industrial Water Supply

The multifarious industrial uses of water impose quality requirements so varied that no meaningful single set of criteria can satisfy a majority of applications. Water treatment technology in its present condition permits utilisation of virtually any available quality of water to create water of any desired quality at the point of use. Such treatment may be costly, however.

This is not to say that the quality of the water supply need not be controlled, but water treatment procedures are in effect established on the basis of the available water characteristics. Market variations in the quality of an industrial water supply can result in deterioration of product quality for some industries, increased costs, modifications of procedures and equipment or other forms of dislocation. Thus, if the quality of the water supply for an established industry at a given site is allowed, on the other hand, by deterioration from its usual range, it can cause undesirable consequences.

❐ Agricultural Uses

Agricultural use of water falls into three major categories: farmstead use, stock watering and irrigation. Water quality criteria for these uses are not always definitively available.

Farmstead Water Supplies

Farmstead water supply includes water for all household purposes, including drinking, washing raw agricultural products and making milk sanitary. Because of the variety of sources utilised and the uncontrolled influences of geographical location and climatic conditions, water quality criteria, realistically, must be presented in terms of acceptable ranges of values.

Livestock Watering Supplies

A single set of water quality criteria for livestock watering is not available because of many important variables including species, age, productivity, diet, behaviour, environment, weather and the interrelationships of all these factors as well as others on livestock. Despite the fact that water quality is not generally regarded as a critical problem, certain trace elements, excess salinity, radionuclides, dissolved organic substances, parasites and pathogens can adversely affect livestock. A dependable source of livestock water of satisfactory quality is necessary for the profitable production of and consumption for animals.

Irrigation Water Supply

As with livestock waters, a single set of criteria to evaluate all water quality requirements for irrigation is impractical. Variations and interactions of soils, plants, water and climate preclude more than general guidelines. The major parameters of concern in irrigation waters are salinity, potentially toxic trace elements, and herbicides. In addition, water having sodium absorption ratio (SAR) values between 8 and 18 may have an adverse effect on the permeability of some clay soils. Table 1.2 suggests water quality criteria for irrigation waters.

❐ Pisciculture

The concept of criteria carries the intrinsic understanding that is concerned with the well-being of those forms that are considered to be desirable. For fish and shellfish, a water quality has to be provided that will keep these aquatic species wholesome and free of disease organisms, toxic substances and other injurious agents capable of being transmitted.

In determining water quality criteria for fish and aquatic life it is essential to recognise that there are not only acute and chronic toxic levels, but also tolerable, favourable and essential levels and regimens of environmental conditions, indirectly through the effects on other forms of life that comprise their food, competitors and predators. Hence the determination of water quality criteria is highly essential. The problem is complicated by the fact that different species and different development life stages of the same or different species may differ widely in their sensitivity or tolerance to different materials, to ranges in environmental conditions, and to the effects of the numbers of factors impinging on the organisms at any given time.

Complete water quality criteria would define upper and lower limits of the various environmental factors as well as optimum values. The criteria cited here are those minima which must be met to ensure a favourable environment for fish and other aquatic life generally. In some instances they will provide ample margins; in others will be inadequate for certain species.

❐ Municipal Water Supply

The use of water for drinking and other domestic purposes by human beings is generally considered to be its highest and most essential use. As a result the water quality criteria that permit this use are those most attentively implemented. Except for sanitary considerations, other uses may have more specific requirements, but, on balance, drinking water represents and is accorded a quality superior to all others.

Table 1.2: Trace Element Tolerances for Irrigation Waters

Element	For water used continuously on all soils	For short-term use on fine textured soil only
	mg/l	mg/l
Aluminium	1.0	20.0
Arsenic	1.0	10.0
Beryllium	0.5	1.0
Boron	0.75	2.0
Cadmium	0.005	0.05
Chromium	5.0	20.0
Cobalt	0.2	10.0
Copper	0.2	5.0
Fluorine	*	*
Iron	**	**
Lead	5.0	20.0
Lithium	5.0	5.0
Manganese	2.0	20.0
Molybdenum	0.005	0.05
Nickel	0.5	2.0
Selenium	0.05	0.05
Tin	***	***
Tungsten	***	***
Vanadium	10.0	10.0
Zinc	5.0	10.0

* The most serious effect of fluorine is on the consuming animal rather than on the plant itself. No limits are proposed at this time.

** Iron is rarely a problem in irrigation waters.

*** Tin and tungsten are effectively excluded by plants.

2

Components of Polluted Water and their Impact

What is the wonder of nature. 'No life without water' is a common saying depending upon the fact that water is one of the naturally occurring essential requirements of all life supportive activities.

Generally, the pollutants come from three different sources:

i. sewage discharged into the river,
ii. industrial effluents discharged into the river, and
iii. surface run off from agricultural land, where chemical fertilisers, pesticides, insecticides, manures are used.

About 1,500 sustenances have been listed as pollutants in fresh water ecosystems and a generalised list of pollutants includes acids and alkalies, detergents, domestic sewage and farm manure, nutrients (phosphates and nitrates), oil and oil dispersants, organic toxic wastes (formaldehydes, phenols), pathogens, pesticides, domestic sewage contains detergents, nutrients, metals, pathogens and a variety of other compounds.

Large number of factors is being used for the study of pollution. Biology of polluted water is being explained by scientists globally. Silicon and nitrate in fresh water has been reported in some of the recent studies. Effluents of large and small scale industries, agricultural run off and city sewage have been marked as a source of pollution during various researches.

Crude agricultural practice is considered as an important source of water pollution. Pesticides in river water have been detected in nearly all the rivers passing through the plains. The nutrient discharges are trapped by micro and macrophytes growing in the water. Industries generate a significant amount of waste water which ultimately finds its way to stream or river. Industrial discharges containing toxic and hazardous substances contribute to the severe kind of pollution in the aquatic system. Industrial development is largely because of the production of chemicals resulting in the generation of toxic and hazardous substances which have been continuously on the increase since the early 1980s. The number of pesticide production had reached 56.20 thousand tonnes during 1986-87 which was only 1.46 thousand tonnes during 1960. Similarly, fertiliser production had reached 7 thousand tonnes during 1986-87, which was only 153 thousand tonnes in 1960. All this contributes to the pollution of water ultimately, either their production or their utilisation. Some of the important pollution components and their effects are now being discussed.

❐ Oil and Derivatives

Two different kinds of oils are encountered as water pollutants. The first type includes animal and vegetable fat, consisting of triglyceride esters formed between glycerol and fatty acids of varying chain lengths. The second type of oil is the liquid fraction of crude petroleum or mineral oil. Crude petroleum is a mixture of hydrocarbons. When petroleum is fractionated by distillation processes, it yields the more commonly recognised products gasoline, kerosene, metor oil, benzene, paraffin and purified mineral oil. None of these fractions is edible or otherwise utilisable as nutrients by higher plants or animals. They are, in many circumstances, highly toxic because of their solvent properties. They also tend to coat cells and tissues, thereby interfering with the normal permeability of cells for nutrient uptake and by-product excretion. Petroleum extracted from the area of continental shelf is transported from one country to another by ships through sea routes. If there is an accident or leakage during transportation, oil is spread hundreds of kilometers on the water surface and causes serious pollution problems. According to an estimate one ton of oil is spilled for every million tons of oil transported, in other words, about 0.0001 per cent of transported oil is lost as spillage. The effluents discharged from the refineries contain plenty of oil and cause pollution of rivers around oil refineries. Oil is washed into rivers from spills on roads and factory floors, from workshops and garages. The oil spill covers the water surface and prevents atmospheric oxygen from mixing with water and consumes much of oxygen itself for its own degradation. The oil film on the surface of water inhibits the photosynthetic activity of aquatic autotrophs and growth of plankton. The reduced availability of oxygen in water, poisoning of food and toxic effect of oil cause death of aquatic animals. Sometimes oil spilled over water surface may catch fire and cause damage to aquatic life.

❐ Carbonic Compounds

It includes detergents and other cleaning materials, surfactants, pesticides and other organic industrial wastes. Many of these materials are poisonous for living organisms and cause serious water pollution problems. Detergents and other cleaning materials form an important source of water pollution. They change the pH of water and thereby the distribution and activities of aquatic life. Synthetic detergents are not easily decomposed by bacteria and are rich source of phosphate that hasten the process of Eutrophication of water with frequent algal blooms which impart colour, odour and unpleasant taste to the water and may cause inconvenience in water supply and fish farming—making the water further unfit for domestic purposes. There is another group of organic pollutants known as phenols in domestic sewage and industrial waste water. These are the hydroxy derivatives of benzene.

Inorganic carbon also affects the eutrophication, which ultimately affects the chemistry of river. Toxic organic contaminants of agricultural origin in water stream are a common topic of discussion nowadays. Organic pesticides in a river of Buenos Aires and Argentina have shown alarming features. Presence of particular organic compounds is responsible for specific odour. Some hydrophytes growing in carbon rich medium have capacity to absorb inorganic carbon for photosynthesis. Seasonal variation in organic content is found in the water bodies. Organic phosphates have also been shown to be absorbed by some selected microorganisms. Dead and decaying plant parts fall in water and increase the organic content of the water body, in addition to the increasing load of the sediments; which is considered to be responsible for the death of most of the modern day lotic ecosystems.

❑ Thermal Pollution

Some industries discharge hot water directly in the water bodies which causes rise in temperature and results in thermal pollution. The important industries which cause thermal pollution are nuclear powers, power generators etc. where water is used as coolant, but nearly all the industries contribute for the above, though they vary in their extent.

Bacterial population reduction in response to thermal pollution has also been reported in some studies. Temperature also affects electrical conductance of water in addition to the oxygen content in water, which is also affected by temperature. Rate of biodegradation of organic compounds increases by increase in temperature, this can be taken as positive as well as a negative contribution of the high temperature of the water body. Distribution of plants in an aquatic system with respect to temperature and light is now a common and well-known phenomenon. DO, BOD and COD, i.e. the oxygen budget, shows large variation in relation to temperature.

❑ pH

pH is the negative log of H^+ concentration present in a sample. A specific pH is essential for the normal survival of any organism. pH affects the enzymatic activity, thus indirectly affects the elemental mobilisation. pH also affects the distribution of plants. The study of changing phytoplanktonic composition as well as the macrophytic diversity with respect to lowering of pH has been reported through the studies in Canada.

❐ Heavy Metals

Heavy metals—which were of no use in human life during a prominent period of evolution—have now encroached into human life to a great extent. Due to Industrial Revolution or industrial based life, the importance of heavy metals has increased a lot. At the same time, the right thing at wrong place has created great problems. Heavy metals are important components of colours and dyes and are also used in various pharmaceuticals and other industries. The excess or surplus or unused heavy metals ultimately find its way into the waterbodies. These components show biological magnification. They are active components, which forms chelates and interfere in biochemical reactions in human body. They are recognised carcinogenic and potent to reduce immunity and also to enhance impotentiality.

Heavy metals are present in a variety of industrial effluents. They are absorbed by hydrophytes—as it has been reported in some of the aquaculture experiments—using some selected plants. These metals also precipitate in the sediments along with the dead and decaying plant parts. Chromium absorption by duckweed was reported. Chromium and Manganese uptake by *Hydrilla* and the same by mosses have also been reported in the recent studies. Mercury in hydrophytes and herbivorous fishes has also been reported in studies; the path of the transmission of the heavy metal from the industrial effluents to the fishes, through the aquatic plants needs no further clarification. Heavy metal content in various strata of rivers also varies. Due to nutrient absorption property of some plants they have been advocated to be the biological filter. This property of the selected plants can be utilised for ecomanagement of the polluted waterbodies.

Accumulation of Copper, Lead, Manganese and Iron by *Hydrodictyon*—an alga—is reported by some Indian scientists. Cadmium and Lead accumulation by rooted aquatic plants have been shown in some of the researches. Mercury, Cadmium, Lead and Thallium have been reported to be present in a nutrient rich lake. Bioaccumulation of Mercury and Chromium by certain blue green algae have been reported. The microorganisms have great tendency to metabolise the heavy metals; this has been possible due to short life span of the microorganisms. Studies regarding the investigation of Lead and Zinc removal by *Azolla* and *Lemna* are also in progress. Zinc and Lead uptake by *Lemna* and any other aquatic plants including *Eichhornia* have been reported. Metals were also reported in composted municipal waste through studies in China. Lichen *Peltigera* has been reported to absorb Cadmium. Chromium accumulation in *Ceratophyllum* was reported in certain landmark researches in India. Cadmium accumulation in *Eichhornia* have been reported. Metals were also reported in composted municipal wate through studies in China. Lichen *Peltigera* has been reported to absorb Cadmium. Chromium accumulation in *Ceratophyllum* was reported in certain landmark researches in India. Cadmium accumulation in *Eichhornia* has been reported in a number of studies. Silver has been reported to be present in the sediments of rivers and estuaries of Africa; the studies report. Study of the behaviour of Lathanide-920-dye complex in water is being studied. Response of metal dye comploxes in waste is being explored in a number of studies.

▢ Biodiversity in Water

"Water is considered as the basis of life" comes true when rich biodiversity is found in waterbodies or the adjoining areas. Biodiversity along riparian corridors have been studied. The biodiversity of any aquatic ecosystem is also affected by pollution or the physicochemical condition of the water body and the adjoining area. Fishes are very sensitive for water pollution and any change in the water quality compels the fishes to migrate. This becomes possible in lotic ecosystem, where the water is free flowing; but this becomes impossible in the case of a lentic ecosystem, where there is no way for the fishes, other than to sacrifice their lives or live diseased.

Occurrence of aquatic fungi in river Satlej which varied seasonally was monitored by a group of scientists and it was also found that its population is affected by the pollution level. The population of bacteria and fungi in aquatic medium also depends upon the physicochemical factors of the waterbody. The slime fungi have been reported in sewage also. Various species of *Eichhornia*, which is an exotic aquatic weed, has been found predominantly growing in polluted waterbodies. *Eichhornia* and other water hyacinths have been reported to absorb nutrients and thus act as pollutant scrubber.

Planktonic studies with respect to varying water quality parameters have been conducted. Limnological studies in fresh water is also attaining prime importance nowadays. Phytosociological study of aquatic plants in light of the phytodiversity is a basic study for sorting the plants as pollution indicator or the pollution scrubber. If a plant is found growing luxuriantly in a polluted condition, this shows that it might be absorbing the pollutants. On the other hand, if a plant is found growing feebly in a mildly polluted area, but totally absent from a heavily polluted zone, this indicates that the plant is pollution sensitive; such plants can be successfully used as the pollution indicators. This finding is subject to certain field trials.

Effect of hyacinths on fish population and also on the algal concentration has shown remarkable results. In the studies regarding the effect of thick hyacinth on water quality, the most remarkable results were found in the case of the oxygen budget, i.e. the DO was found greatly reduced, as compared to the control. Pros and cons of aquatic weeds have been a matter of debate at most of the platforms in seminar and symposia based on the aquatics. Methods to control aquatic weeds are an urgent need of the time to prevent the process of sedimentation. Submerged aquatic plants were advocated to be supporting to the aquatic life as they directly release the dissolved oxygen into the waterbody.

Different macrophytes also behave differently for different pollutants, especially for the metals and the heavy metals. Metals have been detected in few water macrophytes, which were considered to be tolerant for the specific chemical and were found growing luxuriantly in the medium. Response of aquatic weeds on variation in nitrogen level is also interesting. Nitrate and phosphate both promote the phenomenon of eutrophication, thereby blooming of algal community in addition to the macrophytic population. At the same time, the phosphate concentration is considered to be more important than the nitrate concentration for eutrophication.

❒ Suspended Impurities

Particles of an insoluble material may be held in suspension if their size and density are such that they do not settle or float to the surface. The particles can be either organic or inorganic in composition and the ability of a particle to remain in suspension is determined by physical and chemical factors such as chemical composition of the substance, surface charge on the particle, shape, size and density.

❒ Algae and Bacteria

In case of living particles, e.g. bacteria, algae and other microorganisms, the ability to counteract gravity motility is a significant factor, as is the change in buoyant density through production and accumulation of gas in vacuoles within cells. For example, many algae tend to settle from suspension in the dark but produce oxygen in the light (photosynthesis), which gives the cells buoyancy and ability to rise towards the surface.

Any particle suspended in water causes turbidity, which is an expression of the optical property of water. Suspended particles cause light to be absorbed or scattered, or both, rather than transmitted in straight lines. Some of the more commonly encountered suspended materials are a variety of clay types and other soil types, detritus consisting of fragments of previously living organisms and their cells, living microorganisms, phytoplanktons, zooplanktons, and finely dispersed chemical precipitates.

❒ Silts and Sediments

Soil which has been moved by wind, water or ice as the result of erosion and is then deposited in a receiving body of water is considered to be sediment. Based upon size and chemical composition of the particles, sediments are divided into three categories: (i) *Sand*—have a particle size range of 2 to 0.05 mm. It is high in quartz content and is relatively inert. (ii) *Silt*—is usually defined as particles with a size distribution of 0.05 to 0.002 mm. Silt is also high in quartz as well as in feldspar. (iii) *Clays*—consist of aluminium silicates less than 0.002 mm in size. Therefore most clay is of a type that can go into colloidal suspension.

Sedimentation—i.e. the process of particles settling from suspension—is directly proportional to the velocity of the particles in suspension and this is related to its shape, size and density.

Suspended solids, i.e. turbidity, tend to reduce light penetration. This can be either beneficial or detrimental—depending on circumstances and water use. For example, algal growth is generally retarded in highly turbid water caused by suspended silt and clay. If the water is used for drinking it may help in preventing disagreeable flavours and odours originating from by-products of algal metabolism. In contrast, turbidity may be directly caused by high cell density of algae and bacteria, thereby producing disagreeable tastes and odours in the water. When the cells eventually die, they represent an organic load with a high oxygen demand.

Sedimentation is responsible for filling lakes and, over a period of geological time, results in conversion of a lake to a swamp. This process is referred to as lake aging and a dead lake is one that is filled with sediments.

Turbidity of water is affected by Suspended Particulate Matters present in the water. In view of its importance the "river Logger", an instrument to monitor suspended Particulate Matters, has been designed. Trace elements were reported in the Suspended Particulate Matters of many rivers including some of the rivers in India. Suspended Particulate Matters also affects the biotic community as studies indicate that visibility and the turbidity are affected by the Suspended Particulate Matters. Chemistry of water affects the chemistry of Suspended Particulate Matters and sediments, as the selected chemicals get desorbed over the Suspended Particulate Matters.

❐ Oxygen Demanding Wastes

Organic oxygen demanding wastes can be divided into two convenient categories, including those that are of a natural origin produced by biosynthesis, and those that are synthesised chemically. Virtually, all naturally synthesised organic molecules and many synthetic compounds can be attacked or otherwise degraded by the oxidative mechanism of aerobic organisms. The respiratory demand for oxygen by aerobic organisms. The respiratory demand for oxygen by aerobic organisms while they use organic wastes as nutrients is known as biochemical oxygen demand (BOD). The oxygen demand can be enhanced due to domestic sewage, farm animal waste, manufacturing process waste, or any other direct addition of organic matter to water. The practice of aerobic waste treatment is merely an attempt to supply sufficient dissolved oxygen to satisfy the oxygen demand of an increased organic load. Any naturally produced organic compound is capable of being degraded by one organism or another, and, in an aquatic ecosystem, the potential exists for the presence of any specific microorganisms in a mixed population. Many inorganic substances are products of organic degradation or are pollutants added directly to water. Many of these inorganic compounds represent an oxygen demand because they are either metabolised oxidatively by organisms or oxidised chemically under normal atmospheric conditions. In balanced aquatic ecosystem, oxygen demanding substances are always produced but in amounts that allow the available oxygen supply to satisfy the demand. The ecosystem goes out of balance when an external source of oxygen demand is added as the result of human endeavour.

Relationship between DO, BOD and COD in river Ganga and similar comparative study in different other rivers have been conducted. Oxygen budget is directly or indirectly affected by the presence of toxic metals and heavy metals. DO affect the potential of sewage treatment plants. DO of water is also affected by turbidity which restricts the solar radiations. Roots of aquatics contain chloroplast in their root. Any aquatic system is capable enough to balance the oxygen budgent naturally in unmanned condition.

❑ Pesticides

Pesticides are generally categorised in relation to the pest to be controlled, such as insecticides, herbicides, fungicides, rodenticides. The more widely used pesticides are persistent, and their toxicity is of the broad spectrum type. Most of these pesticides are extremely toxic both to fish and to other aquatic organisms. Pesticide in river water was been detected in a number of researches; as they are being used in sufficiently high quantities in agriculture. In some rivers the pesticides are reported to be the major and important water pollutants. Diquate-dibromide, and important pesticide, has also been reported in aquatic ecosystem. The acute toxicity value for aquatic organisms s expressed as a 'Lethal concentration' or LC 50 value, which is a statistical estimate of the pesticide concentration in water necessary to kill 50 percent of the test organisms within a specified time under standardised conditions.

Factors such as temperature, pH, salinity, turbidity and organic content of water may greatly alter the toxicity of a pesticide.

Aquatic plants and animals can accumulate concentrations of certain pesticides many times greater than that in water. The greatest magnification is found with organochlorine insecticides.

Contamination of aquatic environments by pesticides poses a serious threat to equate life forms. Domestic water supplies are frequently the same systems in which aquatic life need to be protected from pesticide contamination. Thus the use of pesticides involves a risk great enough to have surface water criteria for public water supplies (Table 2.1).

Table 2.1: Pesticide Criteria for Public Water Supplies

Pesticide	Permissible Criteria (ppb)	Pesticide	Permissible Criteria (ppb)
Aldrin	17	Heptachlor epoxide	18
Chlordance	3	Lindane	56
DDT	42	Methoxychlor	35
Dieldrin	17	Organophosphates	
Endrin	1	Plus carbamates	100
Heptachlor	18	Toxaphene	5

Pesticides result soil pollution in various ways. Soil pollution assumes major concern in contaminating the crop growth, affecting soil pH, and microbial population, thus affecting the soil fertility.

Use of the less persistent pesticides, development of more target specific pesticides and the potential of biological control (insect parasites, predators and pathogens) might greatly reduce the risk to both man and other organisms.

❐ Disease Causing Agents

Wastes from municipalities sanitories, tanneries, slaughtering houses, sugar mills, dairies, agricultural farms etc. discharged into different waterbodies are the potential sources of different infective and pathogenic agents like bacteria, viruses, protozoans, fungi, platihelminths which cause several fatal and infectious diseases such as typhoid, cholera, hepatitis, scabies, trachoma, sleeping sickness, dysentery, yellow fever, amoebiosis, diorrhea, ascariosis distomatosis etc. in human beings.

Some important diseases of human being and their pathogens transmitted by polluted water are given in Table 2.2.

Microorganisms have been reported to be present in sediments of rivers as well as in ocean. Some microorganism are helpful in removal of nutrients from the waterbodies, but their specific potential is still under investigation. Underground water has also been reported to contain bacteria. Relationship between coliform bacteria and organic pollution level had been studied to facilitate in projecting the water treatment plants. Coliform number and Coli index has also been an important parameter under study.

❐ Nutrients

The elements nitrogen and phosphorus are essential to all life forms. They are also abundant in waste waters as phosphates, nitrates, and ammonia, or combined organic nitrogen. Nitrates and Phosphates which are most often present in the runoff water act as nutrients in the waterbodies and are considered the most important factors for eutrophication. The source of these compounds in waste waters include discharges from domestic sewage treatment plants, wastes from the manufacture and use of fertilisers and wastes from other industries. These compounds, when discharged to streams and lakes, contribute to excessive algal growth and subsequent eutrophication. Excessive algal growth can indirectly contribute to lowering of dissolved oxygen content of the water, due to high oxygen demand represented by the algae remains at the end of the season, or when sunlight is prevented from reaching the algal community by high turbidity in water.

Nitrogen in the unoxidised ammonia state exerts an oxygen demand in waters. Nitrates show a tendency to migrate rapidly through groundwaters. Surface waters containing excess amounts of nitrates are harmful to all animal life. High nitrate concentrations in receiving waters stimulate the growth of plankton and aquatic weeds. High nitrogen content in plant parts retards the rate of biological decomposition. Excessive plant growth, however, can result in eutrophication of

Table 2.2: Some Important Human Diseases and their Pathogens Transmitted by Polluted Water

Disease	Pathogens
Amoebic dysentery	*Entamoeba hystolytica*
Ascariosis	*Ascaris lumbricoides*
Bacillary dysentery	*Bacillus dysenteriae*
Bacterial dysentery	*Shigella serotypes*
Bilharziasis	*Schistostoma ssp.*
Brucillosis	*Brucella spp.*
Cholera	*Vibrio cholerae*
Distomatosis	*Fasciola spp.*
Dracontiasis	*Guinea worm*
Gastroenteritis	*Shigella proteus*
Giardiasis	*Giardia lamblia*
Infantile diarrhea	*Escherichia coli*
Infectious jaundice	*Leptospira interrogans*
Infectious hepatitis	*Liver infecting viruses*
Paratyphoid fever	*Bacillus paratyphosum*
	Salmonella paratyphise
	Salmonella shottmuelleri
	Salmonella typhimurium
Typhoid fever	*Salmonella typhi*
Yellow fever	*Viruses (spread by water borne mosquitoes)*

waters because the death and decay of the plants rob the waters of their dissolved oxygen. In human infants, methemoglobinemia ('Blue babies' disease) results from an increase of methemoglobin in the bloodstream caused by nitrites. Methemoglobin is the blood constituent that is incapable of transporting oxygen.

Phosphorus, in aquatic medium, also plays an important role in controlling its biodiversity. Phosphorus, an active element, does not occur free in nature. It is an essential nutrient for plant and animal growth and—like nitrogen—it passes through cycles of decomposition and photosynthesis. Phosphorus is found in surface and ground waters, principally as phosphates. In water, phosphate ions exist as H_2PO_4- or HPO_4^{2-} depending on the pH. Phosphates are not found in significant concentrations in natural surface waters because they are readily metabolised by plants. Phosphates in receiving waters because they are readily metabolised by plants. Phosphates in receiving water originate especially from municipal sewage as a result of the large usage of synthetic detergents. Phosphates have been considered to be one of the most important key elements to excessive growth of aquatic plants with its deleterious effect on fish life and effect on eutrophication.

Denitrifying bacteria also play an important role in nitrogen concentration of a medium. Biological nitrification and denitrification was studied and is also being studied at length. Detailed investigation of nitrogen level in lotic ecosystem is gaining prime importance nowadays. High nitrogen content in plant parts retards the rate of biological decomposition. Phosphorus in aquatic system is recycled by absorption by plants. Phosphorus in aquatic medium also plays an important role in aquatic plants. Nitrogen and phosphorus accumulation in water hyacinths has been common reporting.

❐ Studies on Effect of Water Pollution

One of the best—rather worst—properties of water is that it is a universal solvent. It dissolves nearly all the things coming in contact of it, excepting some organic compounds. It also has the tendency to keep the dissolved components along with it in the form of solution. Another harmful property is its high permeability. During its course of movement from one place to another it carries the dissolved chemicals along with it. Micro- and macrophytes of the aquatic bodies lodge a lot of harmful chemicals in their body, that which is present in the waterbody. From there hazardous components move into the zoological system via the process of feeding. In this way, ultimately, they reach the human body in a considerable concentration, through the process of eating and being eaten—at the all the trophic level the chemical showing its presence. This is not the only way, but we are so much used to water that no ritual can be completed without water. Further all the civilisations originated at the bank of rivers. Using polluted water in all the walks of life ultimately leads to ill-growth or in the form of a variety of unstudied and unidentified diseases, to human as well as to the cattle and to the plants.

Chemistry of water controls the distribution of the fishes in water bodies. Multidimensional approach for the study of water pollution—rather, environmental pollution and its management—is being promoted globally, as the academic boundaries between the subjects exist no more. Importance of the water quality of bathing water on health is also gaining attention in the higher society.

❐ Seasonal Variation

Distribution of macrophytes, zooplanktons and fishes not only depend on quality of water but also on the climatic condition. Actually, it is the climatic factor which regulates most of the parameters of the water. During summer, due to high temperature, the rate of evaporation is higher; as a result the water in the aquatic systems reduces. The pollutants more or less remain the same. Therefore the waterbodies—lentic or lotic—become highly polluted. On the other hand, during rainy season, dilution of the waterbodies take place by addition of the rain water. The pollutants remain the same, therefore, during rainy seasons, they appear to be comparatively less polluted.

❑ Indicators of Pollution

Plants are more sensitive to pollutants than human or other biotic components. Therefore plants can best be used for the bioindicator of environmental pollution. Sensitive species can serve as indicators and resistant species as accumulators which collect large amount of pollutants without damage. Many chemicals, fertilisers, pesticides and fossil fuels release toxic substance into the environment that are taken up by the plants from their surroundings. Nematodes have been identified as indicator of water pollution in Swartkops river in South Africa. A variety of aquatic macrophytes are recommended to be used as indicator of heavy metal pollution or for indicator of some other component of pollution. Algal community as indicator of organic pollution in river Vishwamitri in Baroda has been recommended. Problems in the filed of locating indicator plants for toxicity testing are tough but rewarding.

3

River Pollution at a Glance

Our very survival on Earth essentially depends on three basic resources—water, air and soil, nature's three valuable gifts to mankind. Water is the most important component as it forms the basic medium for origin of life. Over 97% of all the water on Earth is salty and most of the remaining 3% is frozen in the polar icecaps. The atmosphere, rivers, lakes and underground stores hold less than 1% of all the fresh water and this tiny amount has to provide the fresh water needed to support the Earth's population. Demand of water rose six-fold between 1900 and 1995, more than double the rate of population growth. The first serious effort to take note of the environmental issue at the global level was at U.N. Conference held at Stockholm in June 1972, which was projected towards human environment. Thereafter the concepts like environment, sustainability and carrying capacity of Earth have become the central theme of policy making round the globe.

The advent of the Industrial Revolution since 1760 has irreversibly impacted on the way people across the globe live their daily lives. The 250 year old process of industrialisation has left none untouched, in some way or the other, though in varying measure. While it has influenced both family and society, its impact on humankind's struggle against its environmental after-effects has been most profound. The larger environmental repercussions of our industrial age have to do with the pollution that accompanies it. Pollution accompanies every outshoot of industrialisation, be it industrial production, generation of electric power, or vehicular transport. It has also become a market feature of the lifestyles that have come to mark the beginning of the twenty first century. The varied sources and forms of pollution are only matched by the various technologies developed to control pollution, be it pollution generated from industries, vehicles, use of fuel in generation of power steam, liquid, and solid wastes generated from municipal/residential areas. Indeed, the scientific community all over the world has been giving an extra thrust to researching and designing pollution control mechanisms.

Normally, oxygen is present in water in high quantities, but even a small drop in the level can have a harmful effect on the animals of the rivers. Animals can be listed according to their ability to tolerate low level of oxygen. If the pollutants which act as nutrient become excess they over-stimulate the growth of aquatic plants and algae, the excess growth of which, consequently, clogs our waterways, using up dissolved oxygen as they decompose, and block light to the deeper water. Many fishes and bottom dwelling animals cannot survive when level of dissolved oxygen drops below 2 to 5 ppm (parts per million), this leads to disruption in food chain. Similar incidence needs to be reported here, when mass casualty of thirty quintal fishes took place over a night of July 2009 in Ramgarh lake at Gorakhpur. Reduction in dissolved oxygen was reported to be directly responsible for the episode. Such incidence has taken place many times in Durgakund pond at Varanasi also.

Various resources of water at global level have been studied and explained. Importance of pure water in the near future has been pointed out. Multi-dimensional aspect of water is being studied all over, as it is drawing the attention of the scientists round the globe.

Chemical and biological aspects and their interactions in polluted water have been discussed at length. Urban civilisation requires more water as compared to the rural and the quality of discharged water of the urban area is chemically more toxic as compared to the rural.

❐ River Pollution Studies in India

Water pollution in India has now reached a critical point. Almost every river system in India is now polluted to a considerable extent. As assessed by the scientists of the National Environmental Engineering Research Institute (NEERI), Nagpur, nearly 70% of water in India is polluted. The studies regarding pollution in the river Ganga initiated just few decades after independence, particularly in Varanasi, under the leadership of Professor B. D. Tripathi now the Coordinator of Environmental Science and Technology, Banaras Hindu University. Questions (No. 1464) were raised in the parliament in July 1980 regarding the analytical report of water quality of the river Ganga. The Vice Chancellor of Banaras Hindu University, Varanasi was asked to reply the questions.

"Kindly supply requistie information by 10th July 1980 positively to frame reply to Loksabha Question No. 1464 reproduced below:

(a) *Whether it is a fact that environment pollution compounded by the degrading quality of Air, Water and Soil in and around Varanasi is posing a serious threat to Public Health and Plants according to a survey conducted by a team of Banaras Hindu University Scientist under the supervision of Dr B. D. Tripathi.*

(b) *Whether pollution of the Ganga has created a number of problems and*

(c) *If so the steps which Government proposed to take to prevent pollution of the Ganga at Varanasi." (No.·F. 11016/21/80-EPC)*

Large number of rivers has been studied regarding their pollution status. Some of such rivers are Yamuna at Agra, Okhla and in Delhi; rivers Ganga and

Yamuna both at Allahabad during *Kumbh.* River Gomati in India with respect to blue-green algae was studied, similar studies in river Mahanadi was conducted in Orissa. Pollution in river Bhadra in Mysore was also studied in addition to selected rivers of Andhra Pradesh. Water quality of river Hoogly, river Chambal at Kota, river Godavari, Krishna, Tungbhadra and Kali in addition to the river Gandak river at Samastipur had been studied.

Physico-chemical properties of Sone river and river Kali in Aligarh with respect to biotic community had been studied. Similar studies in river Alaknanda, river Neyyar and river Kanhan in Nagpur were carried out.

❐ River Pollution Studies Abroad

The problem is not only in India, but more or less the same situation prevails in other countries, also; whether they are developed, underdeveloped or developing. It would not be wrong to state that the water quality of the rivers in the developed countries is poorer as compared to the others. Therefore, parallel studies regarding the level of pollution of the rivers and other waterbodies are still in progress or is attaining great importance all over the world. The water quality of river Raisin in Canada, river Glatt in Switzerland, river Nile in Egypt has been done. Chemistry of river Amazon was studied with focus at its microbiological diversity. Nutritional character of river Rhone in France and river Welsh in U.K. had also been conducted. Nutrient analysis in the river Mississippi and limnological studies in the same river along with the river Missouri is being conducted regularly. Studies regarding nutrient pollution in Costal river of Israel and physico-chemical study of lake Mellwaine in Rhodesia have been done.

Multidisciplinary study of river Aliakman in Greece and the chemistry of river Odzi in Zimbabwe were being conducted few years back. Similar study in river Niger was also being carried out. Heavy metal analysis in some estuaries of France and the growth of macrophytes in some lakes of Florida have been done. Similar studies in Detroit river of Michigan, in addition to the analysis of heavy metal pollution in the same river was studied; and its impact on the biotic component of the river were also conducted.

❐ Studies of Industries and Water Pollution

Industries generate a significant quantity of wastewater which ultimately finds its way to stream or rivers. Industrial discharges containing toxic and hazardous substances contribute to the severe kind of pollution in the aquatic systems. Industrial development is largely responsible because of the production of chemicals resulting in the generation of toxic and hazardous substances which have been continuously on the increase during the last decades (e.g. Table 3.1).

There are about 3,200 major industries in India in addition to a large number of small industries. Industrial effluents, though comparatively lesser in volume, cause serious menace to aquatic environment by entering in the food chain. Dairy effluent is rich in microbial population, as it is rich in nutrients also. Distribution of plants—microphytes or macrophytes—in the waterbodies is also regulated

Table 3.1: Toxic Chemical Production in India (during 1960 to 1987)

Industries	Pollutants Released (Thousand tonnes)			
	1960	1970	1980	1986-87
Pesticides	1.46	3.00	40.68	56.20
Dyes & Pigments	1.15	13.55	30.85	—
Organic Chemicals Petrochemicals	580	17,100	24,100	42,500
Fertilisers	153	1059	3005	7000
Stell (Ingots)	1500	3400	8000	9000
Non-ferrous metals	8.5	34.6	82.9	123.4
Caustic soda	101	304	457	764
Pharmaceuticals	1.23	1.79	5.07	—

Source: GOI Publication, India, 1988-89

by the chemistry of the water, which is largely affected by the industrial effluents reaching to the waterbodies. Such studies regarding paper mill effluent, sugar mills, distilleries, chemical distillery and rubber industries have been conducted with prime importance. Industrial effluents affecting BOD and COD have been pointed out. Waste and the effluents of pharmaceutical industries have been reported to be affecting the microbial population in water. Industrial units discharging heavy metals and even the trace elements were found in river water.

We are harming our planet to the point where organisms are dying at an alarming rate. In addition to innocent organism dying off, our drinking water has become greatly affected. About one-fourth of the world population (of 6.7 billion)—1.5 billion people—lack safe drinking water and at least 5 million deaths per year can be attributed to water borne diseases.

Sea has been cited as the limitless dumping site for waste by all the countries round the globe. The most harmful waste for sea is the radioactive waste which is produced from nuclear power plants, industries and also through scientific use of radioactive materials.

In countries like India, religious rituals also contribute to water pollution. Millions of people bathing at the same time in the same water at certain occasions is very harmful. River pollution is hazardous for pilgrims that take bath in the holy river. Nobody knows who suffers from which disease; it could even be a lethal skin disease. Taking a mouthful of water and spitting it back into the river again or urinating while having bath in potentially hazardous. India has a large number of HIV positive cases; the sufferers may be there and leave the affected germs into the water, which others may swallow. All scientific facts remain idle as there is no parameter for *astha* or faith. People will continue to take their holy dips in Ganga even after hundred years by present consensus !

4

Case Study of Varuna: A Tropical River

To conduct a detailed investigation we selected river Varuna, a tributary of river Ganga in Varanasi, Uttar Pradesh, India. Varanasi is among the oldest living cities of the world, where continuity of human habitation and evolution of culture have been uninterrupted since the recorded history available, and its cultural, religious and educational heritage is preserved till date. It is also considered as the cultural capital of India and a famous seat of learning. Varanasi owes its name from Varuna and Assi, which were the two rivers forming the boundary of the city. At present the river Assi has been reduced to a drainage (nala), i.e. the Assi nala, and the river Varuna has maintained its existence. River Varuna originates from Varuna Taal near Phoolpur situated at the border line of Allahabad and Pratapgarh districts. River Varuna at Varanasi is used as a major drainage to carry city sewage. River Varuna, during its flow, receives untreated sewage from twenty-two nalas (Tables 4.1 and 4.2) located in northern and north-western part of the city. Varuna also pollutes the river Ganga when it meets it at about 1 km downstream of Malviya bridge.

Table 4.1: Various nalas and their discharge on Cis Varuna side

Name of nala	Average discharge (mld)
Phulwaria nala	6.80
Imliyaghat nala	0.95
Nala near Clark's Hotel	0.31
Razabazar nala	1.13
Ghausabad nala	1.46
Chaukaghat nala	2.55
Nakkhighat	3.76
Sarya nala	0.81

Table 4.2: Various nalas and their discharge as trans Varuna side

Name of nala	Average discharge (mld)
Central Jail nala	4.38
Orderly Bazar nala	5.95
Chamrautiya nala	2.90
Chazzori nala	0.50
Nala no. 5	0.45
B.P. Agarwal nala	0.72
Colony nala	1.15
Ahiran purwa nala	1.07
Hukulganj nala	1.43
Nari banti nala	3.96
Premchand nala	1.68
Ashok nagar nala	3.25
Nala no. 14	1.21
Narokhar nala	5.45

❐ Sources of Pollution

Rapidly increasing population has led to expansion in urbanisation and industrialisation at a great pace which has created one of the dreaded threats to life on the earth. The development of modern world has created pollutants in almost all the human endeavours. Once the pollutants are discharged into the different environmental components, it becomes difficult to control them.

Thus, in order to control pollution in any system, it is important to know about the following:

- Sources of emission of pollutants
- Nature and intensity of pollutants
- Physico-chemical and biological properties of the receiving aquatic body.

The study of aforesaid information helps in the development of some control devices and ecomanagement of the aquatic ecosystems.

The main sources of pollution of river Varuna at Varanasi includes:

Crude Agricultural Practices

Most of the catchment area of river Varuna along its 15 km flow through Varanasi is agricultural land. The topography of the catchment is such that the land is sloping towards the river. Variety of crops are being grown in the catchment area of river Varuna, consisting of wheat, maize, mustard and vegetables like brinjal, cauliflower, cabbage, etc. In order to get high yield, farmers apply huge quantities of chemical fertilisers, herbicides and pesticides. Major portion of the chemical fertilisers and other chemicals applied remains unutilised and finds its way into the river as surface run-off during rains and overflow.

Disposal of animal dead bodies, cattle washing and cowshed washing add organic matters into the water. They also increase nitrogenous components and promote the growth of pathogenic microorganisms.

City Sewage

The city of Varanasi, through which the river Varuna passes, is a densely populated centre. Huge amount of sewage is produced from this city which is mainly as domestic liquid waste. This waste is rich in organic and inorganic components, soap and detergents, dye and paints, phosphates, nitrogenous wastes and miscellaneous products. It also contains high microbial population, especially the faecal bacteria *E. coli*. Sewage discharges reach the river Varuna through open drainage system like nalas. During their passage the nalas receive some contaminants from local small scale and cottage industries, in addition.

River Varuna has been extensively used for washing activities. At different places Dhobi Ghats have been established on river Varuna. Soaps and detergents are used in significant quantities, which add to the pollution in Varuna.

Industrial Effluents

Varanasi is an industrialised city of the country, having about 5,277 large, basic and small scale industries which are situated in and around the city of Varanasi—manufacturing metal products, chemicals and chemical products, electricals and battery industries, food products, spinning, weaving and finishing of textiles, transport equipments, motor servicing stations, furniture and fixtures, non-metal mineral products, beverages, rubber products including tyres and leather and numerous other products (Table 4.3). Untreated effluents from these industries containing toxic heavy metals, oil and grease, chemicals and other hazardous pollutants are discharged into the rivers Varuna—and thereby into Ganga—directly or indirectly.

In Varanasi, huge quantity of solidwaste is generated. This solidwaste is taken care of by Varanasi Nagar Nigam, which has been entrusted to collect and dispose it off. As very little land is available for the disposal of solidwaste, Varanasi Nagar Nigam has selected some solidwaste disposal sites. Most of the disposal sites are located close to the Varuna river. Two major solidwaste disposal sites are located near Khajuri Colony and Sampurnand bridge. Major part of the solidwaste generated in Varanasi is of putressible nature having high percentage of water. Organic wastes along with water find their way into the river, increasing the pollution load.

In view of the increasing number of polluted rivers, various plans have been developed by the Government for their treatment, such as, Ganga Action Plan for river Ganga, Yamuna Action Plan for river Yamuna; similarly Gomati Action Plan, etc. River Varuna has not been included under any such plan, though it is among one of the highest polluted tributaries of Ganga. No treatment plant has been established to treat the discharges into river Varuna through different drains. It is due to this reason that the sewage discharged into the river Varuna affects

Table 4.3: Nature and Number of Industries situated in and around the City of Varanasi (Industrial Directory, 1991)

Nature of Industries	Number	Percentage
Metal products	1,213	23.0
Chemical and chemical products (candles, agarbatti, cosmetics, soaps, detergents, paints, varnishes, ayurvedic medicines, liquid phenyl, oils, inks, pharmaceutical chemicals, etc.)	633	12.0
Electrical and **battery industries**	596	11.3
Food Products(Ice, Cold drinks, oil and dal mills, salt stuffs, biscuits, bread, etc.).	169	3.2
Finishing of textiles (Hosiery, sarees and **clothes printing and dyeing**, cotton and thread processing, etc.).	164	3.1
Transport equipments and **motor service stations**	117	2.2
Furniture and Fixtures	105	2.0
Non-metallic mineral products (except petroleum and coal)	121	2.3
Wooden and cork (except furniture)	53	1.0
Beverages (Tobacco, Zarda, Pan masala, etc.)	47	0.9
Leather fur, rubber and types, etc.	27	0.5
Printing press and paper products	323	6.1
Miscellaneous (Plastic, polythene, elastic, silk and saree fabrics, metallic yarns, carpets, bricks, cement, tiles, surkhi, sports equipments, pens, photostats, sindur, gulal, etc.)	1,709	32.4
Total	**5,277**	

the water quality of river Ganga and, consequently, is affecting the results of Ganga Action Plan.

Since no provisions have been laid for the treatment of Varuna water and the treatment facilities being too costly to be employed feasibly, in the case of river Varuna alternative treatment practices are required. In this regard, a project had been spearheaded under the title *Studies on the Chemistry of River Varuna Water in Response to the Discharge of Small Scale Industries: Specially Automobile Servicing, Battery and Dyeing Industries*.

Since most of the work which are done in parallel direction includes agricultural runoff, domestic sewage or large scale industries, etc.—where the small scale industries have been totally overlooked—here they have been emphasised. Treatment of Varuna water through chemical and biological processes has been explored.

This project was conducted during year 2001-2002 with the following aims and objectives:

❐ Aims and Objectives

1. To monitor the important small scale industries pouring their effluents in the river Varuna.
2. To monitor the impact of effluents of selected small scale industries on physico-chemical properties and heavy metal concentration in the river water and water sediments at the selected sites throughout the year.
3. To evaluate biological properties of the river water at the selected sites.
4. To conduct laboratory experiments for the control of water pollution through chemical and biological methods.
5. Statistical analysis and computation of data; to check the significance of observed data and to establish their relationships.
6. To suggest economic and feasible management practice for the control of water pollution induced by selected small scale industries.

❐ The Study Sites

The study was conducted in the holy city Varanasi which is situated in the eastern part of Uttar Pradesh, a province of India located in the core of the Indian subcontinent, lying in the middle of Gangetic plain. On the globe Varanasi finds its location at 25°18′ North, 83°1′ East and is situated 76.19 m above the sea level.

River Varuna enters into the domain of Varanasi city near a railway bridge at Varanasi-Lucknow Loop line, which is very close to Imiliya ghat. During 15 km of its flow through Varanasi, the river Varuna receives sewage from twenty two municipal drainage (nalas) located on both the sides (Tables 4.2 and 4.3).

The physico-chemical characteristics of river water near all the nala discharge points were analysed, and their sources were studied. On the basis of variety in sources, i.e. some small scale industries and properties of effluents, four sites were selected for detailed investigation. Detail of the study sites are given in Table 4.4. Five sub-sites were also located at all the sites to collect the true representative of water sample and three sub-sites for sediment sample collection.

Site 2, was located downstream from the Razabazar nala, which drains 1.13 mld of sewage brought from the Nadesar area of the city. The most important additive at this site mainly consisted of discharge from some **battery industries** in addition to domestic sewage. 586 small scale battery industries were located in this area which poured their effluent directly into the Razabazar nala.

Site 3, was the site near Chaukaghat which poured the discharge from Chaukaghat nala. This site was located very close to G.T. (Grand Trunk) Road.

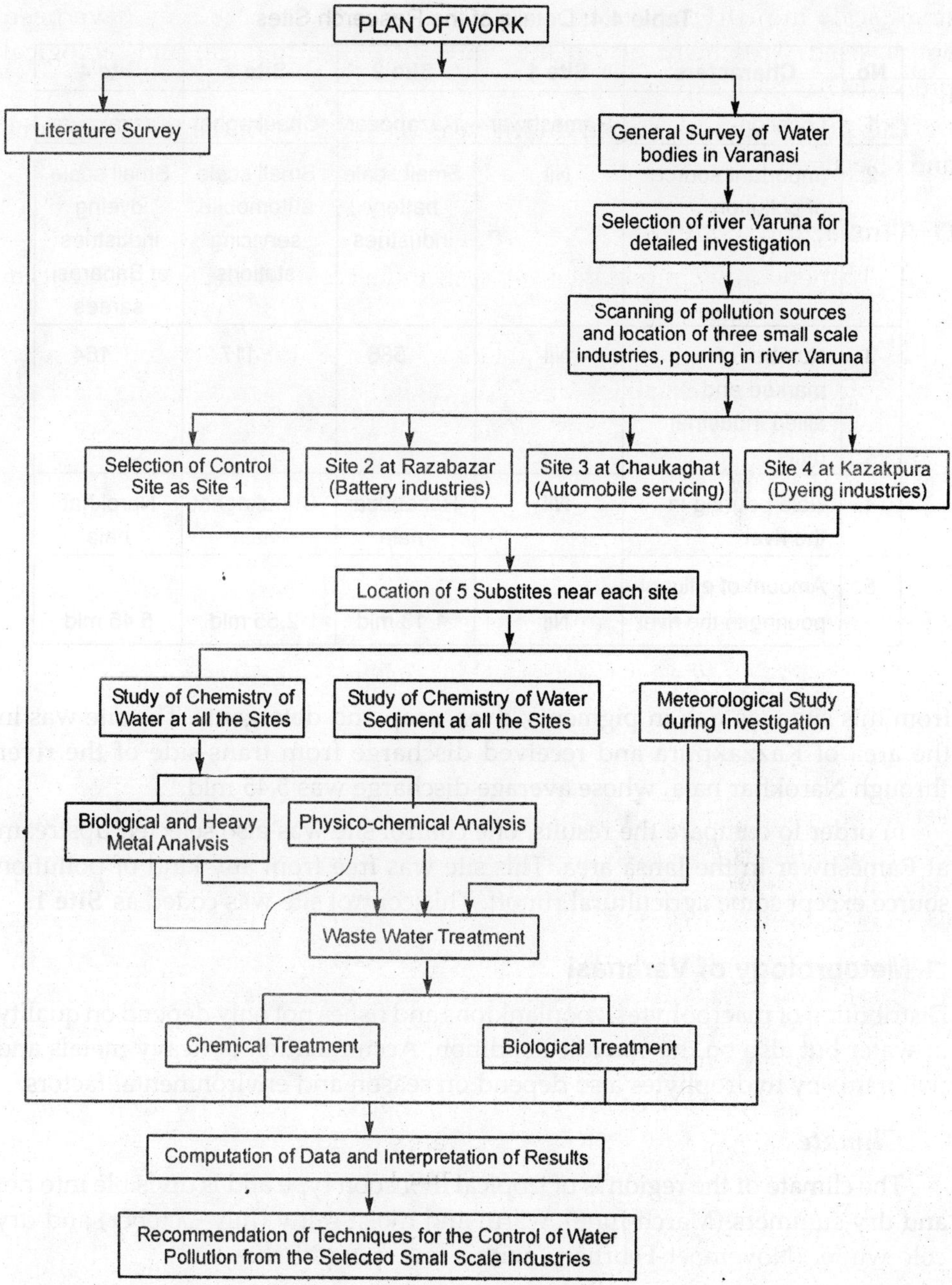

Figure 4.1: Plan of Work

The most common profession in this area was heavy and light **vehicles servicing,** including their washing and painting. Average discharge of Chaukaghat nala was 2.55 mld.

Site 4, located in the area where people are engaged in the processing of Banarsi sarees. This included **washing and dyeing** of the sarees. Thus, discharge

Table 4.4: Details of the Research Sites

No.	Characters	Site 1	Site 2	Site 3	Site 4
1.	Location	Rameshwar	Razabazar	Chaukaghat	Kazzakpura
2.	Important source of pollution	Nil	Small scale battery industries	Small scale automobile servicing stations	Small scale dyeing industries of Banarasi sarees
3.	Number of marked and allied industrial units	Nil	586	117	164
4.	Nala pouring in the river	Nil	Razabazar nala	Chaukaghat nala	Narokhar nala
5.	Amount of effluent pouring in the river	Nil	1.13 mld	2.55 mld	5.45 mld

from this site was rich in pigments, dyes, soap and detergents. The site was in the area of Kazzakpura and received discharge from trans-side of the river through Narokhar nala, whose average discharge was 5.45 mld.

In order to compare the results, one control site was also selected upstream at Rameshwar in the Jansa area. This site was free from any kind of pollution source except some agricultural runoff. This control site was coded as **Site 1**.

❒ Meteorology of Varanasi

Distribution of macrophytes, zooplanktons and fishes not only depend on quality of water but also on the climatic condition. Accumulation of heavy metals and pollutants by hydrophytes also depend on season and environmental factors.

Climate

The climate of the region is of tropical monsoon type and is divisible into hot and dry summers (March-June), warm and moist rainy (July-October) and dry cold winter (November-February) with a few sporadic showers.

Temperature

Monthly mean of minimum and maximum temperature was recorded during the study (April 2001 to March 2002). Lowest minimum temperature (10.03 °C) was recorded during December 2001, but lowest maximum temperature (22.71 °C) was recorded during January 2002, likewise highest minimum temperature (29.65 °C) was recorded during June 2001 and highest maximum temperature (38.16 °C) was found in April 2001. Seasonally, highest temperature was recorded during summer with lowest in winter and intermediate during rainy season. The maximum average temperature gradually starts falling from May 2001 and reaches to the minimum during December when the winter is coldest, then it starts rising from January 2002 and reaches to maximum during April when the summer reaches its peak. The rainy season months, i.e., July to October, normally found warm and wet.

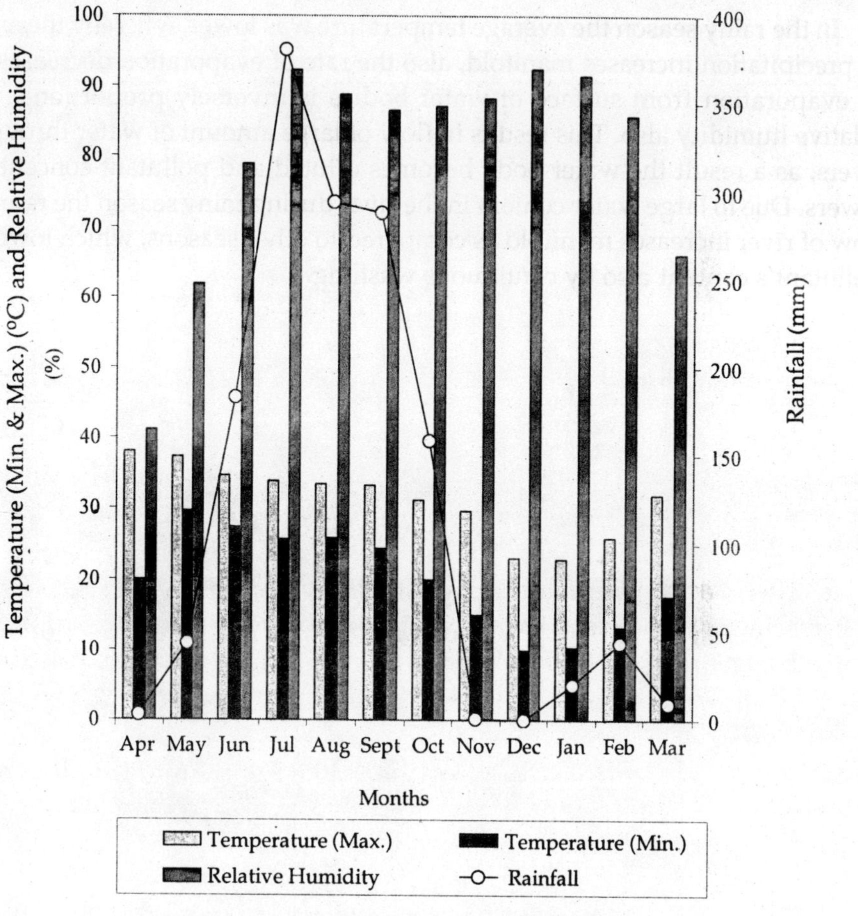

Figure 4.2: Meteorological Information (2001-2002)

Precipitation

During April 2001 to March 2002 highest monthly rainfall was recorded during July 2001 (380.5 mm) while minimum during November 2001 (0.6 mm). Winter season was dry with slight precipitation during summer; rainy season was wet with heavy rainfall (Fig. 4.2).

Humidity

Humidity varies widely in different seasons, maximum being in the rainy and minimum in the summer season. The maximum average relative humidity during study period was in December 2001 (92.54%) while the minimum was in April 2001 (41.26%) (Fig. 4.2).

Studies of meteorological variables are essential because they directly or indirectly affect the concentration of pollutants. During summer season the temperature was recorded much higher, precipitation was also recorded to be low, which ultimately causes high rate of evaporation from the surface of water bodies, due to which the water bodies become concentrated.

In the rainy season the average temperature was lower, whereby the amount of precipitation increases manifold, also the rate of evaporation decreases. Rate of evaporation from surface of water bodies is inversely proportional to the relative humidity also. This results in flow of large amount of water through the rivers, as a result the water body becomes diluted and pollutant concentration lowers. Due to large water content in the river during rainy season the rate of the flow of river increases manifold as compared to other seasons, which lowers the pollutant's content also by continuous washing.

5

VARIATION IN PROPERTIES OF WATER

Physico-chemical properties and heavy metals analysis of the river Varuna water was done fortnightly, from April 2001 to March 2002. The collected data are expressed as monthly mean along with the standard deviations. The same data were analysed for BLOCK ANOVA and correlated to test the significance of variation. All the selected four sites were further subdivided into five sub-sites to collect the true representative sample. Out of the five sub-sites, first and second sub-sites were located very close to the bank at cis and trans sides of the river, sub-sites three, four and five were located in the mid-stream varying vertically. All the sub-sites were located 100 feet downstream from the point of addition of the respective nalas. The parameters analysed during the study are given below:

❐ Temperature

Temperature of the river water was found to be higher at site 4, followed by site 3 and site 2, as an average, the least temperature was recorded at site 1.

At site 1 temperature of the river water was minimum (20.75 ± 0.243 °C) during October 2001 and maximum (32.9 ± 0.276 °C) during April 2001. At site 2 the temperature was found to be minimum (21.00 ± 0.110 °C) during November 2001. Temperature was maximum (33.68 ± 0.893 °C) during April 2001 at this site. At site 3, temperature was recorded to be minimum (21.43 ± 0.083 °C) during November 2001 and it was found to be maximum (33.73 ± 0.121 °C) during the month of May 2001. At site 4, the minimum temperature (21.96 ± 0.118 °C) of the river water was found during November 2001 and maximum (34.35 ± 0.190 °C) during April 2001 (Fig. 5.1). Annual mean temperature of site 1, site 2, site 3 and site 4 was recorded to be 26.371, 26.753, 27.108 and 27.677 °C, respectively.

Comparative study of all the sites show that in river Varuna the minimum temperature of water (20.75 ± 0.243 °C) was recorded during October 2001 at site 1 and the maximum temperature (34.35 ± 0.190 °C) during April 2001 at the site 4. Seasonally, temperature of water was found to be highest during summer followed by rainy season and it was minimum during winter at all the sites.

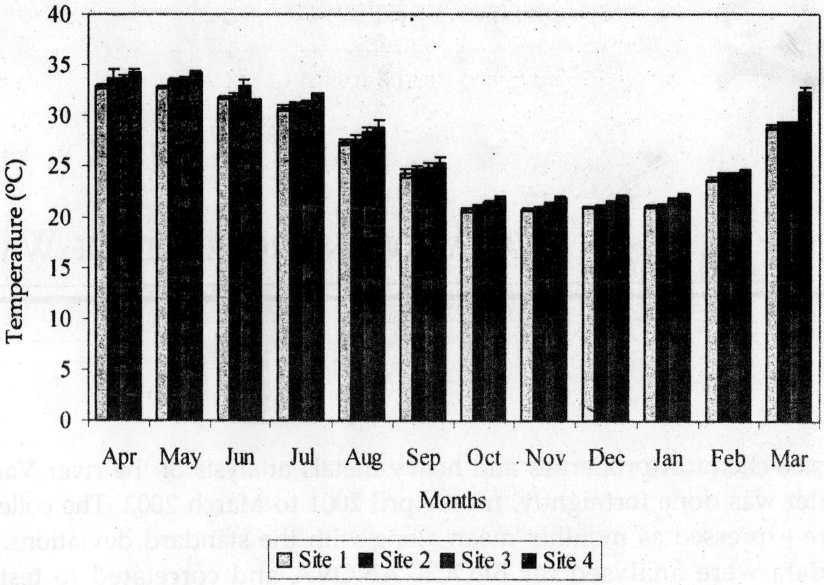

Figure 5.1: Temperature of the River Water (Apr. 2001-Mar. 2002)

Mean level of variance of temperature at the study sites show significant difference among the sites (F = 17.13, p < 0.001) and among the months (F = 469.84, p < 0.001) (Appendix I).

❑ pH

pH of the river water was found to be higher at site 1, followed by site 2 and site 3, as an average the least pH was recorded at site 4 throughout the study.

At site 1, pH of the river water was minimum (8.14 ± 0.07) during April 2001 and maximum (8.66 ± 0.05) during November 2001. At site 2, the pH was found to be minimum (8.11 ± 0.04) during April 2001. pH was maximum (8.50 ± 0.03) during August 2001 at this site. At site 3, pH was recorded to be minimum (7.92 ± 0.07) during March 2002 and it was found to be maximum (8.33 ± 0.03) during the month of September 2001. At site 4, the minimum pH (7.61 ± 0.05) was found during April 2001 and maximum (8.08 ± 0.04) of the river water during June 2001 (Fig. 5.2). Annual mean pH of site 1, site 2, site 3 and site 4 was recorded to be 8.406, 8.325, 8.087 and 7.842, respectively.

Comparative study of all the sites show that in the river Varuna the minimum pH of water (7.61 ± 0.05) was recorded during April 2001 at site 4 and the maximum pH (8.66 ± 0.05) during November 2001 at the site 1. Seasonally, pH was found to be highest during rainy season followed by winter and summer seasons at all the sites.

Mean level of variance of pH at the study sites show significant difference among the sites (F = 67.98, p < 0.001) and among the months (F = 4.71, p < 0.001) (Appendix I).

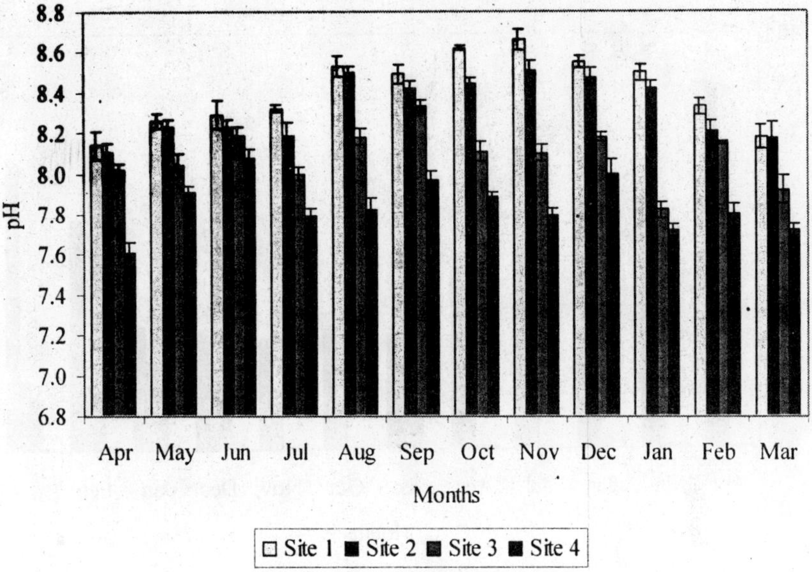

Figure 5.2: pH of the River Water (Apr. 2001-Mar. 2002)

❐ Acidity

Acidity of the river water was found to be higher at site 4, followed by site 3 and site 2, as an average the least acidity was recorded at site 1 throughout the study.

At site 1, acidity of the river water, was minimum (0.21 ± 0.052 mg/l $CaCO_3$) during April 2001 and maximum (0.73 ± 0.075 mg/l $CaCO_3$) during December 2001. At site 2 the acidity was found to be minimum during July and August 2001, and it was 0.25 ± 0.055 and 0.25 ± 0.050 mg/l $CaCO_3$, respectively. At site 2 it was maximum (6.6 ± 0.103 mg/l $CaCO_3$) during December 2001. At site 3 acidity was recorded to be minimum (0.42 ± 0.141 mg/l $CaCO_3$) during July 2001 and it was found to be maximum (8.35 ± 0.187 mg/l $CaCO_3$) during the month of January 2002. At site 4, the maximum acidity (34.46 ± 0.819 mg/l $CaCO_3$) was found during April 2001 and minimum (10.36 ± 0.314 mg/l $CaCO_3$) during November 2001 (Fig. 5.3). Annual mean acidity of site 1, site 2, site 3 and site 4 was recorded to be 0.386, 2.429, 6.526 and 18.516 mg/l $CaCO_3$, respectively.

Comparative study of the river water at all the sites show that minimum acidity (0.21 ± 0.052 mg/l $CaCO_3$) was recorded during April 2001 at site 1 and the maximum acidity (34.46 ± 0.819 mg/l $CaCO_3$) during April 2001 at the site 4. Seasonally, acidity of the river water was found to be highest during summer season followed by rainy and winter season at most of the sites.

Mean level of variance of acidity at the study sites show significant difference among the sites ($F = 42.34$, $p < 0.001$), but among the months the level of variance is non-significant ($F = 0.82$, N.S.) (Appendix I).

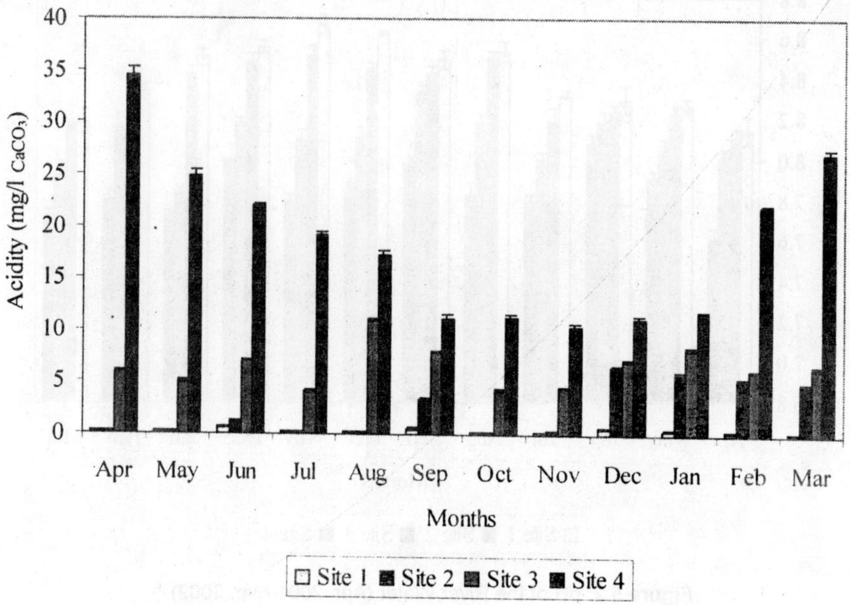

Figure 5.3: Acidity of the River Water (Apr. 2001-Mar. 2002)

❐ Alkalinity

Alkalinity of the river water was found to be higher at site 1, followed by site 2 and site 3, as an average the least alkalinity was recorded at site 4 throughout the study.

At site 1, alkalinity of the river water was minimum (193.66 ± 3.98 mg/l $CaCO_3$) during April 2001 and maximum (461.66 ± 3.14 mg/l $CaCO_3$) during November 2001. At site 2, the alkalinity was found to be minimum (142.33 ± 3.50 mg/l $CaCO_3$) during April 2001. Alkalinity was maximum (347.33 ± 6.18 mg/l $CaCO_3$) during September 2001 at this site. At site 3, alkalinity was recorded to be minimum (126.00 ± 5.85 mg/l $CaCO_3$) during March 2002 and it was found to be maximum (262.83 ± 3.06 mg/l $CaCO_3$) during the month of October 2001. At site 4, the minimum alkalinity (120.83 ± 5.11 mg/l $CaCO_3$) was found during April 2001 and maximum (243.83 ± 7.11 mg/l $CaCO_3$) during February 2002 (Fig. 5.4). Annual mean alkalinity of site 1, site 2, site 3 and site 4 was recorded to be 345.233, 250.316, 218.066 and 193.331 mg/l $CaCO_3$, respectively.

Comparative study of the river water of all the sites show that minimum alkalinity (126.00 ± 5.85 mg/l $CaCO_3$) was recorded during March 2002 at site 3 and the maximum alkalinity (461.66 ± 3.14 mg/l $CaCO_3$) during November 2001 at the site 1. Seasonally, alkalinity of the river water was found to be highest during rainy season followed by winter and summer season at all the sites.

Mean level of variance of alkalinity at the study sites show significant difference among the sites ($F = 44.90$, $p < 0.001$) and among the months ($F = 9.23$, $p < 0.001$) (Appendix I).

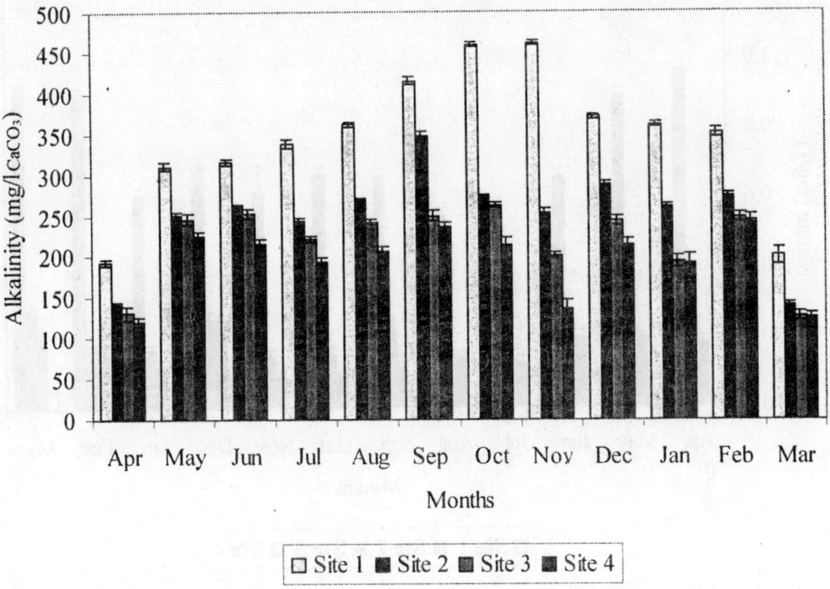

Figure 5.4: Alkalinity of the River Water (Apr. 2001-Mar. 2002)

❐ Nitrate

Nitrate in the river water was found to be higher at site 4, followed by site 3 and site 2, and it was minimum at site 1 throughout the study.

At site 1, nitrate in the river water was minimum (0.023 ± 0.005 mg/l) during May 2001 and January 2002. In both the months the values were same. Maximum nitrate content (0.007 ± 0.014 mg/l) was found during July 2001 at this site. At site 2, the nitrate was found to be minimum (0.092 ± 0.015 mg/l) during November 2001. Nitrate at this site was maximum (0.255 ± 0.014 mg/l) during December 2001. At site 3, nitrate was recorded to be minimum (0.137 ± 0.026 mg/l) during July 2001 and it was found to be maximum (0.292 ± 0.021 mg/l) during the month of March 2002. At site 4, the minimum nitrate (0.517 ± 0.021 mg/l) in the river water was found during July 2001 and maximum (0.968 ± 0.026 mg/l) during April 2001 (Fig. 5.5). Annual mean nitrate of site 1, site 2, site 3 and site 4 was recorded to be 0.041, 0.163, 0.203 and 0.721 mg/l, respectively.

Comparative study of the river water of all the sites show that minimum nitrate (0.023 ± 0.005 mg/l) was recorded during May 2001 and January 2002 at site 1 and the maximum nitrate (0.968 ± 0.028 mg/l) during April 2001 at the site 4. Seasonally, nitrate of the river water was found to be highest during summer season followed by winter and rainy seasons at all the sites.

Mean level of variance of nitrate at the study sites show significant difference among the sites ($F = 184.62$, $p < 0.001$) and among the months ($F = 2.196$, $p < 0.05$) (Appendix I).

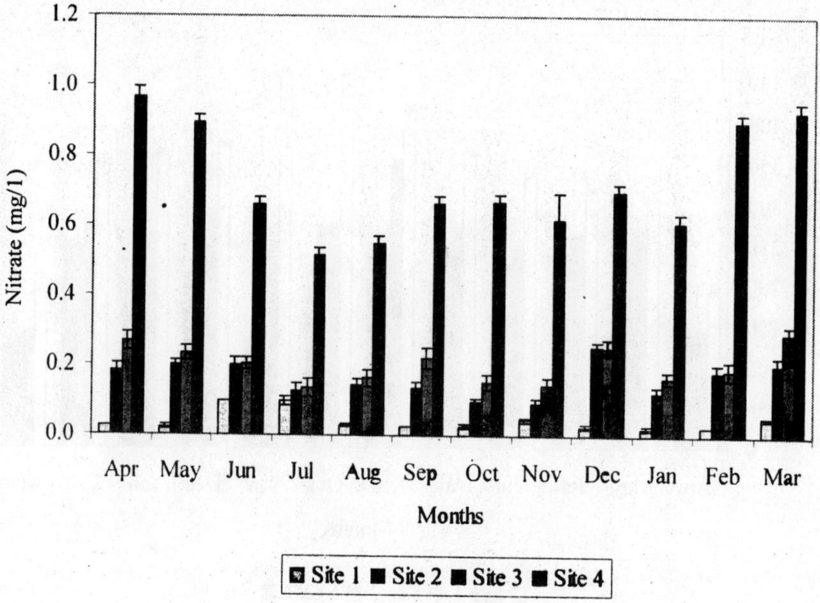

Figure 5.5: Nitrate in the River Water (Apr. 2001-Mar. 2002)

❐ Phosphate

Phosphate content in the river water was found to be higher at site 4, followed by site 3 and site 2, and it was minimum at site 1 throughout the study.

At site 1, phosphate in the river water was minimum (0.015 ± 0.002 mg/l) during August and September 2001. In both the months the values were same. Maximum phosphate content (0.092 ± 0.008 mg/l) in the river water at site 1 was found during December 2001. At site 2, the phosphate was found to be minimum (0.088 ± 0.008 mg/l) during February 2002. Phosphate at this site was maximum (0.652 ± 0.019 mg/l) during April 2001. At site 3, phosphate was recorded to be minimum (0.205 ± 0.019 mg/l) during November 2001 and it was found to be maximum (1.001 ± 0.041 mg/l) during the month of April 2001. At site 4, the minimum phosphate content in water (0.297 ± 0.022 mg/l) was found during November 2001 and maximum (1.565 ± 0.028 mg/l) during April 2001 (Fig. 5.6). Annual mean phosphate of site 1, site 2, site 3 and site 4 was recorded to be 0.034, 0.274, 0.545 and 1.097 mg/l, respectively.

Comparative study of all the sites show that minimum phosphate content (0.015 ± 0.002 mg/l) in water of river Varuna was recorded during August and September 2001 at site 1 and the maximum phosphate (1.565 ± 0.028 mg/l) during April 2001 at site 4. Seasonally, phosphate content in river water was found to be highest during summer season followed by rainy and winter seasons at all the sites.

Mean level of variance of phosphate at the study sites show significant difference among the sites ($F = 71.61$, $p < 0.001$) and among the months ($F = 3.64$, $p < 0.001$) (Appendix I).

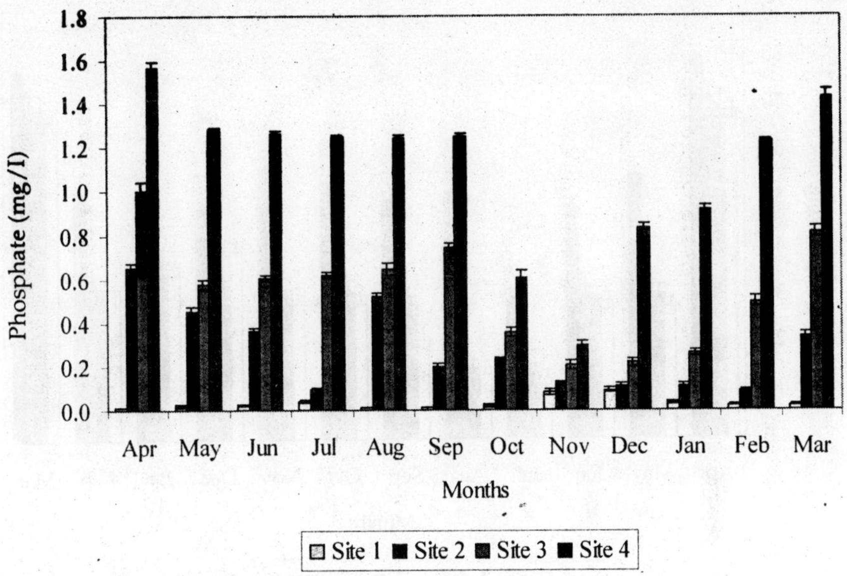

Figure 5.6: Phosphate in the River Water (Apr. 2001-Mar. 2002)

❒ Chloride

Analysis of chloride in the river water shows that the highest value was at site 4 and the lowest at site 1. The same value at site 3 was higher than that at the site 2 throughout the study.

At site 1, chloride in the river water was minimum (12.66 ± 1.63 mg/l) during July 2001 and maximum chloride content (68.66 ± 2.06 mg/l) was found during April 2001. At site 2, the chloride was found to be minimum (14.83 ± 1.63 mg/l) during August 2001. Chloride at this site was maximum (70.00 ± 2.58 mg/l) during April 2001. At site 3, chloride was recorded to be minimum (14.66 ± 1.36 mg/l) during July 2001 and it was found to be maximum (71.5 ± 2.75 mg/l) during the month of April 2001 in the river water. At site 4, the minimum chloride (29.16 ± 1.94 mg/l) was found during July 2001 and maximum (79.5 ± 2.58 mg/l) during April 2001 (Fig. 5.7). Annual mean chloride of site 1, site 2, site 3 and site 4 was recorded to be 34.246, 35.677, 39.053 and 53.872 mg/l, respectively.

Comparative study of the river water of all the sites show that minimum chloride (12.66 ± 1.63 mg/l) was recorded during July 2001 at site 1 and the maximum chloride (79.50 ± 2.58 mg/l) during April 2001 at the site 4. Seasonally, chloride in the river water was found to be highest during summer season followed by winter and rainy season at all the sites.

Mean level of variance of chloride at the study sites show significant difference among the sites ($F = 44.64$, $p < 0.001$) and among the months ($F = 47.10$, $p < 0.001$) (Appendix I).

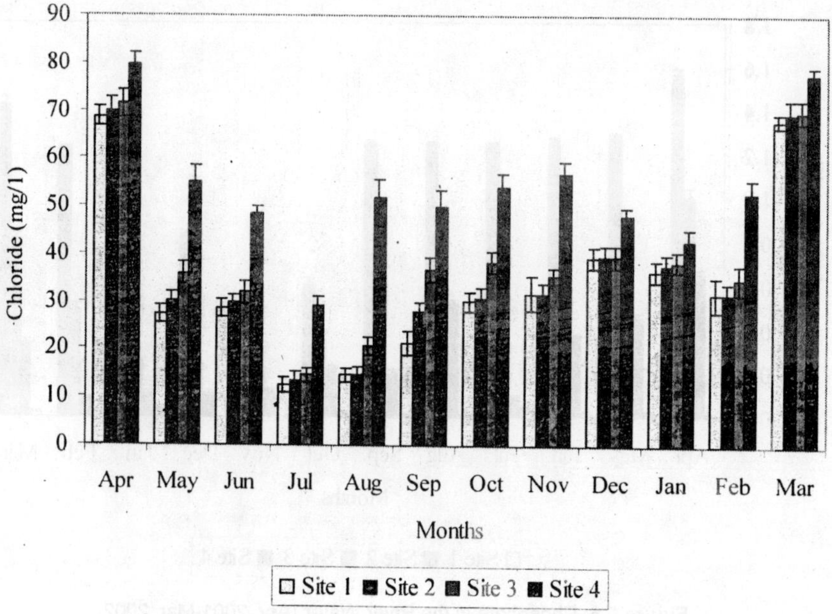

Figure 5.7: Chloride in the River Water (Apr. 2001-Mar. 2002)

❐ Dissolved Oxygen (DO)

Analysis of DO in the river water shows that the highest value was at site 1 and the lowest at site 4. The same value at site 2 was higher than that at the site 3 throughout the study.

At site 1, DO in the river water was minimum (5.80 ± 0.30 mg/l) during April 2001. Maximum DO content (9.16 ± 0.25 mg/l) was found during November 2001 at this site. At site 2, the DO was found to be minimum (4.38 ± 0.21 mg/l) during April 2001. DO at this site was maximum (6.40 ± 0.17 mg/l) during November 2001. At site 3, DO was recorded to be minimum (3.30 ± 0.19 mg/l) during April 2001 and it was found to be maximum (5.28 ± 0.25 mg/l) during the month of November 2001. At site 4, the minimum DO (1.93 ± 0.30 mg/l) was found during April 2001 and maximum (4.48 ± 0.11 mg/l) during November 2001 (Fig. 5.8). Annual mean DO of site 1, site 2, site 3 and site 4 was recorded to be 7.399, 5.358, 4.458 and 3.478 mg/l, respectively.

Comparative study of the river water of all the sites show that minimum DO (1.93 ± 0.30 mg/l) was recorded during April 2001 at site 4 and the maximum DO (9.16 ± 0.25 mg/l) during November 2001 at site 1. Seasonally, DO in the river water was found to be highest during winter season followed by rainy and summer seasons at all the sites.

Mean level of variance of DO at the study sites show significant difference among the sites ($F = 66.40, p < 0.001$) and among the months ($F = 4.74, p < 0.001$) (Appendix I).

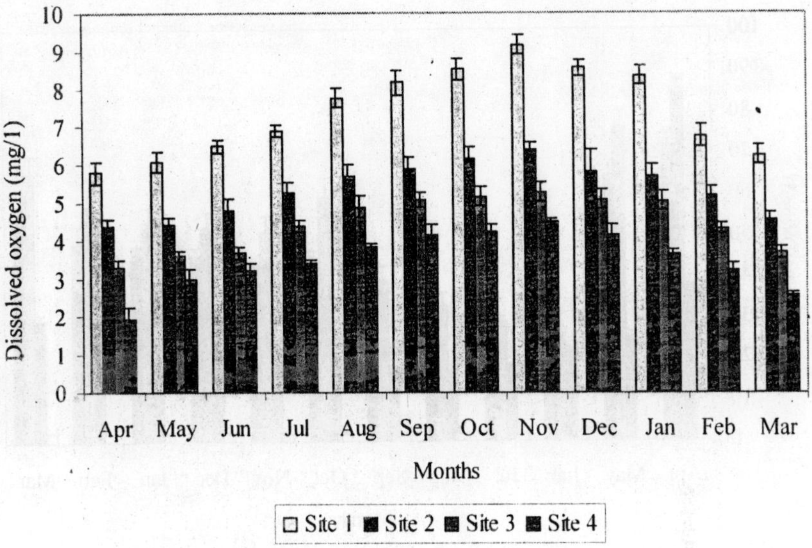

Figure 5.8: Dissolved Oxygen of the River Water (2001-2002)

❐ Biochemical Oxygen Demand (BOD)

Analysis of BOD of the river water shows that the highest value was at site 3 and the lowest at site 1. The same value at site 4 was higher than that at the site 2 throughout the study.

At site 1, BOD of the river water was minimum (1.81 ± 0.07 mg/l) during August 2001 and maximum BOD content (2.96 ± 0.12 mg/l) was found during June 2001. At site 2, the BOD was found to be minimum (16.5 ± 1.04 mg/l) during September 2001. BOD at this site was maximum (38.16 ± 1.94 mg/l) during April 2001. At site 3, BOD was recorded to be minimum (26.00 ± 1.41 mg/l) during June 2001 and it was found to be maximum (84.16 ± 3.40 mg/l) during the month of April 2001. At site 4, the minimum BOD (21.83 ± 1.16 mg/l) was found during June 2001 and maximum (71.68 ± 3.13 mg/l) during April 2001 (Fig. 5.9). Annual mean BOD of site 1, site 2, site 3 and site 4 was recorded to be 2.108, 22.846, 52.108, 42.993 mg/l, respectively.

Comparative study of the river water of all the sites show that minimum BOD (1.81 ± 0.07 mg/l) was recorded during August 2001 at site 1 and the maximum BOD (84.16 ± 3.40 mg/l) during April 2001 at the site 3. Seasonally, BOD of the river water was found to be highest during summer season followed by winter and rainy seasons at all the sites.

Mean level of variance of BOD at the study sites show significant difference among the sites ($F = 73.20$, $p < 0.001$) and among the months ($F = 4.69$, $p < 0.001$) (Appendix I).

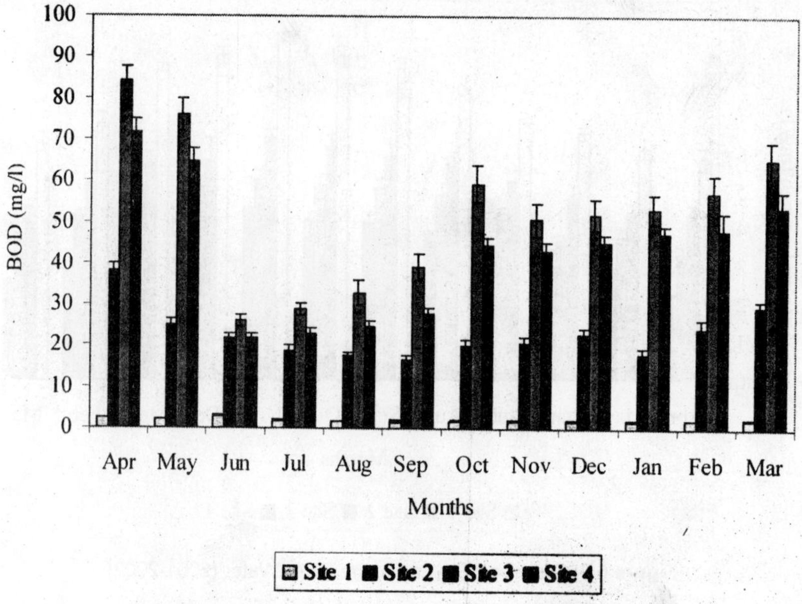

Figure 5.9: BOD of the River Water (Apr. 2001-Mar. 2002)

❑ Chemical Oxygen Demand (COD)

Analysis of COD of the river water shows that the highest value was at site 3 and the lowest at site 1. The same value at site 4 was higher than that at the site 2 throughout the study.

At site 1, COD of the river water was minimum (5.10 ± 0.23 mg/l) during July 2001. Maximum COD content (6.90 ± 0.19 mg/l) was found during April 2001 at site 1. At site 2, the COD was found to be minimum (22.83 ± 2.13 mg/l) during September 2001. COD at this site was maximum (54.00 ± 2.75 mg/l) during April 2001. At site 3, COD was recorded to be minimum (48.50 ± 4.23 mg/l) during June 2001 and it was found to be maximum (136.66 ± 5.46 mg/l) during the month of April 2001. At site 4, the minimum COD (28.16 ± 1.94 mg/l) was found during July 2001 and maximum (114.66 ± 4.22 mg/l) during April 2001 (Fig. 5.10). Annual mean COD of site 1, site 2, site 3 and site 4 was recorded to be 5.766, 32.096, 81.303 and 59.578 mg/l, respectively.

Comparative study of the river water of all the sites show that minimum COD (5.10 ± 0.23 mg/l) was recorded during June 2001 at site 1 and the maximum COD (136.66 ± 5.46 mg/l) during April 2001 at site 3. Seasonally, COD of the river water was found to be highest during summer season followed by winter and rainy seasons at all the sites.

Mean level of variance of COD at the study sites show significant difference among the sites ($F = 60.44, p < 0.001$) and among the months ($F = 4.57, p < 0.001$) (Appendix I).

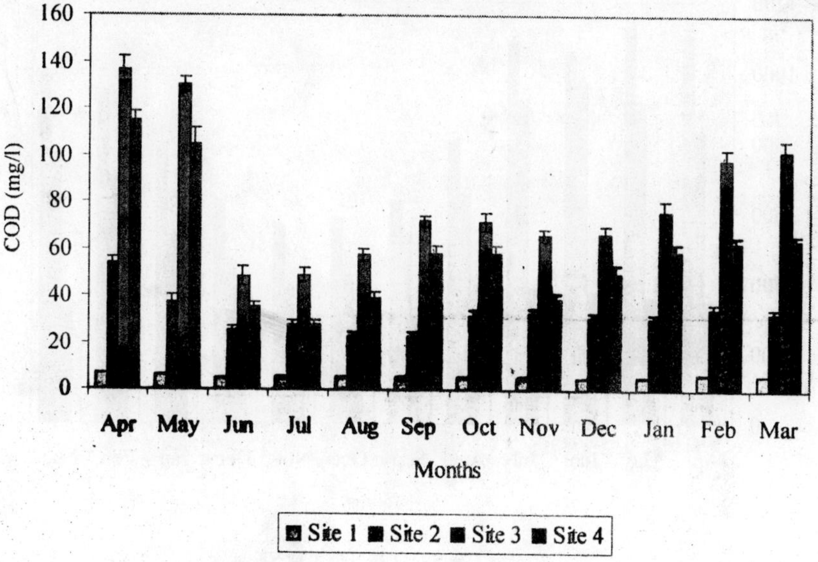

Figure 5.10: COD of the River Water (Apr. 2001-Mar. 2002)

❐ Total Solids

Analysis of total solids in the river water shows that the highest value was at site 4 and the lowest at site 1. The same value at site 3 was higher than that at site 2 throughout the study.

At site 1, total solids in the river water was minimum (193.50 ± 1.41 mg/l) during October 2001 and maximum total solids content (282.16 ± 3.06 mg/l) was found during July 2001. At site 2, the total solids was found to be minimum (284.50 ± 6.25 mg/l) during November 2001. Total solids at this site was maximum (385.00 ± 4.47 mg/l) during July 2001. At site 3, total solids was recorded to be minimum (389.16 ± 6.01 mg/l) during November 2001 and it was found to be maximum (973.50 ± 14.08 mg/l) during the month of June 2001. At site 4, the minimum total solid (563.00 ± 8.53 mg/l) was found during November 2001 and maximum (1128.50 ± 10.80 mg/l) during May 2001 (Fig. 5.11). Annual mean total solids of site 1, site 2, site 3 and site 4 was recorded to be 239.790, 326.096, 672.830 and 856.372 mg/l, respectively.

Comparative study of the river water of all the sites show that minimum total solids (193.50 ± 1.41 mg/l) was recorded during October 2001 at site 1 and the maximum total solids (1128.50 ± 10.80 mg/l) during May 2001 at site 4. Seasonally, total solids in the river water were found to be highest during rainy season followed by summer and winter seasons at all the sites.

Mean level of variance of total solids at the study sites show significant difference among the sites ($F = 85.05$, $p < 0.001$) and among the months ($F = 4.90$, $p < 0.001$) (Appendix I).

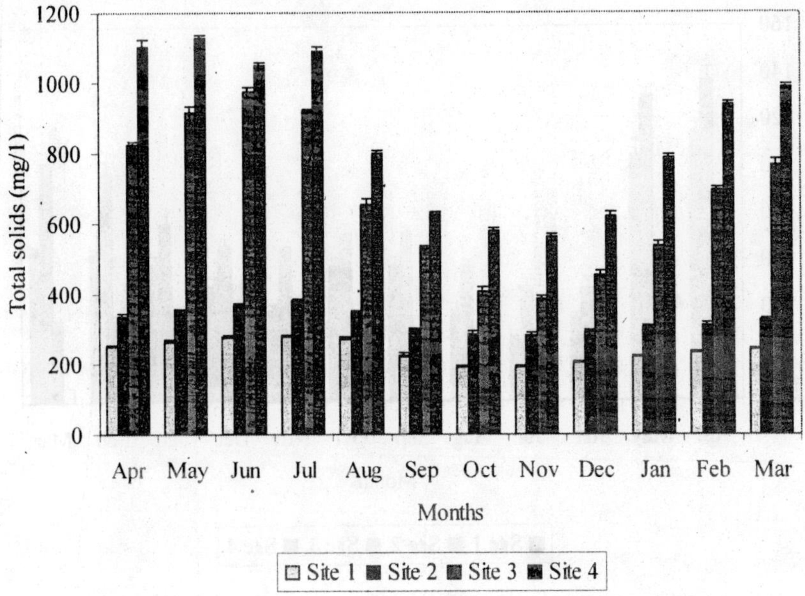

Figure 5.11: Total Solids in the River Water (Apr. 2001-Mar. 2002)

❐ Total Hardness

Analysis of total hardness of the river water shows that the highest value was at site 4 and the lowest at site 1. The same value at site 3 was higher than that at site 2 throughout the study.

At site 1, total hardness of the river water was minimum (38.83 ± 2.31 mg/l $CaCO_3$) during August 2001 and maximum total hardness content (82.50 ± 2.88 mg/l $CaCO_3$) was found during April 2001. At site 2, the total hardness was found to be minimum (159.33 ± 5.40 mg/l $CaCO_3$) during August 2001. Total hardness at this site was maximum (6.44 ± 2.73 mg/l $CaCO_3$) during March 2002. At site 3, total hardness was recorded to be minimum (531.50 ± 3.11 mg/l $CaCO_3$) during June 2001 and it was found to be maximum (911.50 ± 4.11 mg/l $CaCO_3$) during the month of April 2001. At site 4, the minimum total hardness (639.00 ± 2.65 mg/l $CaCO_3$) was found during August 2001 and maximum (963.83 ± 5.56 mg/l $CaCO_3$) during April 2001 (Fig. 5.12). Annual mean total hardness of site 1, site 2, site 3 and site 4 was recorded to be 58.429, 385.483, 672.267 and 737.123 mg/l $CaCO_3$, respectively.

Comparative study of the river water of all the sites show that minimum total hardness (38.83 ± 2.31 mg/l $CaCO_3$) was recorded during August 2001 at site 1 and the maximum total hardness (963.83 ± 5.56 mg/l $CaCO_3$) during April 2001 at site 4. Seasonally, total hardness of the river water was found to be highest during summer season followed by winter and rainy seasons at all the sites.

Mean level of variance of total hardness at the study sites show significant difference among the sites ($F = 191.33$, $p < 0.001$) and among the months ($F = 4.89$, $p < 0.001$) (Appendix I).

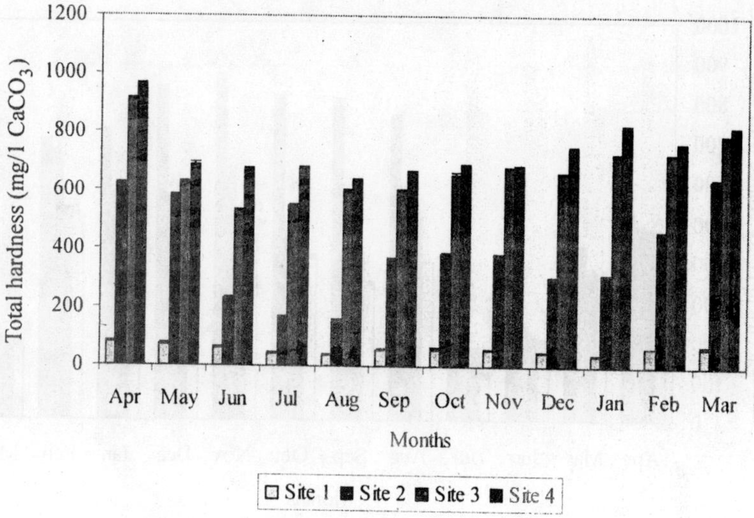

Figure 5.12: Total Hardness of the River Water (Apr. 2001-Mar. 2002)

❐ Electrical Conductance (EC)

Analysis of electrical conductance of the river water shows that the highest value was at site 4 and the lowest at site 1. The same value at site 3 was higher than that at the site 2 throughout the study.

At site 1, electrical conductance of the river water was minimum (114.66 ± 7.29 µS/cm) during July 2001 and maximum electrical conductance content (517.50 ± 4.16 µS/cm) was found during February 2002. At site 2, the electrical conductance was found to be minimum (180.83 ± 5.32 µS/cm) during July 2001. Electrical conductance at this site was maximum (522.66 ± 7.26 µS/cm) during February 2002. At site 3, electrical conductance was recorded to be minimum (215.50 ± 6.31 µS/cm) during March 2002 and it was found to be maximum (669.11 ± 6.51 µS/cm) during the month of February 2002. At site 4, the minimum electrical conductance (315.15 ± 5.26 µS/cm) was found during July 2001 and maximum (857.50 ± 9.13 µS/cm) during November 2001 (Fig. 5.13). Annual mean electrical conductance of site 1, site 2, site 3 and site 4 was recorded to be 363.941, 400.128, 450.685 and 626.830 µS/cm, respectively.

Comparative study of the river water of all the sites show that minimum electrical conductance (114.66 ± 7.29 µS/cm) was recorded during July 2001 at site 1 and the maximum electrical conductance (857.50 ± 9.13 µS/cm) during November 2001 at the site 4. Seasonally, electrical conductance of the river water was found to be highest during winter season followed by rainy and summer seasons at all the sites.

Mean level of variance of electrical conductance at the study sites show significant difference among the sites ($F = 38.86, p < 0.001$) and among the months ($F = 20.64, p < 0.001$) (Appendix I).

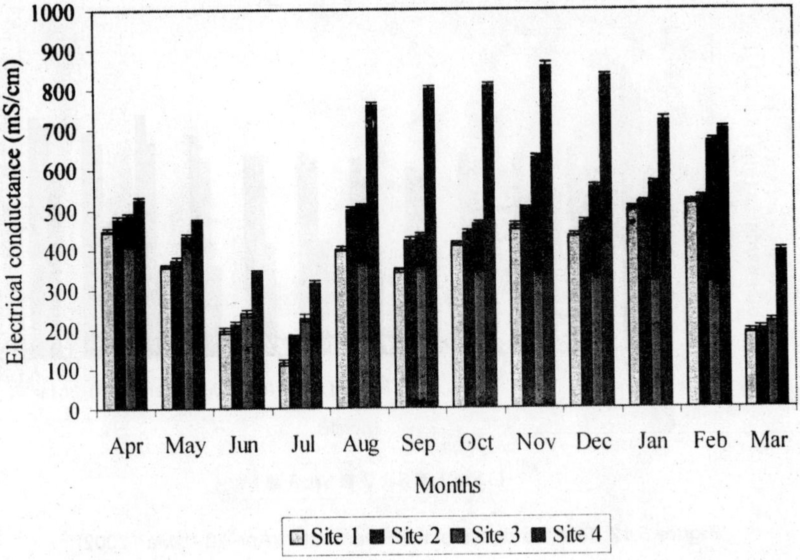

Figure 5.13: Electrical Conductance of the River Water (Apr. 2001-Mar. 2002).

❒ Oil & Grease

Analysis of oil & grease in the river water shows that the highest value was at site 3 and the lowest at site 1. The same value at site 4 was higher than that at site 2 throughout the study.

At site 1, oil & grease was minimum (0.11 ± 0.030 mg/l) in the river water during August 2001 and maximum (0.63 ± 0.021 mg/l) was found during April 2001. At site 2, the oil & grease was found to be minimum (0.35 ± 0.042 mg/l) during August 2001. Oil & grease at this site was maximum (1.89 ± 0.025 mg/l) during April 2001. At site 3, oil & grease was recorded to be minimum (1.09 ± 0.051 mg/l) during August 2001 and it was found to be maximum (6.09 ± 0.09 mg/l) during the month of March 2002. At site 4, the minimum oil & grease (0.95 ± 0.052 mg/l) was found during August 2001 and maximum (3.90 ± 0.063 mg/l) during April 2001 (Fig. 5.14). Annual mean oil & grease of site 1, site 2, site 3 and site 4 was recorded to be 0.420, 1.120, 4.197 and 2.718 mg/l, respectively.

Comparative study of the river water of all the sites show that minimum oil & grease (0.11 ± 0.030 mg/l) was recorded during August 2001 at site 1 and the maximum oil & grease (6.09 ± 0.09 mg/l) during March 2002 at the site 3. Seasonally, oil & grease of the river water was found to be highest during summer season followed by winter and rainy seasons at all the sites.

Mean level of variance of oil & grease at the study sites show significant difference among the sites ($F = 67.96$, $p < 0.001$) and among the months ($F = 6.16$, $p < 0.001$) (Appendix I).

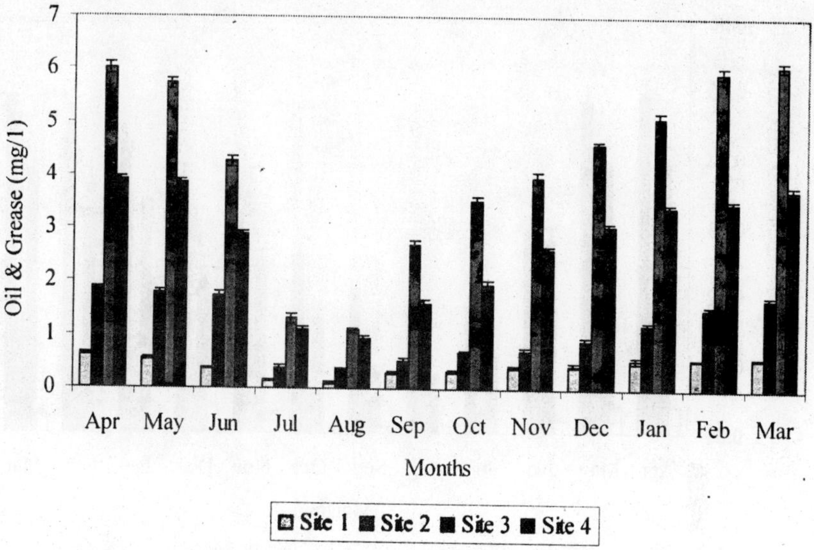

Figure 5.14: Oil & Grease in the River Water (Apr. 2001-Mar. 2002)

❐ Heavy Metal Analysis

Heavy metals analyses in the water of river Varuna at all the four sites were also conducted throughout the year. This was based on analysis of the selected heavy metals which were supposed to be discharged from the small scale industries dominantly being found in the area. Thus, six heavy metals were analysed at the research sites; their results are given below:

❐ Cadmium (Cd)

Analysis of Cd in the river water shows that the highest value was at site 4 and the lowest at site 1. The same value at site 2 was higher than that at the site 3 throughout the study.

At site 1, Cd in the river water was found absolutely absent during June, July and August 2001. Maximum Cd content (0.004 µg/l) at this site was found during April, May, December 2001 and also during January and February 2002. At site 2, the Cd was found to be minimum (0.008 µg/l) during August 2001. Cd at this site was maximum (0.039 µg/l) during April as well as May 2001. At site 3, Cd was recorded to be minimum (0.003 µg/l) during July 2001 and it was found to be maximum (0.020 µg/l) during the month of May 2001. At site 4, the minimum Cd (0.015 µg/l) was found during July 2001 and maximum (0.049 µg/l) during April 2001 and March 2002 (Fig. 5.15). Annual mean Cd of site 1, site 2, site 3 and site 4 was recorded to be 0.002, 0.026, 0.011 and 0.034 µg/l, respectively.

Comparative study of the river water of all the sites show that Cd was not found during June, July and August 2001 at site 1 and the maximum Cd (0.049 mg/l) during April 2001 and March 2002 at site 4. Seasonally, Cd in the river water was found to be highest during summer season followed by winter and rainy seasons at all the sites.

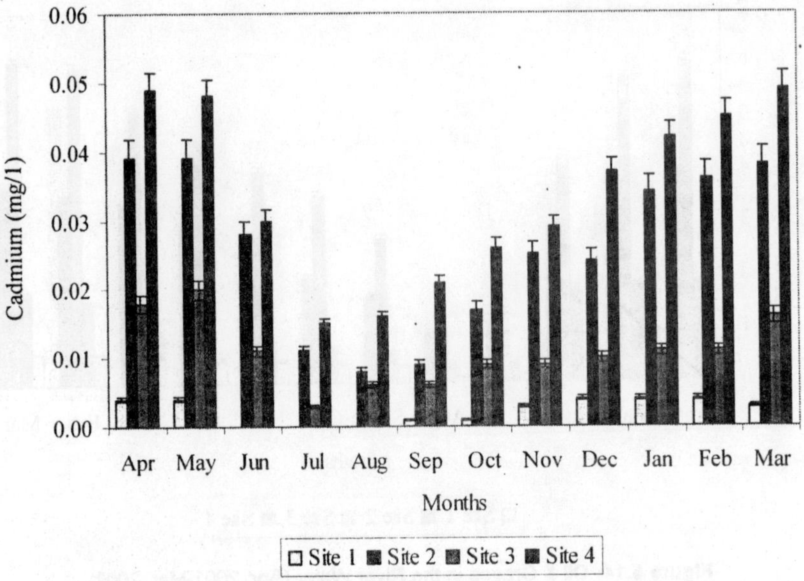

Figure 5.15: Cadmium in the River Water (Apr. 2001-Mar. 2002)

Mean level of variance of Cd at the study sites show significant difference among the sites ($F = 72.53, p < 0.001$) and among the months ($F = 6.97, p < 0.001$) (Appendix I).

❑ Copper (Cu)

Analysis of Cu in the river water shows that the highest value was at site 4 and the lowest at site 1. The same value at site 3 was higher than that at the site 2 throughout the study.

At site 1, Cu in the river water was found absolutely absent during July and September 2001. Maximum Cu content (0.020 mg/l) at this site was found during May 2001. At site 2, the Cu was found to be minimum (0.021 μg/l) during July 2001. Cu at this site was maximum (0.145 μg/l) during May 2001. At site 3, Cu was recorded to be minimum (0.118 μg/l) during September 2001 and it was found to be maximum (0.375 μg/l) during the month of April 2001. At site 4, the minimum Cu (0.113 μg/l) was found during August 2001 and maximum (0.496 μg/l) during May 2001 (Fig. 5.16). Annual mean Cu of site 1, site 2, site 3 and site 4 was recorded to be 0.007, 0.094, 0.262 and 0.332 μg/l, respectively.

Comparative study of all the sites show that Cu was not found during July and September 2001 in the river water at site 1 and the maximum Cu (0.496 μg/l) during May 2001 at site 4. Seasonally, Cu in the river water was found to be highest during summer season followed by winter and rainy seasons at all the sites.

Mean level of variance of Cu at the study sites show significant difference among the sites ($F = 66.40, p < 0.001$) and among the months ($F = 4.74, p < 0.001$) (Appendix I).

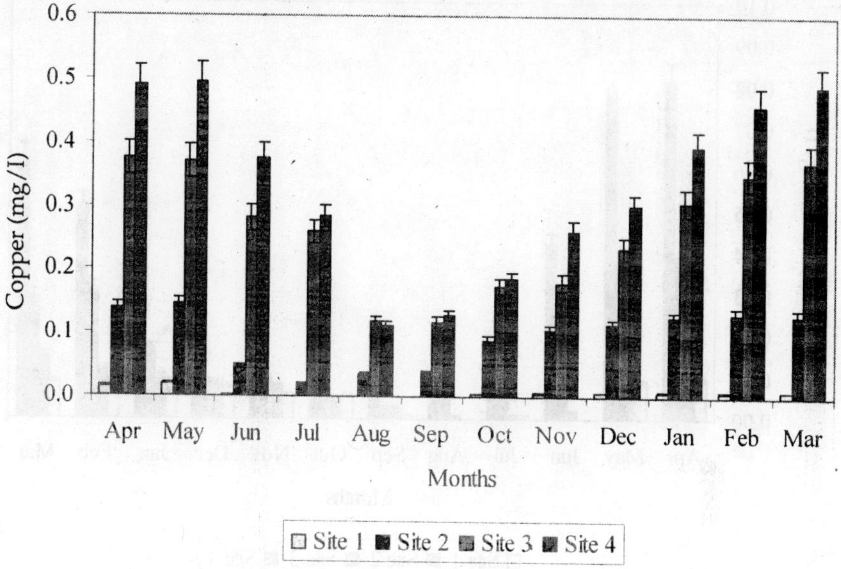

Figure 5.16: Copper in the River Water (Apr. 2001-Mar. 2002)

❐ Chromium (Cr)

Analysis of Cr in the river water shows that the highest value was at site 4 and the lowest at site 1. The same value at site 3 was higher than that at the site 2 throughout the study.

At site 1, Cr in the river water was found absolutely absent during August 2001. Maximum Cr content (0.010 μg/l) at this site was found during April 2001. At site 2, the Cr was found to be minimum (0.001 μg/l) during July and August 2001. Cr at this site was maximum (0.015 μg/l) during April 2001 and March 2002. At site 3, Cr was recorded to be minimum (0.003 μg/l) during September 2001 and it was found to be maximum (0.038 μg/l) during the month of May 2001. At site 4, the minimum Cr (0.006 μg/l) was found during August 2001 and maximum (0.081 μg/l) during April 2001 (Fig. 5.17). Annual mean Cr of site 1, site 2, site 3 and site 4 was recorded to be 0.006, 0.008, 0.019 and 0.041 μg/l, respectively.

Comparative study of all the sites show that Cr was not found during August 2001 at site 1 and the maximum Cr (0.081 μg/l) during April 2001 at site 4 in the river water. Seasonally, Cr was found to be highest during summer season followed by winter and rainy seasons at all the sites.

Mean level of variance of Cr at the study sites show significant difference among the sites ($F = 27.37$, $p < 0.001$) and among the months ($F = 4.20$, $p < 0.001$) (Appendix I).

❐ Nickel (Ni)

Analysis of Ni in the river water shows that the highest value was at site 4 and the lowest at site 1. The same value at site 3 was higher than that at the site 2 throughout the study.

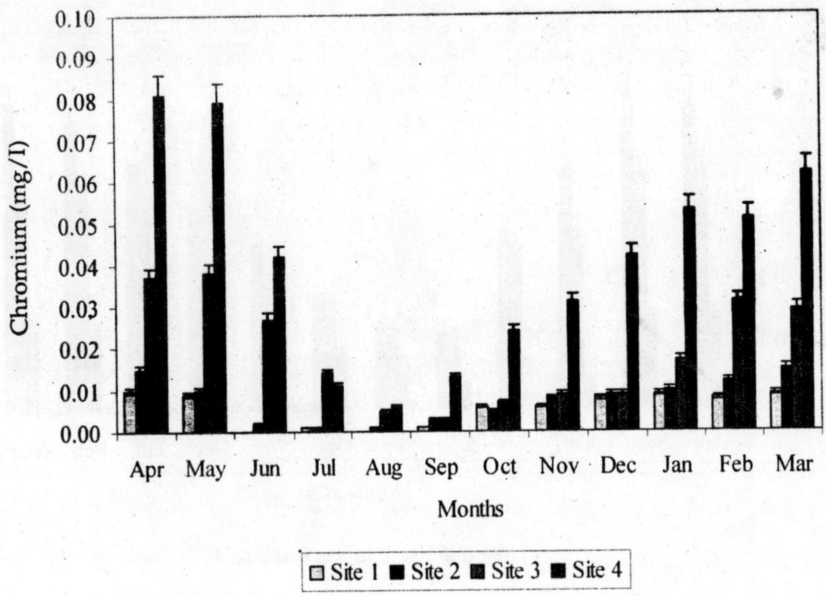

Figure 5.17: Chromium in the River Water (Apr. 2001-Mar. 2002)

At site 1, Ni in the river water was found absolutely absent during August 2001. Maximum Ni content (0.007 µg/l) at this site was found during May 2001, January and March 2002. At site 2, the Ni was found to be minimum (0.001 µg/l) during August and September 2001. Ni at this site was maximum (0.019 µg/l) during April and May 2001. At site 3 Ni was recorded to be minimum (0.001 µg/l) during September 2001 and it was found to be maximum (0.023 µg/l) during the

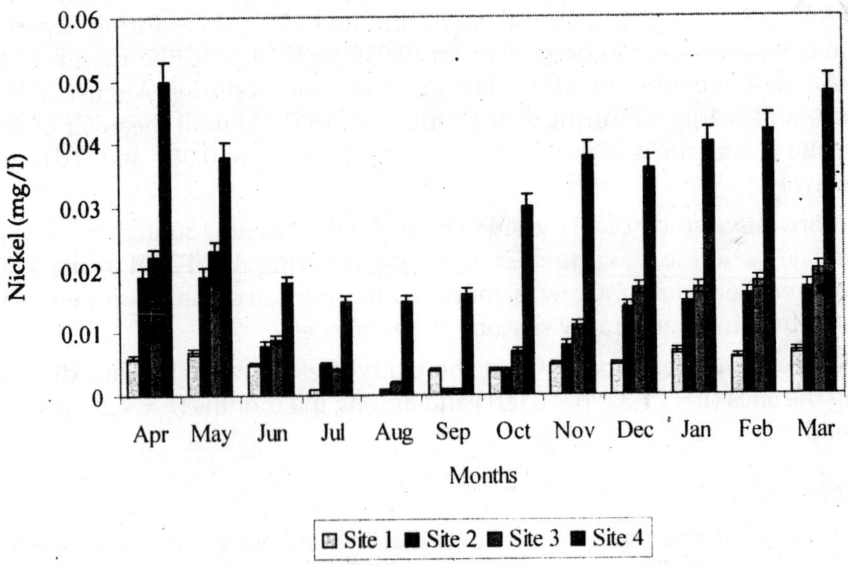

Figure 5.18: Nickel in the River Water (Apr. 2001-Mar. 2002)

month of May 2001. At site 4, the minimum Ni (0.015 µg/l) was found during August 2001 and maximum (0.048 µg/l) during April 2001 (Fig. 5.18). Annual mean Ni of site 1, site 2, site 3 and site 4 was recorded to be 0.005, 0.011, 0.013 and 0.032 µg/l, respectively.

Comparative study of all the sites show that Ni was not found during August 2001 at site 1 and the maximum Ni (0.050 µg/l) during April 2001 at site 4. Seasonally, Ni in the river water was found to be highest during summer season followed by winter and rainy seasons at all the sites.

Mean level of variance of Ni at the study sites show significant difference among the sites ($F = 67.56, p < 0.001$) and among the months ($F = 8.28, p < 0.001$) (Appendix I).

❐ Lead (Pb)

Analysis of Pb in the river water shows that the highest value was at site 2 and the lowest at site 1. The same value at site 4 was higher than that at the site 3 throughout the study.

At site 1, Pb in the river water was found to be minimum (0.001 µg/l) during July 2001. Maximum Pb content (0.015 µg/l) at this site was found during April 2001. At site 2, the Pb was found to be minimum (0.027 µg/l) during August 2001. Pb at this site was maximum (0.021 µg/l) during April 2001. At site 3, Pb was recorded to be minimum (0.010 µg/l) during August 2001 and it was found to be maximum (0.130 µg/l) during the month of March 2002. At site 4, the minimum Pb (0.009 µg/l) was found during August 2001 and maximum (0.139

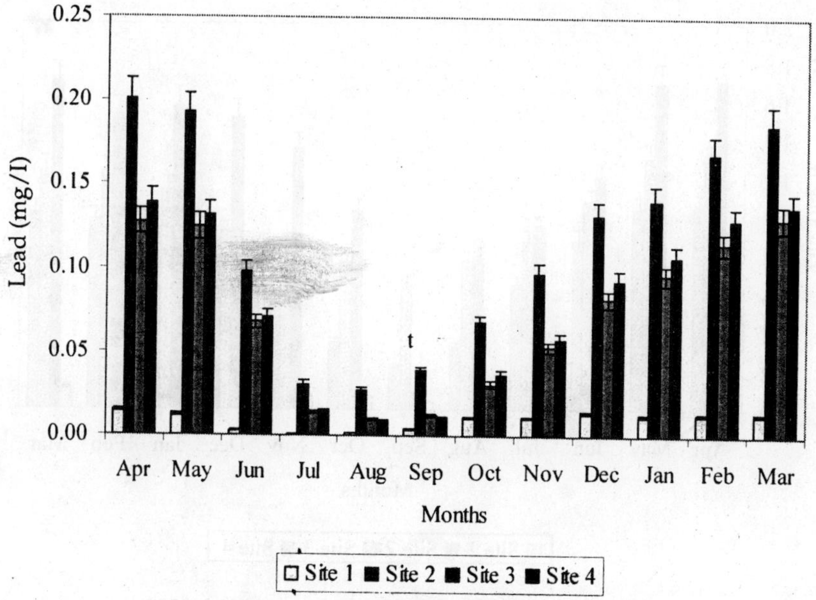

Figure 5.19: Lead in the River Water (Apr. 2001-Mar. 2002)

μg/l) during April 2001 (Fig. 5.19). Annual mean Pb of site 1, site 2, site 3 and site 4 was recorded to be 0.009, 0.115, 0.072 and 0.078 μg/l, respectively.

Comparative study of the river water of all site shows that Pb was minimum (0.001 μg/l) during July 2001 at site 1 and the maximum Pb (0.201 μg/l) during April 2001 at site 2. Seasonally, Pb in the river water was found to be highest during summer season followed by winter and rainy seasons at all the sites.

Mean level of variance of Pb at the study sites show significant difference among the sites ($F = 33.33, p < 0.001$) and among the months ($F = 10.06, p < 0.001$) (Appendix I).

❐ Zinc (Zn)

Analysis of Zn in the river water shows that the highest value was at site 2 and the lowest at site 1. The same value at site 3 was higher than that at the site 4 throughout the study.

At site 1, Zn in the river water was found to be minimum (0.042 μg/l) during September 2001. Maximum Zn content (0.107 μg/l) at this site was found during March 2002. At site 2, the Zn was found to be minimum (0.892 μg/l) during August 2001. Zn at this site was maximum (1.712 μg/l) during April 2001. At site 3, Zn was recorded to be minimum (0.658 μg/l) during September 2001 and it was found to be maximum (1.304 μg/l) during the month of May 2001. At site 4, the minimum Zn (0.228 μg/l) was found during September 2001 and maximum (1.051 μg/l) during April 2001 and March 2002 (Fig. 5.20). Annual mean Zn of site 1, site 2, site 3 and site 4 was recorded to be 0.076, 1.271, 1.004 and 0.744, respectively.

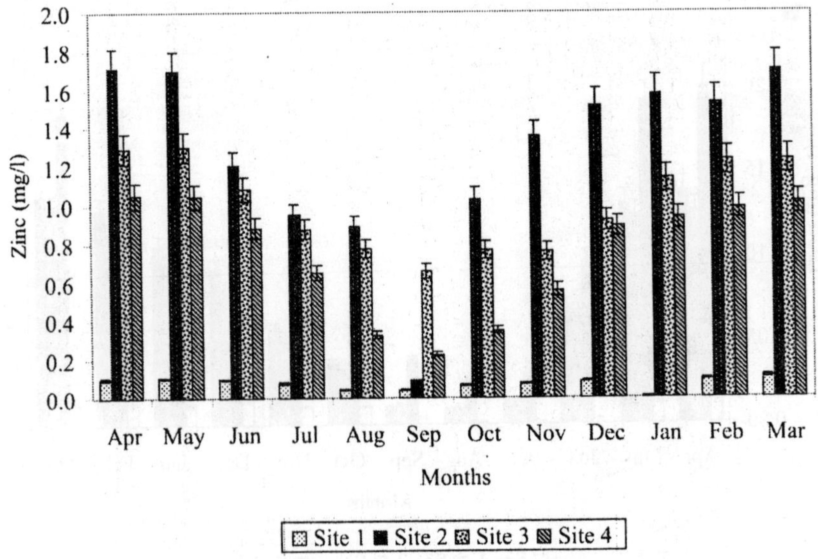

Figure 5.20: Zinc in the River Water (Apr. 2001-Mar. 2002)

Comparative studies of all the sites show that Zn was minimum (0.042 µg/l) during September 2001 at site 1 and the maximum Zn (1.712 µg/l) during April 2001 at site 2 in the river water. Seasonally, Zn in the river water was found to be highest during summer season followed by winter and rainy seasons at all the sites.

Mean level of variance of Zn at the study sites show significant difference among the sites ($F = 71.90, p < 0.001$) and among the months ($F = 5.58, p < 0.001$) (Appendix I).

6

AQUATIC MACROPHYTIC DIVERSITY

The great solvent power of water has been making the creation of absolutely pure water a theoretical rather than a practical goal. Even the highest quality of distilled water has dissolved gases and, to a slight degree, certain solids. The problem, therefore, has been one of determining what quality of water has been required to meet a given purpose and to find practical needs of achieving that quality. The problem is complicated because every use to which water has been put—washing, irrigation, flushing away waste, cooling, industrial use, etc.—has been adding something to the water. Rivers and lakes have been used for dumping human sewage and industrial waste of every conceivable kind, many of which have been highly toxic. They have also been reported to percolate through the soil surface and contaminate the underground water.

Several aquatic macrophytes such as water hyacinth have been found to scavenge inorganic and some organic compounds from the waste water. Study in this regard is in progress regarding investigations on algal communities of the aquatic ecosystem and the occurrence of pollution tolerant algae in a pond, polluted by fertiliser factory effluent. Phycological studies of river Ganga, has recorded the pollution tolerant algae in river Ganga. However, very few researches have been conducted on biological composition of a river with varying levels of pollution load. Some researches on the biological characteristics of river Ganga at Mirzapur and Varanasi have been conducted, however, the studies have been mainly concentrated on phytoplanktonic communities.

Various species of *Eichhornia* has been found predominantly growing in polluted waterbodies. *Eichhornia* is a nuisance aquatic weed which was accidently introduced in West Bengal by queen Victoria during 1889 as an ornamental plant and it has spread all over India due to its explosive growth rate. *Eichhornia* and other water hyacinths have been reported to absorb nutrients—thus acting as a pollutant scrubber.

Regular variation of macrophytic composition of river Varuna with respect to effluents of the selected small scale industries have not been studied yet. So, in order to fill up the gap of knowledge and to provide necessary basic information on the variation of different macrophytic in the lotic ecosystem, the present project had been carried out. It was also essential to find the sensitive and resistant plants. Study of macrophytic composition of the selected research sites were conducted fortnightly and the analysis was done on monthly basis. For this purpose a wooden quadrat of 1 sq. mt. was used.

During this investigation, the following properties of the river at different sites were studied:

1. Macrophytic composition,
2. Similarity and dissimilarity index, and
3. Phytosociological studies:
   - Density of macrophytes
   - Frequency of macrophytes.

❑ Macrophytic Composition

Plants play an important role in all ecosystems. They link the different trophic levels of the ecosystem. Aquatic and terrestrial food chains are linked together by the means of aquatic plants. It has been a regular feature that rivers become nutritionally very rich due to addition of organic and inorganic materials through excessive runoff from the catchment areas and pouring in of sewage leading to the establishment of macrophytic population. A total of 11 aquatic macrophytes were recorded during present investigation at various sampling sites. Site 1 and site 2 were represented by 6 species, site 1 was the control site with no source of river pollution except the agricultural runoff and site 2 consisting of the discharge from battery industries. Site 3—which pours discharge from automobile servicing stations, shows the presence of 5 species, and only 4 species were recorded at site 4 at which the discharge from small scale dyeing industries was discharged.

Apomogeton natans was found to be present at site 1 only. Likewise, *Azolla pinnata* was present only at site 2 and *Potamogeton pectinatus* and *Wolffia* only at site 1. *Hydrilla verticillata* was present at sites 1, 2 and 3 but was not found at sites 4. *Ipomoea aquatica* was present only at site 3, however, it was not reported at sites 1, 3 and 4. *Eichhornia crassipes* was present only at sites 3 and 4, however, it was absent at sites 1 and 2. Contrary to it, *Salvenia natans* was preset only at sites 1 and 2 but not at sites 3 and 4. *Salvenia molesta* was present at sites 2, 3 and 4 but was not recorded at site 1. *Pistia stratiotes* were present only at sites 1 and 2, however, it was not found at sites 3 and 4. *Lemna minor* was not present at site 1 but it was recorded at sites 2, 3 and 4 (Table 6.1).

Seasonal distribution of the macrophytes is presented in Table 6.2. *Aponogeton natan,* which was present only at site 1, was found during summer and winter seasons. *Azilla pinnata* was also found during the same season at site 2. *Eichhornia crassipes* was recorded in summer and winter seasons at site 3 and at site 4 it was present during summer, winter and earlier part of the rainy season. *Hydrilla verticillata,* which was present at sites 1, 2 and 3, was recorded from site 2 during all the seasons except late rainy season, however, at sites 1 and 3 it was not

Table 6.1: Distribution of aquatic macrophytes at the research sites

Plant species	Site 1	Site 2	Site 3	Site 4
Aponogeton natans	+	–	–	–
Azolla pinnata	–	+	–	–
Eichhornia crassipes	–	–	+	+
Hydrilla verticellata	+	+	+	–
Ipomoea aquatica	–	–	+	–
Lemna minor	–	+	+	+
Pistia stratiotes	+	+	–	–
Potamogeton pectinatus	+	–	–	+
Salvenia molesta	–	+	+	+
Salvenia natans	+	+	–	–
Wolffia sps.	+	–	–	–
Total	**6**	**6**	**5**	**4**

recorded during rainy season but was found to be present during summer and winter. *Ipomoea aquatica* was observed only during summer and winter season at site 3. *Lemna minor* was recorded during summer and winter seasons of sites 2, 3 and 4. Likewise, *Pistia stratiotes* were found to be present only during summer and winter seasons at sites 1 and 2. *Potamogeton pectinatus* was recorded during summer and winter seasons at sites 1 and 4. *Salvenia molesta* was not found at site 1 during any season but it was reported at all the other three sites during summer,

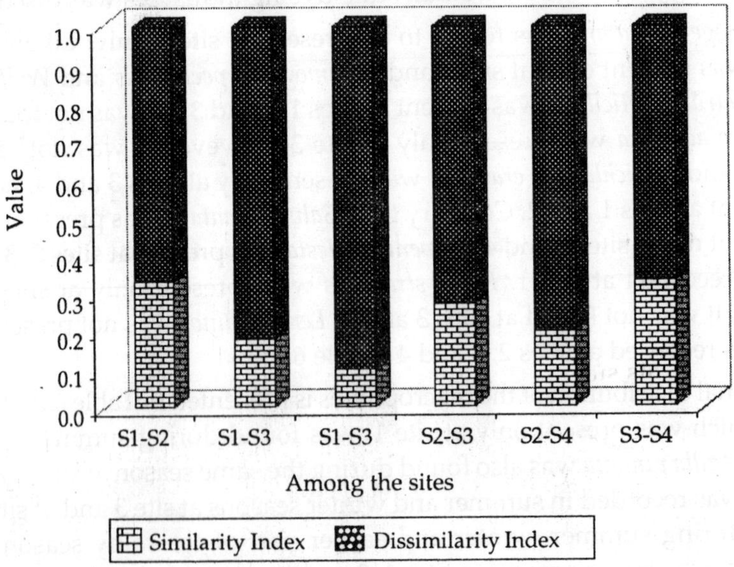

Figure 6.1: Similarity and dissimilarity index of aquatic macrophytes between different study sites

Table 6.2: Seasonal distribution of aquatic macrophytes at the research sites

Plant species	Site 1			Site 2			Site 3			Site 4		
	1	2	3	1	2	3	1	2	3	1	2	3
Aponogeton natans	+	-	+	-	-	-	-	-	-	-	-	-
Azolla pinnata	-	-	-	+	-	+	-	-	-	-	-	-
Eichhornia crassipes	-	-	-	-	-	-	+	-	+	+	+	+
Hydrilla verticellata	+	-	+	+	+	+	+	-	+	-	-	-
Ipomoea aquatica	-	-	-	-	-	-	+	-	+	-	-	-
Lemna minor	-	-	-	+	-	+	+	-	+	+	-	+
Pistia stratiotes	+	-	+	+	-	+	-	-	-	-	-	-
Potamogeton pectinatus	+	-	+	-	-	-	-	-	-	+	-	+
Salvenia molesta	-	-	-	+	+	+	+	+	+	+	+	+
Salvenia natans	+	-	+	+	-	+	-	-	-	-	-	-
Wolffia sps.	+	-	+	-	-	-	-	-	-	-	-	-

1 = Summer, 2 = Rainy and 3 = Winter seasons

winter and in the early rainy season. *Salvenia natans* were reported during summer and winter seasons at sites 1 and 2. *Wolffia* was also present only at site 1 and that too during summer and winter season.

Similarity and Dissimilarity Index

By the study of similarity and dissimilarity index, different habitat conditions, quality and quantity of pollutants at the respective sites and response of the plants growing in the area can be interpreted. The same values with respect to the aquatic plant were calculated (Table 6.1). The results indicate that maximum dissimilarity was found between site 1 and sites 4 (0.9). Similarity index between site 1 and site 2 and also between site 3 and site 4 were highest and the value was 0.33. Least value of similarity index (0.1) was recorded between site 1 and site 4.

❐ Phytosociological Studies

Among phytosocioloical studies, density and frequency of the plant species present at the sites were studied.

Macrophytic Density

Site 1: At this site six plants were recorded with *Hydrilla verticellata* as the most dominant flora followed by *Pistia stratiotes*. Density of *Hydrilla verticellata* was found to be maximum (20.467 plants per m^2) during January 2002; however, no *Hydrilla verticellata* was recorded during June to September 2001. The density of *Pistia stratiotes* was found to be maximum (20.467 plants per m^2), but it was not recorded during July, August and September 2001. *Aponogeton natans* showed maximum density (2.168 plants per m^2) during January 2002. *Salvenia* *natans* showed maximum density (5.738 plants per m^2) during January 2002. *Potamogeton pectinatus* also showed maximum density (6.11 plants per m^2) during January 2002, similar to *Wolffia sps.* with maximum density (6.38 plants per m^2) during January. In case of most of the plants no species were recorded during rainy season (Fig. 6.2).

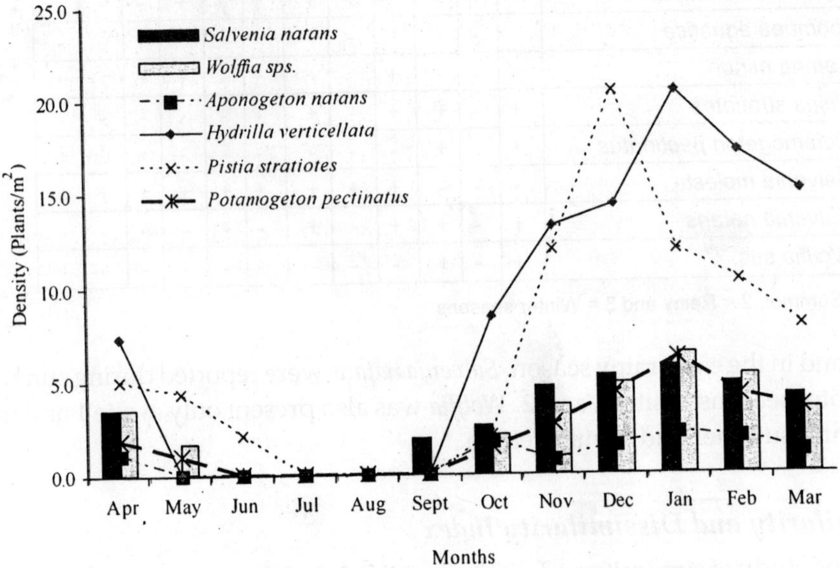

Figure 6.2: Macrophytic density at Site 1 (Mean values from April 2001 to March 2002)

Site 2: At this site also only six plants were recorded. *Hydrilla verticellata* with maximum density (19.521 plants per m^2) during December 2001; however, no *Hydrilla verticellata* was recorded during July to September 2001. *Salvenia natans* showed maximum density (5.731 plants per m^2) during January 2002. *Azolla pinnata* was recorded with maximum density (41.332 plants per m^2) during January 2002, this plant was not recorded during May to September 2001. *Salvenia molesta* was recorded with maximum density (47.368 plants per m^2) and *Lemna minor* (42.633 plants per m^2) during January 2002. Maximum density of *Pistia stratiotes* (16.31 plants per m^2) was recorded during December 2001. No plants were recorded during July and August 2001 (Fig. 6.3).

Site 3: At site 3, five plants were recorded during the study period (April 2001 to March 2002). *Salvenia molesta* and *Eichhornia crassipes* were found to be the most dominant flora of the site throughout the study. Density of *Salvenia molesta* was found to be maximum (52.72 plants per m^2) during January 2002; in the same month *Eichhornia crassipes*

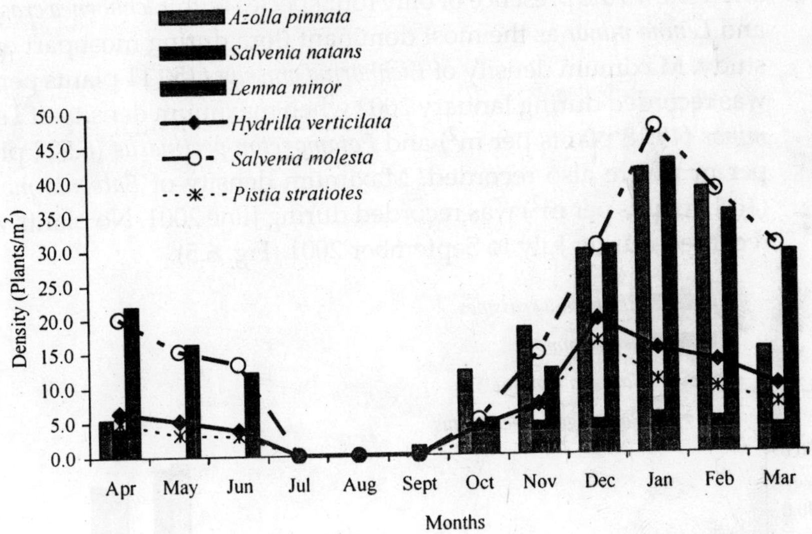

Figure 6.3: Macrophytic density at Site 2 (Mean values from April 2001 to March 2002)

also showed maximum density (47.338 plants per m^2). The third most dominant flora was *Lemna minor* with maximum density (13.91 plants per m^2) during June 2001. *Hydrilla verticillata*, a submerged macrophyte, showed maximum density (3.81 plants per m^2) during January 2002. *Ipomoea aquatica* also was with maximum density (6.38 plants per m^2) during January 2002. No plants were recorded during July to September 2001, except *Ipomoea aquatica* with density 2.368 plants per m^2 during September (Fig. 6.4).

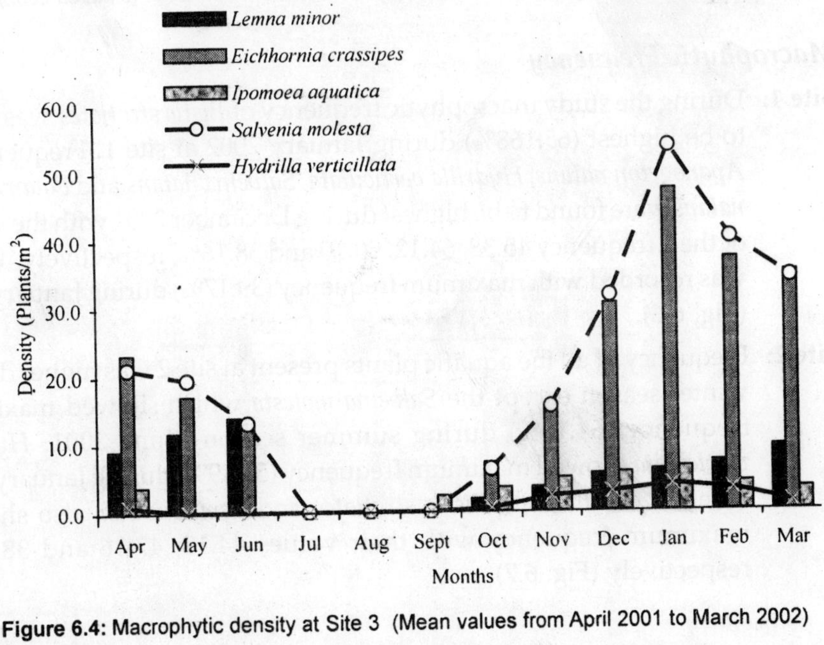

Figure 6.4: Macrophytic density at Site 3 (Mean values from April 2001 to March 2002)

Site 4: Site 4 shows the presence of only four species with *Eichhornea crassipes* and *Lemna minor* as the most dominant flora during most part of the study. Maximum density of *Eichhornia crassipes* (50.11 plants per m^2) was recorded during January 2002 when maximum density of *Lemna minor* (49.18 plants per m^2) and *Potamogeton pectinatus* (6.527 plants per m^2) were also recorded. Maximum density of *Salvenia molesta* (16.11 plants per m^2) was recorded during June 2001. No plants were recorded during July to September 2001 (Fig. 6.5).

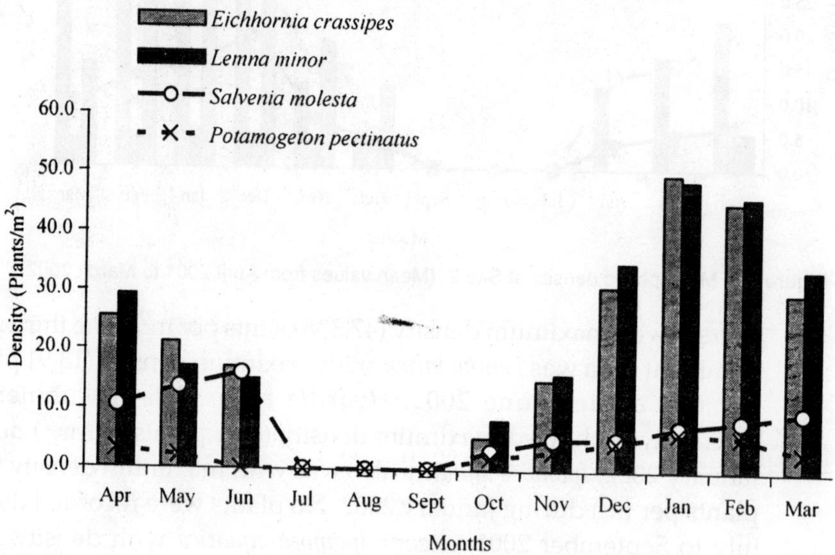

Figure 6.5: Macrophytic density at Site 4 (Mean values from April 2001 to March 2002)

Macrophytic Frequency

Site 1: During the study macrophytic frequency of *Pistia stratiotes* was found to be highest (65.168%) during January 2002 at site 1. Frequency of *Aponogeton natans, Hydrilla verticillata, Salvenia natans* and *Potamogeton natans* were found to be highest during December 2001 with the values of their frequency 45.38, 64.12, 50.10 and 38.16%, respectively. *Wolffia* was recorded with maximum frequency (39.17%) during January 2002 (Fig. 6.6).

Site 2: Frequency of all the aquatic plants present at site 2 was higher during winter season except the *Salvenia molesta* which showed maximum frequency (64.15%) during summer season—June 2001. *Hydrilla verticillata* showed maximum frequency (58.19%) during January 2002 when *Azolla pinnata, Pistia stratiotes* and *Lemna minor* also showed maximum frequency with their values 44.19, 47.16 and 38.19%, respectively (Fig. 6.7).

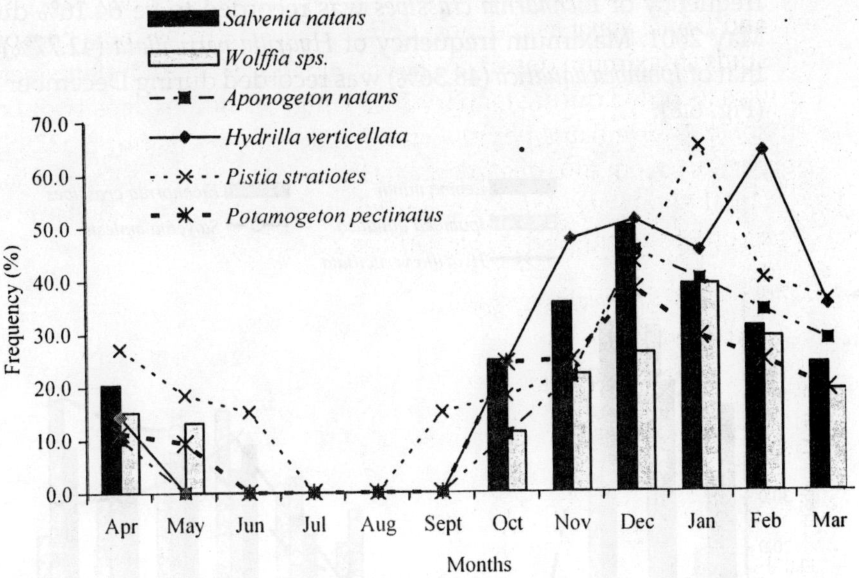

Figure 6.6: Macrophytic frequency at Site 1 (Mean values from April 2001 to March 2002)

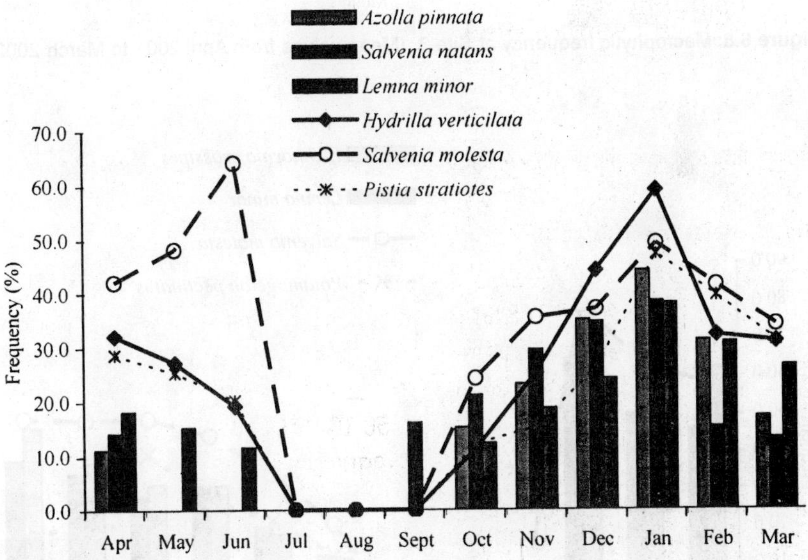

Figure 6.7: Macrophytic frequency at Site 2 (Mean values from April 2001 to March 2002)

Site 3: At this site, 5 plants were recorded out of which *Lemna minor* showed maximum frequency (64.98%) during June 2001. *Salvenia molesta* was also present with the same value of frequency (54.19%), which was maximum for this plant, and it was recorded in June 2001. Maximum frequency of *Eichhornia crassipes* was recorded to be 64.16% during May 2001. Maximum frequency of *Hydrilla verticillata* (42.77%) and that of *Ipomoea aquatica* (48.36%) was recorded during December 2001 (Fig. 6.8).

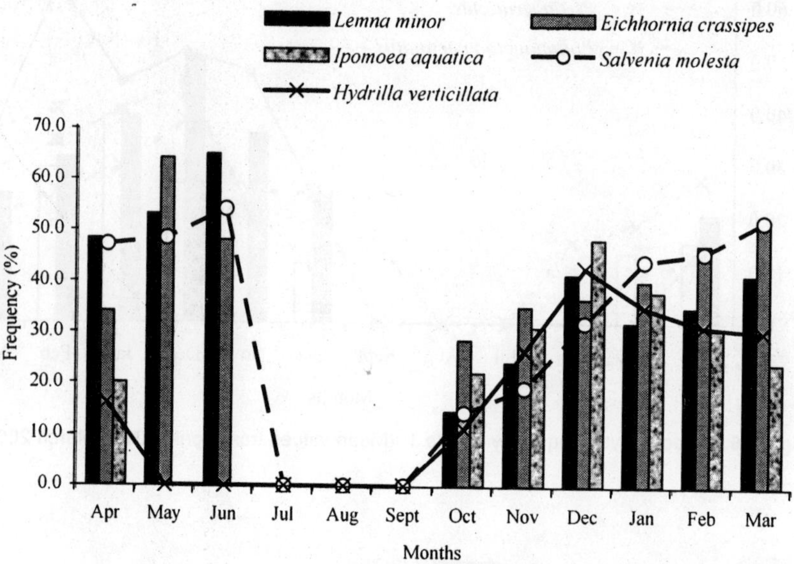

Figure 6.8: Macrophytic frequency at Site 3 (Mean values from April 2001 to March 2002)

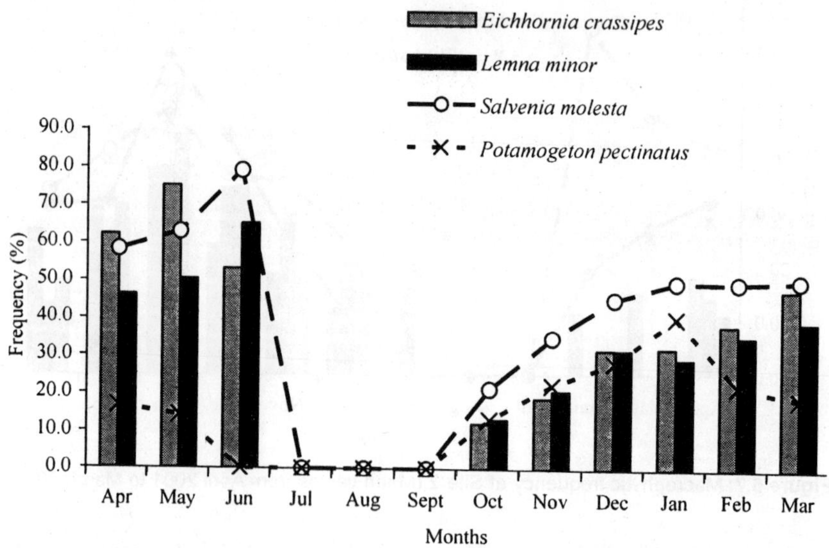

Figure 6.9: Macrophytic frequency at Site 4 (Mean values from April 2001 to March 2002)

Site 4: At this site, only four plants were recorded during the study. *Salvenia molesta* showed maximum frequency (79.13%) during June 2001. Maximum frequency of *Eichhornia crassipes* (75.15%) was recorded during May 2001 and that of *Lemna minor* (65.11%) was also recorded but in June 2001. The fourth plant *Potamogeton pectinus* showed maximum frequency (40.19%) during January 2002, however, this plant was absent from the site during June 2001 when all the other plants were with their maximum frequency (Fig. 6.9).

7

Quality of Water Sediments

Pollution load in a river not only affects the properties of water but the properties of sediments are also affected. The undesirable chemical components direct the composition of micro- as well as macroflora of the water bodies, thereby the organic components being added in the sediments is changed. Reduced microbial population delays decomposition of dead plant parts. Therefore, not only the dry and wet colour but also the texture of the water sediments changed. The properties of water are not static, rather it shows regular variation, as a result the properties of water sediments also change regularly. In addition to the mechanical properties, physico-chemical properties of the water sediments also show regular variation. Sick water sediments is a symbol showing that the water body is badly polluted. In order to learn the pollution load of the river Varuna, the soil sediments were also analysed.

❑ Mechanical Properties of Sediments

In the study of the properties of sediment, colour of the sediment in wet as well as in dry condition was examined. Composition of sediment was analysed which mainly consisted of the percentage of sand, clay and silt (Table 7.1) on the basis of which the textural class of the water sediment was determined. The properties like colour and texture of water sediments from all the four sites which were studied throughout the year (April 2001 to March 2002) are expressed in Table 7.2.

In the month of April, the colour of the dry sediment was light grey and light brown for the wet sediment at site 1 whereas site 2 showed the dark grey colour for dry sediment and dark brown for wet sediment. Site 3 and site 4 showed the same result as site 2. Texture of sediment was silt clay, same for all four sites, i.e. site 1, site 2, site 3 and site 4.

During May, the colour of the dry sediment was light grey and light brown for wet sediment at site 1. Site 2 and 4 showed dark grey and dark brown colour of the dry sediment and wet sediment, respectively. The texture of the sediment was same as in April for all the four sites—silt clay.

Colour of the dry sediment was light grey, olive grey, olive grey, dark grey at site 1, site 2, site 3 and site 4, respectively in the month of June. During this

Table 7.1: Mechanical composition of water sediments at various sites

Month	Components	Site 1	Site 2	Site 3	Site 4
April	Sand %	15.91	14.86	14.21	14.15
	Clay %	42.61	44.10	43.25	43.11
	Silt %	41.35	41.07	42.44	42.51
May	Sand %	15.11	14.61	13.25	14.31
	Clay %	43.25	42.72	42.68	41.79
	Silt %	41.96	44.25	43.05	44.68
June	Sand %	17.26	13.08	14.22	14.11
	Clay %	38.77	40.21	41.51	40.81
	Silt %	43.63	47.51	44.72	45.32
July	Sand %	19.06	12.92	15.71	17.35
	Clay %	30.51	37.52	34.12	35.26
	Silt %	48.91	50.61	48.65	48.65
August	Sand %	19.78	15.42	16.36	18.11
	Clay %	33.72	34.76	35.21	36.71
	Silt %	47.26	50.15	48.63	46.36
September	Sand %	18.52	14.31	15.11	17.96
	Clay %	31.52	56.19	33.71	35.12
	Silt %	50.11	48.87	51.25	47.51
October	Sand %	13.25	13.76	13.25	17.13
	Clay %	40.61	40.31	38.13	37.08
	Silt %	46.37	45.16	49.11	44.36
November	Sand %	13.81	13.02	14.15	14.25
	Clay %	41.51	42.15	40.56	40.11
	Silt %	44.33	45.25	45.78	45.37
December	Sand %	14.08	13.56	13.76	13.21
	Clay %	42.31	42.72	41.91	42.15
	Silt %	43.72	44.36	44.37	44.38
January	Sand %	13.76	14.11	13.21	13.86
	Clay %	42.51	42.29	42.46	42.68
	Silt %	43.22	43.71	44.15	43.12
February	Sand %	13.21	13.76	13.15	13.60
	Clay %	41.61	43.86	43.27	43.81
	Silt %	45.32	43.11	43.15	42.96
March	Sand %	12.98	13.41	14.27	14.12
	Clay %	42.51	43.51	43.81	43.82
	Silt %	45.16	42.72	42.66	42.11

Table 7.2: Colour and texture of water sediments at various sites

Month	Parameters		Site 1	Site 2	Site 3	Site 4
April	Colour	Dry	Light grey	Dark grey	Dark grey	Dark grey
		Wet	Light brown	Dark brown	Dark brown	Dark brown
	Texture		Silty clay	Silty clay	Silty clay	Silty clay
May	Colour	Dry	Light grey	Dark grey	Dark grey	Dark grey
		Wet	Light brown	Dark brown	Light brown	Dark brown
	Texture		Silty clay	Silty clay	Silty clay	Silty clay
June	Colour	Dry	Light grey	Olive grey	Olive grey	Dark grey
		Wet	Olive brown	Light brown	Light brown	Dark brown
	Texture		Silty clay loam	Silty clay	Silty clay	Silty clay
July	Colour	Dry	Olive grey	Light grey	Olive grey	Olive grey
		Wet	Olive brown	Light brown	Light brown	Light brown
	Texture		Silty clay loam	Silty clay loam	Silty clay loam	Silty clay loam
August	Colour	Dry	Olive grey	Light grey	Olive grey	Olive grey
		Wet	Olive brown	Olive brown	Olive brown	Light brown
	Texture		Silty clay loam	Silty clay loam	Silty clay loam	Silty clay loam
Sep.	Colour	Dry	Olive grey	Olive grey	Olive grey	Light grey
		Wet	Olive brown	Olive brown	Olive brown	Light brown
	Texture		Silty clay loam	Silty clay loam	Silty clay loam	Silty clay loam
October	Colour	Dry	Olive grey	Olive grey	Light grey	Light grey
		Wet	Olive brown	Olive brown	Light brown	Olive brown
	Texture		Silty clay	Silty clay	Silty clay loam	Silty clay loam
Nov.	Colour	Dry	Light grey	Light grey	Light grey	Light grey
		Wet	Olive brown	Light brown	Light brown	Olive brown
	Texture		Silty clay	Silty clay	Silty clay	Silty clay
Dec.	Colour	Dry	Light grey	Dark grey	Dark grey	Dark grey
		Wet	Olive brown	Light brown	Light brown	Dark brown
	Texture		Silty clay	Silty clay	Silty clay	Silty clay
Jan.	Colour	Dry	Light grey	Dark grey	Dark grey	Dark grey
		Wet	Olive brown	Light brown	Light brown	Dark brown
	Texture		Silty clay	Silty clay	Silty clay	Silty clay
Feb.	Colour	Dry	Light grey	Dark grey	Dark grey	Dark grey
		Wet	Light brown	Dark brown	Dark brown	Dark brown
	Texture		Silty clay	Silty clay	Silty clay	Silty clay
March	Colour	Dry	Light grey	Dark grey	Dark grey	Dark grey
		Wet	Light brown	Dark brown	Dark brown	Dark brown
	Texture		Silty clay	Silty clay	Silty clay	Silty clay

month the colour of wet sediment was olive brown at site 1, site 2 and site 3 showed light brown colour, while site 4 showed dark brown colour. Texture of sediment was silty clay loam for site 1 and silty clay for site 2, site 3 and site 4.

Colour of dry sediment was olive grey and light grey, olive grey, olive grey for sites 1, 2, 3 and 4, respectively in the month of July and August. The wet sediment colour was olive brown for site 1 in both the months, i.e. July and August, whereas, at site 2, the wet sediment showed light brown colour in July and olive brown in August. Site 3 also showed different colours of the wet sediment during July and August, i.e. light brown in July and olive brown in August. Light brown colour of the wet sediment was observed in both the months at site 4. Texture of the sediment was silty clay loam for all the four sites in both the months.

Olive grey colour of the dry sediment was observed at site 1 and 2 during the months of September and October. At site 3, colour of the dry sediment was olive grey during September and light grey during October. Light grey colour was observed at site 4 in September as well as in October. Olive brown colour of the wet sediment was observed at site 1 and site 2 during September and October. Wet sediment of site 3 showed olive brown colour in September and site 4 showed light brown colour in October. Light brown and olive brown colour was observed in the months of September and October, at site 3. Silty clay loam texture of the sediment was observed during September at all the four sites. In October, texture of the sediment was silty clay at sites 1 and 2 and silty clay loam at sites 3 and 4.

Colour of the dry sediment in November was recorded to be light grey at all the four sites, and that of wet sediment was olive brown at site 1 and site 4, likewise at site 2 and site 3 it was light brown. Texture of the sediment during November at all the sites was silty clay.

During December, colour of the dry sediment of site 1 was light grey and at all the remaining three sites—i.e. site 2, site 3 and site 4 it was dark grey. Wet colour of sediment was olive brown at site 1, light brown at sites 2 and 3 both, and at site 4 the colour was dark brown. Texture of the sediment during December was silty clay at all the four sites.

During January, colour of dry sediment was light grey at site 1 and dark grey at all the remaining three sites, that of wet sediment was olive brown at site 1, light brown at sites 2 and 3, and at site 4 it was dark brown. Texture of the water sediment of all the four sites was silty clay.

Colour of dry sediment during February was light grey at site 1 and dark grey at the remaining three sites; and that of wet colour it was light brown for site 1 and dark brown at all the remaining three sites. Texture of the water sediment of all the four sites was silty clay. During March also, colour of the water sediment for dry and wet conditions followed the same trend as February. Texture also remained the same at all the four sites and it was silty clay. Heavy metals settling in sediments of contaminated water was reported. Pollutants concentrating in the sediments have been also highlighted.

❐ Physico-chemical Properties of the Water Sediments

Study of physico-chemical properties of the water sediments was conducted at all the selected four sites in river Varuna. The analysis was done fortnightly. The sample of water sediments were collected from three points from each site, two points were located at cis and trans side of the river while the third from the mid-stream of the river. Expression of the results was done on monthly basis starting from April 2001 to March 2002.

pH

pH of the water sediments of the river was found to be higher at site 4, followed by site 3 and site 2, as an average the least pH was recorded at site 1 during most of the time, sometime pH of site 2 was found lower than site 1.

At site 1, pH of the water sediments of the river was minimum (6.8) during June and August 2001 and maximum (8.0) during April 2001. At site 2, the pH was found to be minimum (6.9) during July and August 2001. pH was maximum (7.9) during April 2001 at this site. At site 3, pH was recorded to be minimum (7.0) during August 2001 and it was found to be maximum (8.9) during the month of April 2001. At site 4, the minimum pH (7.2) was found during August and September 2001, it was maximum (9.0) of the water sediments of the river during April 2001 (Table 7.3).

Comparative study of all the sites show that in the river Varuna the minimum pH of water sediments (6.8) was recorded during June and August 2001 at site 1 and maximum pH (9.0) during April 2001 at site 4. Seasonally, pH was found to be highest during summer season. The value of pH was nearly uniform during rainy and winter seasons at sites 1 and 2, however, it was higher at sites 3 and 4 during rainy season as compared to winter.

Potassium

Potassium of the water sediments of the river was found to be higher at site 2, followed by site 1 and site 3, as an average the least potassium was recorded at site 4 throughout the study.

At site 1, potassium of the water sediments of the river was minimum (0.584 μg/g) during March 2002 and maximum (0.798 μg/g) during August 2001. At site 2, the potassium was found to be minimum (0.762 μg/g) during February 2002, and it was maximum (0.926 μg/g) during August 2001. At site 3, potassium was recorded to be minimum (0.460 μg/g) during March 2002 and it was found to be maximum (0.569 μg/g) during the month of August 2001. At site 4, the minimum potassium (0.440 μg/g) was found during April 2001 and maximum (0.491 μg/g) during September 2001 (Table 7.3).

Comparative study of the water sediments of the river at all the sites show that minimum potassium (0.440 μg/g) was recorded during April 2001 at site 4 and the maximum potassium value (0.926 μg/g) during August 2001 at site 2. Seasonally, potassium of the water sediments of the river was found to be higher during rainy season followed by summer and winter seasons at most of the sites.

Table 7.3: Physico-chemical properties of water sediments

	Apr	May	Jun	Jul	Aug	Sep	Oct	Nov	Dec	Jan	Feb	Mar
pH												
Site 1	8.0	7.5	6.8	6.9	6.8	7.1	7.1	7.3	7.3	7.4	7.6	7.8
Site 2	7.9	7.7	7.1	6.9	6.9	7	7.1	7.2	7.2	7.3	7.4	7.6
Site 3	8.9	8.2	7.4	7.1	7	7.2	7.3	7.3	7.5	7.7	8.1	8.5
Site 4	9.0	8.6	8.1	7.6	7.2	7.2	7.3	7.5	7.7	7.7	8.3	8.6
Potassium (µg/g)												
Site 1	0.59	0.613	0.685	0.721	0.798	0.756	0.695	0.631	0.6	0.59	0.596	0.584
Site 2	0.788	0.811	0.881	0.898	0.926	0.903	0.875	0.861	0.816	0.796	0.762	0.793
Site 3	0.471	0.498	0.509	0.531	0.569	0.55	0.511	0.505	0.499	0.49	0.485	0.46
Site 4	0.44	0.448	0.459	0.471	0.481	0.491	0.49	0.475	0.48	0.465	0.45	0.443
Sodium (µg/g)												
Site 1	0.51	0.496	0.48	0.471	0.46	0.471	0.478	0.481	0.48	0.49	0.493	0.485
Site 2	0.663	0.669	0.661	0.65	0.643	0.631	0.639	0.64	0.647	0.653	0.651	0.659
Site 3	0.209	0.199	0.189	0.183	0.173	0.17	0.178	0.184	0.19	0.195	0.191	0.203
Site 4	0.329	0.339	0.336	0.329	0.321	0.308	0.301	0.309	0.317	0.316	0.312	0.32
Calcium (µg/g)												
Site 1	2.557	2.413	2.292	1.905	1.764	1.826	1.961	2.04	2.183	2.251	2.031	2.398
Site 2	4.693	4.615	4.481	4.016	3.869	3.802	3.955	4.054	4.251	4.252	4.321	4.153
Site 3	5.493	5.406	5.255	5.2	4.814	4.731	4.802	4.886	4.951	4.981	4.917	5.052
Site 4	7.022	7.012	7.001	6.934	6.713	6.363	6.557	6.571	6.71	6.851	6.361	6.683
Phosphorus (µg/g)												
Site 1	0.065	0.064	0.07	0.06	0.054	0.053	0.057	0.057	0.059	0.06	0.059	0.061
Site 2	0.068	0.07	0.07	0.068	0.065	0.061	0.061	0.063	0.065	0.065	0.065	0.066
Site 3	0.102	0.106	0.098	0.092	0.087	0.085	0.085	0.088	0.09	0.091	0.089	0.094
Site 4	0.111	0.119	0.115	0.108	0.101	0.097	0.096	0.098	0.1	0.1	0.101	0.107
Total Nitrogen (µg/g)												
Site 1	0.159	0.169	0.161	0.153	0.14	0.138	0.141	0.145	0.149	0.15	0.147	0.152
Site 2	0.091	0.103	0.099	0.094	0.08	0.079	0.078	0.081	0.083	0.084	0.082	0.087
Site 3	0.06	0.067	0.066	0.059	0.051	0.046	0.046	0.049	0.05	0.053	0.049	0.054
Site 4	0.067	0.073	0.073	0.067	0.06	0.052	0.053	0.056	0.059	0.058	0.057	0.061
Organic Carbon (%)												
Site 1	0.461	0.469	0.463	0.446	0.438	0.435	0.439	0.441	0.441	0.439	0.44	0.452
Site 2	0.445	0.459	0.44	0.421	0.411	0.413	0.417	0.417	0.422	0.421	0.42	0.432
Site 3	0.71	0.715	0.711	0.702	0.691	0.685	0.688	0.691	0.693	0.692	0.692	0.701
Site 4	0.629	0.642	0.636	0.624	0.606	0.602	0.604	0.604	0.61	0.612	0.61	0.621

Sodium

Sodium of the water sediments of the river was found to be higher at site 2, followed by site 1 and site 4, as an average the least sodium was recorded at site 3 throughout the study.

At site 1, sodium of the water sediments of the river was minimum (0.460 µg/g) during August 2001 and maximum (0.510 µg/g) during April 2001. At site 2, the sodium was found to be minimum (0.631 µg/g) during September 2001, and it was maximum (0.669 µg/g) during May 2001. At site 3, sodium was recorded to be minimum (0.170 µg/g) during September 2001 and it was found to be maximum (0.209 µg/g) during April 2001. At site 4, the minimum sodium (0.301 µg/g) was found during October 2001 and maximum (0.339 µg/g) during May 2001 (Table 7.3).

Comparative study of the water sediments of the river at all the sites show that minimum sodium (0.170 µg/g) was recorded during September 2001 at site 3 and the maximum sodium value (0.669 µg/g) during May 2001 at site 2. Seasonally, sodium of the water sediments of the river was found to be higher during summer season followed by winter and rainy seasons at most of the sites.

Calcium

Calcium of the water sediments of the river was found to be higher at site 4, followed by site 3 and site 2, as an average the least calcium was recorded at site 1 throughout the study.

At site 1, calcium of the water sediments of the river was minimum (1.764 µg/g) during August 2001 and maximum (2.557 µg/g) during April 2001. At site 2, the calcium was found to be minimum (3.802 µg/g) during September 2001, and it was maximum (4.693 µg/g) during April 2001. At site 3, calcium was recorded to be minimum (4.731 µg/g) during September 2001 and it was found to be maximum (5.493 µg/g) during the month of April 2001. At site 4, the minimum calcium (6.361 µg/g) was found during February 2002 and maximum (7.022 µg/g) during April 2001 (Table 7.3).

Comparative study of the water sediments of the river at all the sites show that minimum calcium (1.764 µg/g) was recorded during August 2001 at site 1 and the maximum calcium value (7.022 mg/g) during April 2001 at site 4. Seasonally, calcium of the water sediments of the river was found to be higher during summer season followed by winter and rainy seasons at most of the sites.

Phosphorus

Phosphorus content in the water sediments of the river was found to be higher at site 4, followed by site 3 and site 2 and it was minimum at site 1 throughout the study.

At site 1, phosphorus in the water sediments of the river was minimum (0.053 mg/g) during September 2001. Maximum phosphorus content (0.070 mg/g) in the water sediments of the river at site 1 was found during June 2001. At site 2 the phosphorus was found to be minimum (0.061 mg/g) during September and October 2001. Phosphorus at this site was maximum (0.070 mg/g) during May and June 2001. At site 3, phosphorus was recorded to be minimum (0.085 mg/g) during September and October 2001 and it was found to be maximum (0.106 mg/g) during the month of May 2001. At site 4, the minimum phosphorus content in water sediments (0.096 mg/g) was found during October 2001 and maximum (0.119 mg/g) during May 2001 (Table 7.3).

Comparative study of all the sites shows that minimum phosphorus content (0.053 mg/g) in water sediments of river Varuna was recorded during September 2001 at site 1 and the maximum phosphorus (0.119 mg/g) during May 2001 at site 4. Seasonally, phosphorus content in water sediments of the river was found to be highest during summer season followed by winter and rainy seasons at all the sites.

Total Nitrogen

Analysis of total nitrogen in the water sediments of the river shows that the highest value was at site 1 and the lowest at site 3. The same value at site 2 was higher than that at the site 4 throughout the study.

At site 1, total nitrogen in the water sediments of the river was minimum (0.138 mg/g) during September 2001 and maximum total nitrogen content (0.169 mg/g) was found during May 2001. At site 2, the total nitrogen was found to be minimum (0.079 mg/g) during September and October 2001. Total nitrogen at this site was maximum (0.103 mg/g) during May 2001. At site 3, total nitrogen was recorded to be minimum (0.046 mg/g) during September and October 2001 and it was found to be maximum (0.067 mg/g) during the month of May 2001 in the river water. At site 4, the minimum total nitrogen (0.052 mg/g) was found during September 2001 and maximum (0.073 mg/g) during May and June 2001 (Table 7.3).

Comparative study of the water sediments of the river of all the sites shows that minimum total nitrogen (0.046 mg/g) was recorded during September and October 2001 at site 3 and the maximum total nitrogen (0.169 mg/g) during May 2001 at site 1. Seasonally, total nitrogen in the water sediments of the river was found to be highest during summer season followed by winter and rainy seasons at all the sites.

Organic Carbon

Analysis of Organic Carbon in the water sediments of the river shows that the highest value was at site 3 and the lowest at site 2. The same value at site 4 was higher than that at the site 1 throughout the study.

At site 1, organic carbon in the water sediments of the river was found to be minimum (0.435%) during September 2001. Maximum organic carbon content (0.469%) at this site was found during May 2001. At site 2, the organic carbon was found to be minimum (0.411%) during August 2001. Organic carbon at this site was maximum (0.459%) during May 2001. At site 3, organic carbon was recorded to be minimum (0.685%) during September 2001 and it was found to be maximum (0.715%) during the month of May 2001. At site 4, the minimum organic carbon (0.602%) was found during September 2001 and maximum (0.642%) during May 2001 (Table 7.3).

Comparative study of the water sediments of the river of all the sites shows that organic carbon was found to be minimum (0.411%) during August 2001 at site 2 and the maximum organic carbon (0.715%) during May 2001 at site 3. Seasonally, organic carbon in the water sediments of the river was found to be highest during summer season followed by winter and rainy seasons at all the sites, showing slight fluctuation.

8

Traditional Waste Water Treatment

Water treatment process has been required to be operated immediately after man realised that the water is not fit for consumption. Traditional waste water treatment is directed towards the treatment processes which include specially the reduction of suspended matters, biochemical oxygen demand, and bacterial concentration.

❒ Oil and Grease Removal

The terms 'grease' and 'oil' as used in waste water treatment denote a variety of materials, including fats, waxes, free fatty acids, calcium and magnesium soaps, mineral oil and other non-volatile materials that are soluble in water, and can be extracted by hexane from an acidified sample. In average domestic waste, grease constitutes 10% of the total organic matter. Dairy, laundry, garage-machine shop and oil refinery wastes also have high grease-oil content.

It is usually required to reduce the grease content of the industrial wastes below 100mg/litre before it is discharged to a municipal system. Under quiescent condition, some portion of the grease settles with the sludge and some floats to the surface, i.e. as scum, where it may be removed by skimming.

(a) ***Grease Traps and Grease Interceptors:*** These are used to collect grease and floating material from households, garages, restaurants, small hotels, hospitals, and the like. Owing to the danger of explosion or fire, motor oil, gasoline and similar light mineral oils should not be allowed to enter sewer systems.

Where the wastewater contains large amount of greasy kitchen waste, grease traps should be used. Commercial grease interceptors are also available for restaurants and smaller industrial establishments which are connected to public sewer systems.

(b) ***Grease Removal by Air-Aided Flotation (Flotation Units):*** Grease and finely divided suspended solids may be converted to floating matter by air or gas-aided flotation units with or without flotation aids.

Gas-particle Contact

The particles must be contacted by gas before floatation of the suspended solid is accomplished.

❒ Aeration Type Units

1. ***Aerated Skimming Tanks, Pre-aeration: (Aeration before primary treatment):*** This treatment also facilitates sedimentation and helps to refresh septic waste which—in combination with increased floating and suspended solid removal—improves the BOD reduction.

   For grease removal, 5 to 15 minutes' aeration, using 0.01 to 0.1 ft^3 per gallon (0.075 to 0.75 m^3 per 100 liters) of air is usually sufficient.
2. ***Manufactured Skimming Tanks:*** Pressure and vacuum flotation techniques generate air bubbles by reducing the pressure of supersaturated air waste mixture or by applying vacuum to the mixture. The liberated minute bubbles tend to form around and attach themselves to suspended particles in the waste. With this type of equipment, capital and operating costs are both relatively high. Therefore, this type of flotation unit is most popular for pretreatment of industrial wastes at the source—where the flow rate is less and the concentration is high.

❒ Pressure Type Units

This process consists of pressurising the wastewater with air, usually in a separate air-saturation tank, to 1-3 atm. and venting the tank to the atmosphere. This type of flotation involves high operating power costs.

❒ Vacuum Type Units

This process consists of saturating the waste water with air by aerating in a tank or by permitting air to enter on the suction side of the waste transfer feed pump. Under vacuum the solubility of air in the waste is decreased and air is released in minute bubbles. The rising air bubbles attach themselves to the solid particles in the waste, carrying them to the surface.

Because of the fairly high vacuum level involved, this type of flotation unit requires an expensive, air-tight construction.

❒ Skimming Devices

Scum collecting and removal facilities, including baffling are desirable ahead of the outlet weirs, on all settling tanks. Horizontal spraying with water under pressure may be employed to collect the scum for hand removal if no mechanical skimmers are installed.

❒ Square Settling Tanks

The straight scum baffle is installed ahead of the effluent weir-troughs and is submerged to a minimum depth of 18 inches (45 cm). Scum collectors usually move the scum towards the effluent side of the tank. Treatment plants are often equipped with hand-operated revolving slotted pipe skimmers installed horizontally across the tank ahead of the scum baffle. If the scum is to be removed mechanically, cross-collectors consisting of endless chains above the surface are used.

❐ Circular Settling Tanks

The circular scum baffle is installed ahead of the circular effluent weir-trough and is submerged to a depth of at least 18 inches (45 cm). Scum removal is usually performed by a radial arm skimmer, which is attached to and rotates with the sludge-removal equipment.

❐ Air Skimmers

They may be used to serve small treatment plants. They work on the same principle as airlifts. They are provided with a funnel type extension to collect the scum.

❐ Scum Disposal

The scum is generally collected in a separate sump, which can be provided with dewatering facilities. The scum is usually combined with the primary sludge and is disposed off by

(1) Digestion, yielding gas with high fuel value;
(2) By vacuum filtration or incineration; and
(3) By Burial.

❐ Soluble Organics Removal

Soluble organics are very harmful from the physico-chemical characteristic point of view for water as they directly affect other properties. Therefore, their removal is of utmost consideration.

❐ Treatment Characteristics

1. *Septic Tanks:* Septic tanks received raw sewage, allow it to settle and pass the relatively clear liquid on to the adsorption field which is the next stage of treatment. The remaining solids digest slowly in the bottom of the tank. They are inexpensive but, because of their incomplete treatment, they are suitable only for small flows.

   The anaerobic decomposition, which takes place in the absence of free O_2 in the septic tank, is a slow process. In order to maintain practical detention times the reactions cannot be carried far. Therefore, the effluent is often malodorous; containing a multitude of microorganisms and organic materials, it requires further decomposition. Efficiency of this method is 15 to 25% reduction of BOD and removal of 40 to 60% suspended solids.

2. *Imhoff Tanks:* The process that takes place in this tank is similar to septic tank, except that the tank is so designed that the flow through the upper chamber is separated from the lower digestion chamber, resulting in a two-storey tank. The upper compartment acts only as a settling zone where little or no decomposition takes place. This chamber often remains aerobic, and its effluent has a lower BOD than the effluent from a septic tank. In the lower chamber, anaerobic digestion takes place. Since the effluent is of a higher quality, the process is suitable for communities and small cities.

Additional treatment for further decomposition of the organic matter in the effluent is required. The efficiency of Imhoff tank is 25 to 35% reduction in BOD and 40 to 60% removal of suspended solids.

❒ Suspended Solids Removal (Settling or Clarification)

Suspended solids removal from wastewater is traditionally by settling tanks or clarifiers—either longitudinal or circular. In either case, the design for domestic wastes is often based on overflow rate, a term relating to the flow per surface area which is equivalent to the settling velocity of the critical particle. The removal of suspended solids (in wastewater treatment) is almost always accomplished by gravity settling. These units are known as settling tanks, clarifiers or sedimentation tanks. Removal of the solid matter from the liquid is accomplished by allowing the (heavier) solids to sink to the bottom of the tank while the clear liquid flows over weirs. If the size of the solid particles does not change and if they are not influenced by their neighbours, then the process can be called *discrete particle settling*. However, in most wastewater applications, the solids do undergo some flocculation with their neighbours—and the process must thus be classified as *flocculent settling*.

An ideal settling tank is shown in (Fig. 8.1). The basin is divided into four zones: the inlet, outlet, sludge and settling zones. In the inlet zone, the incoming flow is assumed to be evenly distributed so as to afford uniform horizontal flow through the settling zone. The outlet zone is used to collect the effluent for discharge over the weir. It is assumed that no settling occurs in these two zones. The sludge zone is provided for the collection and storage of the solids. The settling zone is where the actual gravitational separation is assumed to occur.

❒ Types of Settling Tanks

The most common type of device is the circular clarifier. This clarifier is relatively inexpensive to instal and requires low maintenance. The central pier holds the sludge scraping mechanism which pushes the sludge to a central well from which it is pumped or drawn out by gravity.

The rectangular tank has the disadvantage of requiring submerged gears and chains, and these need more maintenance. It has often been suggested, however, that the rectangular tank has superior settling characteristics for similar overflow rates. One design that eliminates the problem of submerged moving parts involves

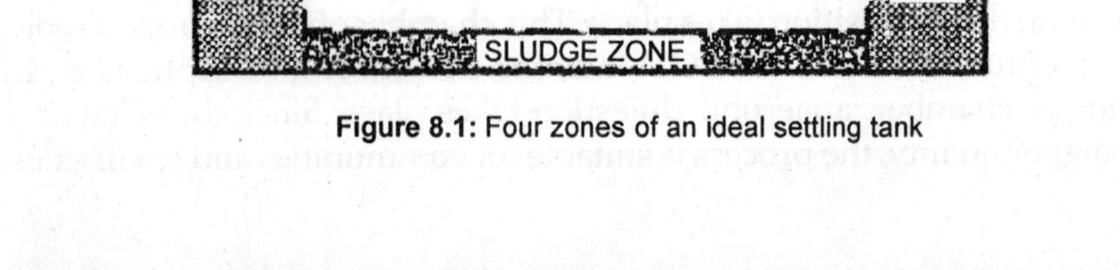

Figure 8.1: Four zones of an ideal settling tank

the use of a trolley with a submerged squeegee which moves back and forth, thus scraping the sludge to the sludge well. Settling tanks provide for the removal of material, which floats as well as sinks. Primary clarifiers are all equipped with scum removal mechanism which forces the solids to a separate well.

Tube Settler

Its basic aim is to provide a great increase in the surface area and thus increase the efficiency. Tube settlers have been used successfully in water treatment plants for alum sludge and in final clarifiers for attaining greater suspended solids removal.

❒ Ocean Dumping

The concept of an infinite ocean (a mile and a half—2.4 km—deep on the average around the whole world) has given way to the concept of the ocean as a limited and valuable resource. The resource must be protected—otherwise it may go the way of Lake Erie and the Baltic Sea, and the irreversible oceanic life systems may create an uninhabitable environment for people as well as for marine life.

Methods of Disposal

The most common method of ocean disposal is to thicken the waste to a sludge or solid and submerge it to the point of disposal. When the waste is toxic it is usually put in containers and dropped in more remote places. There are so-called approved areas on the East gulf and Atlantic coasts for waste disposal.

The sludge can also be disposed-off at sea through a pipeline—either by diluting the digested sludge with the treated effluent from the plant or by reducing the solids content and allowing the solids to be diffused into the ocean together will the sewage. The advantage in removing the solids and digesting them in advance of disposal is that this treatment results in as much as 80% reduction of volatile solids and as much as 99% removal of coliform and pathogenic bacteria. It appears that a low-cost alternative to ocean disposal is the disposal of digested sludge on croplands.

Ecology

The environment of the sea is changed by the addition of wastes. Some authorities argue that organic compounds and nutrients benefit the sea and cite statistics on increased yield of fish per acre per year. The classical concept is that as long as oxygen is not depleted to the point at which fish are killed, wastes can be safely disposed-off in the sea. Neither the level of dissolved O_2 nor the waste assimilating capacity of a body of water can be a safe criterion because both have serious limitations in a changing environment. In addition to the quantity of wastes there is a question as to the synergistic effects of many chemicals (synthetic) being discharged into the ocean.

Abstracts appearing regularly in the journals of water pollution control give a vivid picture of the need for stricter regulations for ocean dumping as well as in pollution abatement on a world scale.

❐ Conventional Sewage Treatment Plants

Conventional sewage treatment plants can probably be best identified by what they do not achieve, namely nutrient removal, demineralisation and removal of trace organics. Therefore, the conventional plant's performance is usually measured by reductions in suspended matter, biochemical oxygen demand (BOD), and bacteria.

Conventional Sewage Treatment Processes

Processes found in conventional plants include:

(1) Pretreatment

(2) Settling

(3) Chemical treatment

(4) Biological Oxidation

(5) Disinfection

(6) Sludge conditioning and disposal processes.

Selection of Specific Processes

Selection of specific processes and plant design must take into consideration the existing and potential regulatory standards; plant operators' requirements and availability; existing and projected sewage flow; the flow pattern and waste characteristics; climate, topography and availability of land; plant location within community; and all aspects of cost. Land availability and wise plant layout are two basic considerations.

Pre-Treatment Activities

To protect pumping equipment, control and monitor instruments, and to avoid clogging filters, chemical feeders, valves and overflow devices, physical pretreatment processes are routinely included in all plants. Pre-treatment equipment includes screens, grinders, skimmers and grit chambers. Flow equalisation is also considered to be a pretreatment process. Equalisation can assist in controlling hydraulic overloads that may occur during some period of the day and can also balance the incoming waste strength.

Precipitation (Settling)

Settling processes are used to remove settlable solids by gravity settling either prior to or after biological or chemical treatment and in-between multiple-stage biological or chemical treatment steps. The solids are accumulated at an underflow withdrawal point by mechanical scrapers in larger tanks, whereas smaller and some older systems have a hopper bottom for solids collection. Solids move down the sloped tank bottom by gravity in hopper bottom tanks. Both circular and rectangular tank shapes are used. A rectangular or square tank makes more efficient use of land area and can save construction costs by nesting units and using common walls. Settling tanks are commonly designed on *overflow rate*, the unit volume of flow per unit of time divided by the unit of tank area (gallons per day per square foot).

Chemical Treatment

Traditional chemical precipitation uses either iron or aluminium salts to form a floc which is then settled. Lime also clarifies. Suspended solids reduction up to 85% can be accomplished in this process. The accumulated chemical sludge is removed by gravity flow or pumping to conditioning or disposal or both. The chemicals and sewage are flash-mixed in a mixing tank that has only a few minutes' detention time followed by 30 to 90 minutes' detention in a flocculation tank, which is slowly agitated to aid in the growth of floc. Thus, settling follows the flocculation tank.

Biological Oxidation

Two basic techniques—the fixed bed and fluid bed—are utilised in conventional biological treatment. The trickling filter employs a fixed bed of stone or plastic packing materials to provide a surface for the growth of the zooglea, bacteria and other organisms. The intermittent sand filter and the spray irrigation systems are other examples of the fixed-bed technique.

The various activated sludge processes and sewage lagoons are fluid-bed systems. The activated sludge process uses mechanical aeration and return of a percentage of the active sludge to the process of influent. Lagoons or stabalisation ponds and the oxidation ditch do not routinely waste sludge, but multipond systems may have recirculation. Septic tanks and Imhoff tanks combine, in a single tank, for the settling and biological oxidation processes.

❐ Activated Sludge

Processes that use continuous agitation and artificially supplied aeration of settled sewage, together with recirculation of a portion of the active sludge which settles in a separate clarifier back to the aeration tanks, are classified as activated sludge processes. There are variations as to detention time, method of mixing and aeration and the technique of introducing the waste and recirculated sludge into the aeration tank.

❐ Trickling Filters

These are the most common treatment units used by municipalities to provide aerobic biological treatment. They are classified by the hydraulic and organic loading applied. Sludge from the final clarifier is usually recirculated to a point ahead of the primary settling tank. Single-stage and multistage filter arrangements are both utilised because there are many recirculation schemes and many options of intermediate settling between multistage filters. All returned sludge from the intermediate and final clarifiers that is not wasted (excess) is returned ahead of the primary settling tanks.

❐ Lagoon and Oxidation Ponds

The lagoon refers to a pond of engineering design that receives waste which has not been settled or exposed to biological oxidation prior to entering the lagoon. Simplicity is the main feature of the raw sewage lagoon. The oxidation pond, as opposed to the raw sewage lagoon, receives an influent that has undergone primary treatment. The maturation pond provides a final, polishing treatment step that follows some form of secondary treatment. The oxidation pond may be mechanically aerated to improve treatment and reduce pond size. There are many applications for lagoons and ponds, ranging from complete treatment of raw waste to polishing of secondary plant's effluents.

❒ Septic Tank

It continues to serve as the wastewater disposal system for millions of household and for numerous small industries. The system combines settling and anaerobic surface disposal, usually by open jointed tile under drain network. Since the septic tank almost always operates without power, an automatic siphon is used for dosing by discharging the chamber contents each time the level reaches a fixed point.

Imhoff Tank

A two storey tank uses the upper chamber for settling and the lower chamber for sludge digestion. It can be followed by additinal process steps to improve the quality of the plant effluent. The intermittent sand filter furnishes additional treatment to an Imhoff tank effluent.

Selection of the sand filters to be dosed is usually a manual operation controlled by valves. 3 to 4 inches (7.5-10 cm) of sand is normally laid over about 6 to 12 inches (15-30 cm) of gravel. Tile under drains collect the effluent, which is discharged to the receiving waters. Uniform distribution of flow to the sand filters is important and is usually achieved by distribution or by a rotary arm distribution device.

Disinfection

Conventional treatment plants use chlorination as the final treatment process to reduce the concentration of bacteria. Pre-chlorination, performed on the plant influent, is used if the incoming sewage is septic or if the flows are low and the holdup time in the plant is such that the waste will become septic. Pre-chlorination is usually at a fixed dosage, and a residual chlorine level is not maintained. For post-chlorination 15 to 30 minutes detention time in a baffled, closed tank to prevent short circuiting and dissipation of the chorine is provided. Chlorination is not frequently used to reduce the BOD in the plant effluent. Ordinarily, a combined chlorine residue between 0.2 and 1 mg per litre is the target for the final effluent.

Sludge Treatment

The settled solids material from the various treatment processes is called sludge. For the excess quantities of sludge to be disposed-off economically and with a minimum of objection, the raw sludge is digested and dewatered. Controlled digestion reduces the quantity of complex organic materials, increases the number of ultimate sludge disposal alternatives and decreases the undesirability of the sludge.

Sludge Storage

Excess quantities of activated sludge and sediments from primary, intermediate and final clarifiers are routed through the steps of mixing, digestion, dewatering and/or conditioning.

Some form of short term storage is essential to prevent overloading, regulate sludge flow to the digesters and allow collection and mixing of the sludge. Some plants mix in some final effluent with the sludge (in the mixing tank) to improve its thickening characteristics. Storage tank should be open to avoid gas buildup in the tank.

Sludge Thickening

Gravity thickening in a deep circular open tank is frequently used ahead of anaerobic digestion; polyelectrolyte have also been used but their use is not widespread. Air floatation thickening of activated sludge is an alternative. Dissolved or diffused air and, in some cases, a coagulant are used to float the sludge to the surface where it is removed by a mechanically driven skimmer. The effluent draw-off near the tank bottom is combined with incoming plant influent and passes through the treatment cycle.

Sludge Digesters

Anaerobic digestion is more common than aerobic digestion because the anaerobic process does not require an air supply and generally produces enough gas to provide digester with fuel for heating. It can be classified as low rate, high rate and secondary units. The low-rate system merely holds the sludge for long periods (30 days or more). The high-rate system employs some form of mixing and heating to accelerate digestion and, consequently, has shorter detention periods (10 to 20 days) and can accommodate increased solid loadings. The high rate unit is typically followed by a larger secondary digester that furnishes stratification of supernatant and sludge.

Aerobic sludge digestion requires an extensive air supply to maintain a dissolved oxygen surplus in the digester. Aerobic tanks have the advantage of not being subject to upsets and of producing a more treatable supernatant but the costs of air make the operating cost of aerobic digestion higher than that of anaerobic digestion.

Sludge Conditioning

Eluciration and chemical addition are the two sludge conditioning alternatives. Conditioning is an intermediate process between primary and secondary anaerobic digesters and also improves dewatering on digested sludge. Iron and aluminium salts and lime are the most popular chemicals for conditioning.

Eluciration is the washing of suspended sludge held in suspension by air or by stirring. It reduces the alkalinity and makes the sludge more filterable. Single and multitank (countercurrent) eluciration are both used. The single tank system uses repeated washing of the sludge, whereas in the countercurrent system the fresh wash water is added to the last sludge tank.

Sludge Dewatering

Rotating drum vacuum filters serve as the conventional sludge dewatering equipment. The filtrate is returned to the plant influent and the sludge cake is disposed-off. Sludge drying beds are common in smaller plants for disposal. Weather conditions are an important controlling factor when open drying beds are used. Drying beds have under-drain networks of tile fields laid in sand and gravel. The discharge from this network should be disinfected if it is not returned to the treatment plant. Sludge treatment and disposal are usually carried out in separate treatment plants.

9

ADVANCED WASTE WATER TREATMENT

Advanced waste water treatment basically deals with the removal of nutrients, minerals and trace organics in addition to the reduction of suspended solids, BOD, and bacterial content of the waste water. However, the advanced waste water treatment process can further be designated as modified traditional or conventional waste water treatment processes.

❒ Oil and Grease Removal

Oil Source

The two principal sites of oil waste are at the oil field and at the oil refinery. At the former, drilling techniques frequently involve the use of water under pressure to bring oil to the surface with the drilling mud being removed from the drill hole.

At the refinery nearly all the sources of oil wastages are the result of spills. The prime sources of spills are at the loading and unloading sites. These areas should be separately sewered with provisions for separating the oil from the surface water run off.

Many other sources of oil reach the environment due to man's activities. Many are related to the transportation of oils. The machine tool industry uses considerable volumes of oil for both lubrication and cutting. In the steel industry fabricated metals frequently are dipped in oil to prevent rust during storage. Numerous natural sources of oils also exist.

Properties of Oils

Mostly the oils are insoluble in water and majority of these are lighter than water—thus, they float on its surface. The oils creating the greatest problems are those the density of which is very close to that of water. They separate from the water very slowly. The soluble oil may be naturally soluble but generally are rendered soluble or miscible owing to man's activities.

❐ Treatment

Chemical

Chemicals may be added to improve the separation of oils the density of which is very close to that of water or to oils that are slightly soluble. As a general rule, oils are rendered less soluble under both extreme acidic, and extreme basic conditions. Most commonly sulphuric acid (H_2SO_4) is used; however, lime at a pH of 8.4 has also been shown to be effective.

Truly soluble oils are difficult to render insoluble with acids or bases alone and chemical coagulation at an appropriate pH is usually required. Studies show that alum in the range of pH 8.0-9.0 and ferrous sulphate ($FeSO_4$) in the pH range of 8.0-10.0 are effective in coagulating soluble oil. Soda ash (Na_2CO_3) is generally utilised to raise the pH to the desired level, since it is more difficult to control the pH in this range with lime.

In the interest of recycling, a system is there that recovers both the chemicals added and the oil separated. In this system, Ferric chloride ($FeCl_3$), lime, ferrice sulphate [$Fe_2(SO_4)_3$] and a polymer are added to the oily liquid waste. The precipitated sludge containing the oils is treated with sulphuric acid at 90 °F (32.2 °C) which releases the oil from the sludge. This oil is then separated and reused, whereas the ferric sulphate is also reclaimed from the sludge.

Physical

Insoluble oils lighter than water may be separated easily in a settling tank provided with an adjustable skimming weir. These oils readily float to the surface and the depth of the weir is adjusted according to the amount of oil in the water. Insoluble oils heavier than water can be recovered in a settling basin provided with a bottom sludge separator. All coagulation techniques use the settling principle so that oil may be removed by plain settling with appropriate sludge removal.

For coagulated solids, filtration through various media is practiced. Sand provides a satisfactory filter medium but diatomaceous earth is more commonly used. Continuous centrifuging for the separation of the oils from the water may also be practiced, but this is an expensive technique.

Dispersed air floatation is also effective in separating the oil from water. This has been practiced both with and without prior chemical coagulation. In some instances, it is difficult to breakdown the foam after it has carried the oil from the water. Dispersants may be used to breakdown the foam so that the oil may be properly disposed-off.

Disposal

Ultimate disposal of the oil frequently creates a problem. Occasionally the reclaimed oil may be reprocessed in a refinery. In other instances, reclamation is uneconomical. Disposal on land has been practiced but proper precautions must be made to prevent the oils from contaminating the groundwater. Up to a limit, soil microorganisms are capable of breaking down oil and rendering it inoffensive. Facilities for burning the waste oil are also available. Problems may arise owing to the differing volatilities of the various oils collected.

❐ Typical Treatment System

In a typical combination treatment system for soluble and insoluble oil removal the soluble oils are precipitated by coagulants, elevated pH and coagulant aids. Both the soluble and insoluble oils are separated in the combination, floatation and settling tank. Proper application of chemical treatment methods can result in satisfactory separation and removal of oil from liquid wastes.

❐ Soluble Organics Removal Using Special Aerators

(a) ***U-tube Aeration Systems:*** The U-tube concept was introduced to aerate water in a water treatment plant. The U-tube technique is simple as it uses no moving parts for achieving increased aeration. It consists of an air feeder and of a vertical U-shaped flowpath (Fig. 9.1). Water enters on one side of the U-tube and flows downward underneath the baffle and back up the other side. Air is injected just below the surface of the incoming stream. The U-tube system operates above atmospheric pressure due to the hydrostatic head of the liquid. The dissolved oxygen saturation concentration is thereby temporarily increased, resulting in an increased rate of oxygen transfer into the DO-deficient water. This method of aeration

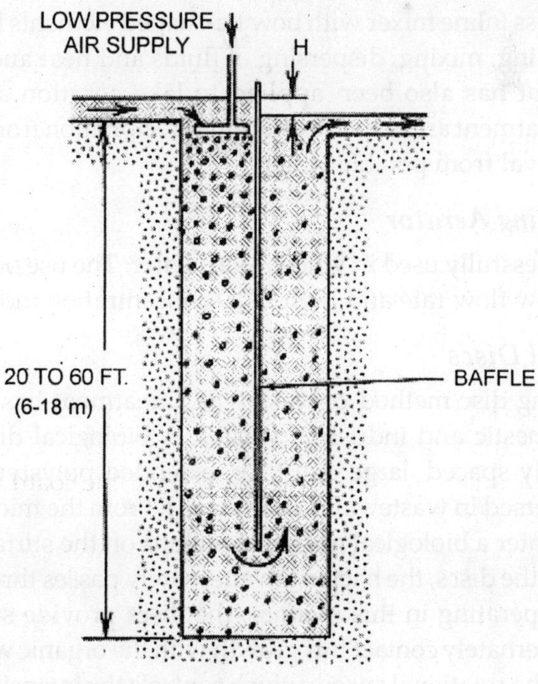

Figure 9.1: U-tube aeration system

is particularly well suited to raise the dissolved oxygen concentration in moving streams.

(b) ***Jet Aerators:*** Jet aeration is used for treating organic wastes. The air is introduced through a water jet injector for the purpose of treating sewage. The jet type aerator is also used on industrial wastes from the manufacture of organic intermediates, polymers and fibres. The jet aerator achieves aeration by utilising both bubble diffusion and hydraulic shear. It functions using a high velocity stream of water through an orifice to draw the air in, that is supplied (by blower) to the throat of the orifice.

The aerators would normally be located near the basin bottom with the wastewater being recirculated by a centrifugal pump through the jet orifice. The compressed air is sheared by the liquid and fine air-water dispersion is released at the bottom of the basin. Studies of jet aerators indicate that an optimum relationship exists between air and water flow rates in order to achieve maximum oxygen transfer efficiency. The oxygen transfer efficiency of these aeration systems depends on the compressor to pump power ratio and on the submergence depth.

Draft Tube Type Air Lifts

Several variations of these air lift devices are available for air motivation, water pumping, mixing and aerating.

Air Lift with Bow Tie Mixer

A motionless inline mixer with bow tie-shaped elements has been successfully used for blending, mixing, dispersing of fluids and heat and mass transfer. This mixing concept has also been applied to lake aeration and in several other wastewater treatment areas such as sulphur precipitation from hydrogen sulphide and iron removal from potable water.

Self-Priming Aerator

It was successfully used in vinegar fermenter. The use of self-priming aerator is limited to low flow rate and high BOD concentration industrial wastes.

Biological Discs

The rotating disc method of wastewater treatment has been used to treat a variety of domestic and industrial wastes. A biological disc unit consists of a series of closely spaced, large diameter, extended polystyrene discs which are partially immersed in wastewater and rotated. From the microorganisms present in the wastewater a biological growth develops on the surface of the discs. With the rotation of the discs, the bacterium alternately passes through the wastewater and the air. Operating in this manner, the discs provide support for microbial growth and alternately contact this growth with the organic wastewater pollutions and with air. The rotational speed, which controls the intensity of contact between the biomass and the wastewater, and the rate of aeration can be adjusted according to the organic load in the wastewater. The residence time of the wastewater in the disc sections and the rotational speed of the discs determine the BOD removal efficiency of the unit.

Staged operation is especially advantageous when the wastewater contains several types of biodegradable materials because staging enhances the natural development of different biological cultures in each stage.

Suspended Solids Removal

Filtration Enhanced by Applied Chemical Coagulants

Completely clear filter effluents can only be obtained by feeding chemical coagulants such as alum, iron or polyelectrolytes to the wastewater prior to filtration. Addition of chemicals to the clarifiers reduces the solids load on the clarifier overflow effluent filters. When chemical coagulation takes place it results in 100% solid removal including colloidal particle sizes as small as 0.05 micron. When stain free filter effluent is required, chemical feeds are absolutely necessary. Without chemical feeds the suspended solids removal efficiency of filters generally ranges from 50-80%. However, the addition of chemical coagulants increases the solids load and therefore filter runs will be shortened. Surface type and ultra high rate filters are drastically affected in this regard.

In multilayered or in-depth filter applications the influent must contain flocculant particles. The larger flocs are removed by the coarse filter layers and the smaller particles are removed by the fine (sand) layers below.

Selection and Operation of Filters

There are cyclic variations in waste flows. Surge basins are needed as part of the filter system design to accommodate these flow variations. When domestic waste is mixed with industrial waste (which contains metals or inorganic salts e.g. Cu, Al, Fe, etc.) the filtration characteristics of secondary effluents may be enhanced. In such cases fewer colloidal particles and larger or stronger flocs can be expected, allowing for high-rate filtration or surface type micro-screening with removal efficiencies of over 80%, without the use of additional chemical coagulants.

General Design Parameters

Pressure filters—horizontal or vertical—are recommended in wastewater applications because they handle higher solids loads, higher pressure heads, and are more compact and less costly.

Diatomaceous Earth Filters

The diatomaceous earth filter is available both as a vacuum and as a pressure filter. Diatomaceous earth filtration produces clear effluents with removal efficiencies of over 90%. Colloidal substances are usually not removed (as in the case with ordinary granular filters) unless coagulants are added. Coagulants are seldom added to diatomaceous earth filter influents because this drastically shortens the runs.

Microscreening

It has been applied in domestic water treatment, sewage wastewater filtration and in filtering industrial effluents. Microscreening utilises a special woven metallic or plastic filter fabric, which is mounted on the periphery of a revolving drum provided with continuous backwashing. Wastewater enters through the open upstream end of the drum and flows radially outward through the microfabric leaving behind the suspended solids. The stainless steel wire cloth used in microstrainers has generally been more successful.

Moving Bed Filters

Moving bed filters have also been applied to wastewater filtration. The filter involves the intermittent removal of the most heavily clogged portion of the sand filter media from the filtration zone without interrupting the filtration process.

The moving bed filters is reported to be able to remove 70 to 90% of the suspended solids from secondary, primary, and rural wastewaters.

Because the intermittent movement of sand creates periodic upsets in the effluent quality and suspended solid content, these units are classed as rough filtration or straining devices.

Membrane Filtration

Surface filtration at relatively high pressures and low flow rates through thin films or through dynamically formed membranes is termed membrane filtration. In membrane filtration, the 0.45m membrane is used in evaluating filter effluents for trace concentrations of colloids, colour, metallic oxides and bacteria.

In ultrafiltration, tighter or less porous ultramembranes are capable of rejecting high molecular weight soluble organic substances, but not salt. In hyperfiltration, specially prepared membranes affect the salt, soluble organic matter, colloidal or soluble silica and phosphate removal at 80 to 95% efficiency.

All of the membrane processes described are considered to be final polishing filters, with the common property of affecting particulate removals in excess of 99%. In so doing, they tend to foul easily, and their flux flow rate tends to decline. Therefore membrane filters must be protected from fouling by pretreatment of the feeds utilising coagulation and rough filtration.

❑ Nutrients and Inorganics Removal

Chemical Precipitation of Phosphorus

Phosphorus that occurs in wastewater is principally in the form of orthophosphate ion, polyphosphates or condensed phosphates and organic phosphorus compounds. The predominant phosphorus species is orthophosphate, which can occur in varying chemical forms, depending on the pH of the wastewater.

Many ionic forms are effective in the precipitation of phosphorus from solution such as aluminium, calcium and iron. Ionic Iron, Aluminium and Calcium form insoluble precipitates with phosphorus.

❐ Electrodialysis of Phosphorus and Nitrogen

Electrodialysis is a membrane separation process utilising a voltage impressed across cation-anion membrane pairs to remove dissolved solids from aqueous solutions.

The electrodialysis processes are used for the removal of specific ions of nitrogen and phosphorus from wastewater effluents. Pretreatment requirements and ion selectivity are especially important for this application. The nutrients and other dissolved salts removed from the feedstream are concentrated in a waste stream leaving the electrodialysis cell. The overall nutrient removal process must provide for treatment or disposal of this concentrated waste stream. Many wastewater effluents are characterised by extreme variability in composition and flow.

Biological Nitrification and Denitrification

The two successive steps involved in the biological removal of Nitrogen are:

(1) Nitrification; and

(2) Denitrification.

Nitrification

The oxidation of ammonia to nitrate is a two step process. Initially ammonia is oxidised to nitrite by *Nitrosomonas*—an aerobic autotrophic bacteria—and the second step is the conversion of nitrite to nitrate accomplished by the *Nitrobacter*.

The overall nitrification reaction is represented as:

$$2NH_4^+ + 3O_2 \rightarrow 2NO_2^- + 2H_2O + 4H^+ \quad (1)$$

$$2NO_2^- + O_2 \rightarrow 2NO_3^- + 2\,NO_3^- \quad (2)$$

$$NH_4^+ + 2O_2 \rightarrow NO_3^- + 2H^+ + H_2O \quad (3)$$

The optimum pH for nitrification is 8.4 and 90% of the optimum rate can be achieved in the 9.8 to 8.9 range.

Denitrification

Biological denitrification is achieved under anaerobic conditions by heterotrophic microorganisms that utilise nitrate. The specific denitrifying capacity of these microorganisms may differ, with some only reducing nitrites to molecular nitrogen and some achieving reduction of both nitrates and nitrites to molecular nitrogen.

❐ Nitrogen Removal by Ion Exchange

The process that can be successfully employed for the removal of relatively high concentrations of nitrogenous compounds from the industrial wastewater discharges, especially by the ammonium nitrate fertiliser industry, is none other than ion exchange process.

The principle of ion exchange is used widely to soften or demineralise water and to recover useful by-products from industrial wastes. Ion exchange is defined as a reversible interchange of ions between a liquid and a solid, involving no radical change in the structure of the solid. A number of natural materials such as zeolites as well as certain synthetic resins can exchange ions with ions in water solution.

❐ Chemical Treatment

Neutralisation Agents and Processes

Neutralisation means the restoration of the hydrogen (H^+) or hydroxyl (OH^-) ion balance in solution, such that the ionic concentrations of each are equal. Conventionally, the notation pH describes the hydrogen ion concentration present in a given solution, i.e.

$$pH = -\log_{10} [H+]$$

where, $[H^+]$ = hydrogen ion concentration, g mol per litre

At neutrality, the concentration of hydrogen and hydroxyl ions is equal.

The physical well-being of all forms of life depends on not only the absolute value of pH but on the frequency of pH variation of environmental waters as well.

Common Neutralisation Reagents

The hydrogen or hydroxyl ion imbalance present in a given waste effluent must be countered by the addition of a material that will restore the ion balance. Thus, if the waste effluent is acidic, i.e. its pH is less than 9.0, a reagent having basic characteristic must be blended with the waste to achieve neutrality.

Lime as a Neutraliser

Chemical lime is produced by the calcinations of high quality limestone to produce either high calcium quicklime or dolomite quicklime. They are further treated to produce their hydrated counterparts. The difference in chemical composition between the two types of quicklimes result in varying reaction rates and reactivities when these materials are used to treat the same wastewater.

Lime as neutralising reagent is normally supplied in slurries or as a dry feed along with water to small agitated holding containers that overflows to the neutralisation process. The chemical reactions associated with hydrated limes will depend on the type of acid being neutralised:

$$H_2SO_4 + Ca(OH)_2 \rightarrow CaSO_4 \downarrow + 2H_2O$$

$$2H_2SO_4 + Ca(OH)_2 + MgO \rightarrow CaSO_4 + MgSO_4 \downarrow + 3H_2O$$

Limestone

Limestone ($CaCO_3$) is an effective means of neutralising waste acids. The process involves the flowing of the waste acids (mixture of HCl and H_2SO_4) through a bed of limestone granules. The main reason for decreased reliability is the contamination of the limestone by materials such as oil and grease.

Caustic

Sodium hydroxide (Caustic) ranks about equal in popularity with lime as a neutralising agent. Although it is more expensive than lime, its reaction characteristics and handling convenience are factors behind its widespread use.

The efficacy of NaOH, particularly in solution form, is virtually instantaneous. Ease of delivery to the neutralisation process is another advantage. However, NaOH solutions are corrosive.

The neutralisation reactions depend on the acid being neutralised:

$$2\,NaOH + H_2SO_4 \rightarrow Na_2SO_4 + 2H_2O$$

$$NaOH + HCl \rightarrow NaCl + H_2O$$

$$NaOH + HNO_3 \rightarrow NaNO_3 + H_2O$$

Ammonia

It is not a prime neutralising reagent. It is the most toxic of all the alkaline neutralising reagents and is expensive too. It finds widespread use in the petroleum industry but the most serious disadvantage is that it produces ammonium salts, which, in turn, supply nutrients (nitrogen) for algal growth.

Generally, when large volumes of waste are to be treated, lime will be the reagent of choice but for the small wastewater treatment plant, a single tank filled with caustic solution by a local chemical supplier is the logical selection.

Acidic Reagents

Although five acids—H_2SO_4, HCl, HNO_3, SO_2, and CO_2—have been listed for possible use as reagents, sulphuric acid, especially 93.2% H_2SO_4, is the most popular. It is the cheapest, and in highly concentrated solutions, and it is also very efficient.

HCl and HNO_3 are more costly than H_2SO_4 and are highly corrosive, requiring special materials for construction. CO_2 and SO_2, besides being relatively expensive, must also usually be dissolved in the wastewater to produce carbonic acid and sulphurous acid, respectively.

❒ pH Control

The pH control problem is the most demanding in the entire spectrum of industrial process control. In order to cope with the chemistry of the process, an exhaustive investigation must be undertaken of the characteristics of the material to be treated to determine the measurable ion load on the process. It is important to know how much the pH of the treatable material varies, the frequency with which the load changes and the representative titration curves at various ion loadings. The titration data obtained will reflect the difficulty of the control problem and will show whether the control problem becomes more or less severe with ion loading. Ion loading is high when the solution pH is far from neutrality. A strong acid or base is a compound that is completely dissociated in aqueous solutions. A buffered aqueous solution is one that resists a change in its hydrogen ion concentration when either an acid or alkali is added to the solution. The buffered solutions were prepared with HCl and potassium acid phthalate ($KHC_8H_4O_4$).

Reagent Addition Requirements

Reagent addition requirements can be handled in diverse ways, depending on the process loads (flow of wastewater to be neutralised) into the neutralisation facility and the variation of the hydrogen or hydroxyl ion concentration—or both—in that flow. It should be recognised that because of the logarithmic nature of the pH measurement, a pH change of one unit is a ten-fold change in load. Thus the consequences of flow variations in waste streams can be relatively minor in comparison to ion concentration variation.

The choice of equipment to deliver reagents to the process under automatic control includes a metering device or a control valve. Metering devices as a choice for reagent delivery are very accurate; however, delivery range ability capability is limited to about 10 to 1. This means that for pH variations greater than $\pm$ 0.5 they will cycle or be inadequate. When pH load variations are minor (0.2 or less) and flow variations are less than 5 to 1, the choice of a metering pump is sufficient.

Control valves have limited range ability. In this category there are two types of internal plug forms. They are the linear and the equal percentage throttling characteristics.

Disinfection

Disinfection ideally should kill not only all pathogenic bacteria but also the viruses in the water. Sterilisation is not always necessary. The removal of contaminants that impart colour and objectionable taste and odour to the water improves the water's palatability. These contaminants are usually present in such low concentration that their detection and identification is often difficult. Few disinfection treatment techniques are successful in accomplishing the objectives of disinfection coupled with colour, taste, and odour removal. Ozonation is the most effective technique in this regard.

Ozonation

Ozone is an unstable triatomic allotrope of oxygen. It is a powerful oxidising agent, having the highest oxidation potential of all commonly used oxidising agents (Table 9.1).

It effectively destroys most organic compounds in the water, thereby controlling odour, taste and colour. The bactericidal action of ozone efficiently destroys bacteria and viruses in wastewater treatment effluents. The oxidation products of ozonation are usually non-poisonous and biodegradable.

Ozone is generated on the site of application from dry air or from oxygen in an electric discharge field generator. There are basically two ozone generator designs—the plate and the tube types.

Table 9.1: Oxidation Potentials of Chemical Disinfectants

Disinfectant	Oxidation Potential (Volts)
Ozone	2.07
Permanganate	1.67
Hypobromous acid	1.59
Chlorine dioxide	1.50
Hypochlorous acid	1.49
Hypoiodous acid	1.45
Chlorine gas	1.36
Oxygen	1.23
Bromine	1.09
Hypochlorite	0.94
Chlorite	0.76
Iodine	0.54

The disinfection is faster with ozone and less influenced by pH and temperature variations than with chlorine.

The ozone concentration needed for disinfection is dependent on the chemicals and contaminants in the water and on the concentration of microorganisms.

Heat Treatment

Prolonged heating, especially under pressure, is effective in killing most bacteria and viruses. It is similar to pasteurisation and rarely used on a large scale.

Ultraviolet Radiation

The irradiation of water by ultraviolet light kills bacteria and viruses in the water. This bactericidal action of ultraviolet light is most effective in the wavelength range of 250 to 260 mm. The disinfection is carried out by passing the water between batteries of powerful mercury vapour lamps.

The water must be pretreated to remove its colour and turbidity. Ultraviolet disinfection introduces no bactericidal chemicals into the water and, therefore, it can immediately be recontaminated after it has passed through the germicidal lamp.

Lime Treatment

Lime treatment is primarily for water softening so as to remove Ca and Mg salts. By the addition of lime or soda ash the calcium salts are precipitated as calcium carbonate and the magnesium salts as magnesium hydroxide.

When excess lime is used, leading to pH values in excess of 9 and adequate settling time is allowed, the lime treatment also has bactericidal effect because pathogenic bacteria do not survive in strongly alkaline water.

Miscellaneous Disinfection Processes

Ultrasonic waves with a frequency of approx 40,000 Hz kill both bacteria and spores. Metal ions, e.g. Cu, Hg and Ag, are also effective bactericides in minute concentrations. This action of metal ions is called Oligo-dynamic action. The application of this method has been limited to small scale specialised cases of treatment such as the water treatment in the food and beverage industry.

❐ Advanced Wastewater Treatment Unit

Advanced wastewater treatment plants usually consist of several unit processes operating in series. Each unit process represents an additional treatment step on the way to a treated, reusable effluent. By combining differing unit processes, almost any purity of effluent can be attained to meet the ultimate use of the treated wastewater.

The treatment processes can be broken down into categories according to the degree of treatment required. Advanced treatment plants are designed to have high treatment efficiencies, i.e. to produce water suitable for reuse or for non-polluting disposal. One of the most widely used indicators of treatment efficiency is BOD (Biochemical Oxygen Demand). Organic material usually exerts the largest component of BOD and, thus, BOD removal is a direct measure of organic material removed from the wastewater. Another important parameter is phosphate removal. Phosphates promote the growth of algae and plants. Such growth ultimately leads to anaerobic and polluted conditions.

The common categories of treatment level are primary, secondary and tertiary and their combinations such as the physicochemical treatment which combines primary and tertiary processes. Conventional treatment usually consists of the primary (suspended solids removal) and secondary (BOD reduction) steps, while advanced treatment refers to specialised or tertiary processes.

Secondary Equivalent (80 to 90 per cent BOD Reduction)

Conventional primary and secondary treatment implies a primary stage of settling followed by biological treatment of a trickling filter or of the activated sludge process type. The biological stage is usually followed by another settling step and sludge disposal is by incineration, biological digestion or landfill.

Primary-Secondary Wastewater Treatment

Sludge treatment is an important part of this system. Sludge from the primary clarifier gravity is thickened. The biological sludges are more difficult to concentrate and can be thickened by floatation. The sludges can be conditioned by heat treatment to prepare them for the final dewatering step which can be done by vacuum filtration. Finally, the organic sludge with a moisture content of 60 to 75 per cent can be further compacted into an inert and harmless ash by incinerators which need no supplemental fuel except during startup if the sludge concentration is high enough.

Pure Oxygen

Conventional secondary treatment usually involves an extensive aeration step in which the wastewater is mixed with a bacterial seed. The use of pure oxygen makes the aeration steps more efficient by carrying out the entire process in oxygen-rich environment.

Moving Carbon Bed Absorption

The wastewater—after suspended solids removal—flows through beds of activated carbon, which absorbs a large portion of the soluble organic molecules. This is a physicochemical treatment process which does not rely on bacteria for the degrading of organic matter. For industrial wastewaters, in which no suspended solids are present, the coagulation-flocculation step can be deleted and the water can be treated only with activated carbon.

Phosphate Removal

These processes produce an effluent with 80 to 90% BOD reduction, together with phosphate removal, by inserting chemical and physical treatment steps either in place of or in addition to the secondary treatment. The quality of effluent produced is often suitable for reuse in industry. The processes are generally more specialised and must be selected and designed for the specific wastewater influents to be treated and for the effluents required.

Lime Precipitation of Phosphorus

This is a phosphate precipitation system which is a modification of the primary settling step in a primary-secondary treatment plant. The raw wastewater is mixed with lime and flocculated to precipitate the phosphate in the form of an insoluble calcium salt. The lime tends to soften the water. The lime can be reclaimed from the sludge by incinerating the solids. The process is reported to provide between 80% and 95% phosphate removal together with substantial BOD removal.

Ferrous Precipitation of Phosphorus

Metal ion such as ferrous converts the soluble phosphate in the wastewater into an insoluble form. A polyelectrolyte flocculants is used to help settle out the phosphate complexes in the primary settling basin. The process itself is capable of removing from 70 to 80% of the influent phosphate. In combination with biological treatment, removals as high as 90% have been observed.

The ferrous chloride, a waste from steel plants, is economical if it does not need to be transported far from its source. This process also reduces the BOD load on the secondary treatment units. Corrosion resistant sludge handling equipment is required due to the ferrous sludge. The chemical sludge produced is not compatible with all methods of dewatering and the chloride ion content of the effluent is increased as a result of this treatment process.

Alum and Ferric Precipitation of Phosphate

The metal salts (alum or ferric) are added to the secondary effluent, producing phosphate precipitates that are trapped in the granular media filter. Periodic backwashing of the filter yields a waste phosphorus sludge that is uniformly mixed in an equalisation tank and is then recycled proportional to the plant influent flow rate back to primary settling basin. The waste sludge acts to absorb more phosphorus and thereby reduces the phosphate load on the filters.

Wet Air Oxidation

The wet air oxidation process treats the sludge by oxidising the organic material while the sludge is still in a water solution or suspension. It can treat the sludge from the digester and improve its dewatering characteristics. Usually, both raw and digested sludge can be treated by this process and the need for chemical additives to improve dewatering is eliminated.

Thermal Treatment for Sludge

Heat treatment of sludge is done to facilitate dewatering. After the sludge has been conditioned with heat and pressure, it has a lower COD and can be readily dewatered without chemical in a decanting and vacuum filter unit. The sludge is ground and pumped through a heat exchanger into a reactor where it is held for 30 to 60 minutes while steam heats it to 380 °F and maintains a high pressure. The system is a continuous process, and the high temperature sludge leaving the reactor is used to heat the incoming sludge. There are no chemical additives required to make the treated sludge compatible with vacuum filtering.

Physicochemical Treatment Process

In physicochemical treatment the two most important unit processes are chemical coagulation and adsorption on activated carbon. Coagulation is similar to phosphate removal methods as metal ions are added to the wastewater flow. Flocculation utilises polyelectrolyte to form the heavy organic floc which easily settles out. Activated carbon is a product of the combustion of some type of carbonaceous material (bituminous coal; coconut shells) at a high temperature in the absence of oxygen. This char has large surface area which accounts for the carbon's great adsorptive capacity.

Granular carbon is used in the form of a bed in the treatment. The wastewater flows through this bed much like a sand filter. Organic molecules are attracted by the carbon and adsorbed on its surface. When the carbon becomes loaded with the adsorbed molecules and loses its adsorptive ability, it is removed from the system and regenerated.

Following pretreatment—which includes screening and grit removal—a coagulant such as lime is added and mixed. Part of the lime coagulant dosage needed can be supplied by re-calcifying the sludge in a furnace. The supernatant from the clarifier passes through a multimedia filter of sand and anthracite coal to remove the remaining suspended solids. The activated carbon beds remove refractory colloidal and also some of the soluble organic molecules. After disinfection with chlorine the treated effluent can be discharged. The removal efficiencies of this type of plant are 97% to 99% of organic material and 85% to 99% of phosphorus.

Hydrolysis-Adsorption Process

This process uses lime to hydrolyse large organic molecules into small enough to be adsorbed by activated carbon. This process can operate at 90% BOD and COD removal efficiencies and at 97% phosphorus removal. The physicochemical treatment plants are not subject to upsets and loss of efficiency from toxic wastes and they can make use of many recycle methods to recover some of the chemical treatment agents. Their land requirements are also less and phosphorus removal is part of their total treatment performance.

Sludge disposal problems associated with the large quantities of chemicals used can be reduced by the recycling of calcium in the sludge. Heavy metals are also precipitated into the lime sludge.

Tertiary Equivalent

A tertiary treatment plant removes practically all solid and organic contaminants from wastewater, thereby producing potable water directly from the sewage.

10

EXSITU TREATMENT OF RIVER WATER

According to analysis of river water, water sediments and biodiversity of river Varuna, the river appears to be highly polluted. At one or the other research site many of its parameters have even crossed the threshold level (e.g. oil & grease, DO, BOD, COD, Phosphate, Total hardness, Cr, Pb, etc.) or are about to (e.g. Total solids, Heavy metals such as Ni, Zn, Cu, etc.). In addition to above, neither any treatment plant is operating to control the pollution nor is any planning for it in progress. Though, it is a great loophole in the GAP (Ganga Action Plan) and a matter of question for the MoEn (Ministry of Environment and Forests). But to protect the natural resources is a matter of public concern and our fundamental duty. Therefore, measures to control the pollution of river Varuna was taken into consideration.

During the study (from April 2001 to March 2002) the water samples at the research sites were found to be most polluted during summer season, especially in the month of April 2001. In correlating the obtained data, it was found that, owing to extreme hot climate, traces of rainfall and extremely low relative humidity, water content of the river decreases. The effluents being added to the river remains unchanged. The rate of evaporation of water from the lotic water body would also have been higher. As a result, the the river becomes concentrated during summer, and most polluted during this season—especially in April.

❐ Recommended Methods for Treatment of Polluted Water

Chemical Methods

Various methods of treatment of waste water and sludge have been studied by different workers. Process of heavy metal removal and its recovery from the sewage sludge has been experimented in Japan. Radio tracer technique was used to study the removal of Ba and Sr by titanate powder by a group. Removal of Ni (II) and Mo (VI) from water by adsorption technique has been studied. Different types of wetlands constructed for waste water treatment in Europe have been disucssed at length allover. Extensive use of artificial wetlands in field of nutrient and heavy metal removing from the polluted water is being planned. Problems in the path of disposal of industrial effluents is also gaining importance, as the ignorance of which may lead to total failure of the project. This would not only destroy the labour and budget input but also the precious time of the great brains involved in the process. Activated sludge treatment for industrial waste is also being tried for a variety of waste. Use of metal chelators has been studied for the treatment of metal and heavy metal affected pollutants. Disinfection of organic pollutants by photo-oxidation in sunlight has also been reported.

Ionising radiation technique is also being considered at a smaller scale in laboratory for the sludge treatment. Different methods for treatment of the distillery effluents are being tried.

Removal of heavy metal by Perth sands has been done, with positive recommendation by phallus process. Removal of Ni(II) from polluted water using decaying leaves has been studied in laboratories.

Importance of aeration in treatment was studied by a group of scientists which showed that the presence of oxygen in the medium promotes the process of treatment, except in the case of reducing reactions. Percolation through sand column and red mud column had been found useful for nutrient removal and also as antimicrobial.

A very interesting difference in lotic and lentic ecosystem regarding automatic pollutant removal has been reported. Some pollutants are automatically removed in the river system during flow, while in ponds they are arrested.

Anaerobic fixed beds packed with Fe containers were reported for phosphorus removal from domestic waste.

❒ Biological Method

Vegetated submerged beds can also be used to eradicate pollution. Watershed management is being discussed allover.

Water hyacinth is being employed for treatment of waste water of different sources. High rate algal pond has been used for the treatment of waste from tomato concentrate industry. Same had been used for treatment of effluent of a fertiliser factory and also for phosphate removal.

Eichhornia has been found to accumulate fluorides. Impact of aquaculture of *Lemna* on the quality of sewage is being studied by many scientists. The same on river water and in pond is reported. Nitrogen metabolism and Cu toxicity of phytoplankton was studied by a group; the has also reported the nitrate removal by macrophytes. Nitrate and phosphate uptake by duckweed in sewage lagoons has also been reported.

Macrophytes have been reported to absorb heavy metals from polluted water. In another study, Cu, Zn, Cd and Pb absorption is reported by some selected macrophytes growing as a resistant plant in the polluted medium. Similar studies around metal smelter have been conducted.

Duck Weed Water Treatment design for wastewater treatment has been recommended to be an inexpensive water treatment plant. Diatoms have been studied for pollutant accumulation in lotic system. Role of denitrifying bacteria in nitrate removal from aquatic system is also being explored. Cd accumulation by an alga *Scendesmus* and by moss has been reported by a team of scientists.

❒ Use of Aquatic Plants

Multidimensional studies for the use of aquatic plants have been conducted by many scientists. They have explored the further use of aquatic macrophytes in various aspects. If the aquatic macrophytes are being used for aquaculture, as phytoremediation, then what shall be the fate of the recovered plants was a question before the scientists. Efforts are being made for the proper, safe and judicious use of such plants, by the scientists in laboratory. Also, the safe disposal of the treated water is needed. Water hyacinth to be used for paper making is also advocated. Development of artificial rivers by recycling of the waste water after treatment has been suggested by a group of scientists in the dry areas. Water hyacinths also adsorb various chemicals on their surface which can be extracted and can be used as important raw material in various industries. Production of N_2O gas from floating plants in brakish water was suggested.

Use of aquatic vascular plants for pollution scrubber, food and energy production has been explored. Aquatic weeds have been recommended as foodstuff or fodder for the animals on the basis of protein content and the nutritional explained.

Derivation of energy from the plants used in wastewater treatment was explained as also a constructive alternative. Energy generation from all such wastes including agricultural waste has been explained. Methane gas is an ecofriendly fuel and methods of production of this gas from decomposition of aquatic plants are studied.

❒ Laboratory Experiments

Laboratory experiments were conducted to control pollution of the river Varuna. As a result of complete one year study of physico-chemical properties and heavy metal analysis of river water and the water sediments at selected study sites, in addition to the meteorological analysis for year 2001 and 2002, April was found to be the most polluted month for the river. Meteorological variables of April 2001 and 2002 (Table 10.1) also closely resemble; therefore, April 2002 was selected as pollution treatment month in the present study.

300 litres of water sample were collected from each of the polluted site (site 2, site 3 and site 4) during the second half of April 2002 at around 8 a.m. in the morning. Samples were collected from site 2 on 21 April (Sunday), from site 3 on 25 April (Thursday, the Mahavir Jayanti) and from site 4 on 28 April (Sunday). Spot testing of some of the parameters was applied and remaining parameters were analysed in laboratory on the same day, i.e. on the day of collection to get the initial reading.

Table 10.1: Meteorology of April 2002

Parameters		Value
Rainfall (mm)		Trace
Temperature (^oC)	Maximum	38.68
	Minimum	22.49
Relative Humidity (%)		66.62

The laboratory experiments consisted of basically two treatments (Fig. 10.1):

- Chemical; and
- Biological.

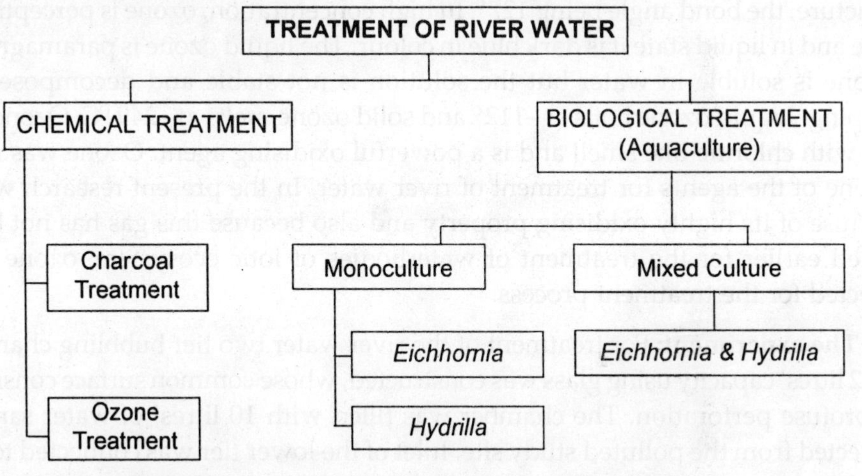

Figure 10.1: Laboratory Experiments for River Water Treatment

Chemical Treatment

Charcoal Adsorption Process: Charcoal is an amorphous form of carbon. It is obtained by heating of wood, bone or sugar in limited supply of air through the process called destructive distillation. It is black, soft, porous and brittle solid which ignites at temperature 340 ºC. It is heavier than water having specific gravity 1.5 but floats on it as it has the capacity to hold air in its pores. It is a bad conductor of heat and electricity and a good absorbent. Generally, charcoal contains about 10-12% amorphous carbon, which is deposited on a porous framework consisting of calcium phosphate. Charcoal is further activated by heating it for a long time in a current of steam as this process removes most of the absorbed gases.

Charcoal is the most reactive of the forms of carbon and its activity is due to its enormous surface area. For this purpose it has been used in gas masks or respirators. It has also been used in decolourising of sugar syrups and potable water purifiers.

Since its potential has not ever been tested in the case of river pollution treatment; the study of river pollution treatment by charcoal was conducted.

The experiment: 50 litres of water sample was maintained in a 100 litre aquarium. In the setup 10 small packets of tissue paper containing 1 gm activated charcoal each were sinked with the help of weight. Initial reading of all the variables was recorded and the same was analysed on 24 hour basis for 5 days. Maximum pollutant removal was recorded on the fourth day. Thus, the value of variables on the 4th day is expressed in the records.

The same experiment was conducted for water samples of all the three polluted sites. Results obtained from the samples of site 2, site 3 and site 4 are expressed in Appendix II.

Ozone Treatment: The molecule of ozone possesses an open chain bent structure, the bond angle being 127°. In high concentration, ozone is perceptively blue and in liquid state it is dark blue in colour. The liquid ozone is paramagnetic. Ozone is soluble in water but the solution is not stable and decomposes on keeping. Liquid ozone boils at –112° and solid ozone melts at –249 °C. Ozone is a gas with chlorine like smell and is a powerful oxidising agent. Ozone was used as one of the agents for treatment of river water. In the present research work, because of its highly oxidising property and also because this gas has not been tested earlier for the treatment of waterbodies of lotic ecosystem, ozone was selected for the treatment process.

The experiment: For treatment of the river water two tier bubbling chamber of 12 litres' capacity using glass was constructed, whose common surface consisted of profuse perforation. The chamber was filled with 10 litres' of water sample collected from the polluted study site. Inlet of the lower tier was connected to the modified Siemen-Halske Ozoniser, which consisted of earthed cast iron box and a number of aluminium rods surrounded by glass cylinders cooled by water. The rods are charged to high potential and the air passing through the annular space gets ozonised.

Ozonised gas was passed through the bubbler which comes above, crossing the water in the form of minute bubbles. Change in the parameters was recorded hourly and the maximum pollution removal was found after 6 hours' treatment, thus, only this value is expressed in the record.

This experiment was conducted for all the three polluted sites; results obtained from the samples of site 2, site 3 and site 4 are expressed in Appendix II.

***Biological Treatment*:** Many plants have been used for the treatment of waste water coming from different sources; the important plants are *Lemna, Spirodella, Wolffia, Eichhornia, Pistia, Salvinia, Hydrilla,* etc. On the basis of study of quality and quantity of pollutants in river water at the various study sites, in addition to the biological parameters *Eichhornia crassipes* and *Hydrilla verticillata* were the two macrophytes selected for the biological treatment process.

The biological treatment process consisted of two basic experiments

- Monoculture; and
- Mixed culture.

The experiment: Three aquaria of 100 litre capacity were prepared for the study of river water treatment for each polluted site through biological process. Thus, in total, 9 aquaria were maintained by 50 litre of water sample, three samples from each site. Healthy plants of *Eichhornia crassipes* and *Hydrilla verticillata* were collected from the agro pond of Institute of Technology, B.H.U. In the first aquarium of each site only *Eichhornia*, which is a floating macrophyte, was cultured. In the second aquarium of each site only *Hydrilla* was cultured—which is a submerged macrophyte; and in the third aquarium of each site *Eichhornia* and *Hydrilla* both were maintained. Constant density of the aquatic macrophytes (*Eichhornia* and *Hydrilla*) was maintained in all the aquaria.

Change in various parameters in all the nine aquaria was recorded on alternate days and the process of analysis continued till 18 days for each culture. Water loss in aquaria due to evaporation and transpiration were maintained by distilled water. Maximum pollutant removal was recorded during 16th day of inoculation in nearly all the aquaria. So, the level of various parameters recorded only on 16th day is expressed in the record (Appendix II).

During the treatment studies selected parameters were analysed. Only those characters were selected which were found to be much higher in the water samples of the study sites. The same variables were analysed in all the five treatments such as charcoal treatment, ozone treatment, monoculture *Eichhornia* treatment, monoculture *Hydrilla* treatment as well as in the mixed culture of *Eichhornia* and *Hydrilla*. The selected parameters were:

- Acidity
- Nitrate
- Phosphate
- DO
- BOD
- COD
- Total Solids
- Total Hardness
- Oil & Grease
- Cd
- Cu
- Cr
- Ni
- Pb
- Zn

❑ Result of the Treatment Processes

Acidity

Out of the five treatments of water sample, the charcoal treatment shows reduction of acidity by 64.647%, by ozone treatment 99.088%, *Eichhornia* monoculture by 51.706%, *Hydrilla* monoculture by 49.636% and mixed culture of *Eichhornia* and *Hydrilla* showed the reduction of acidity by 74.971% (Table 10.2).

The reduction of acidity was found to be highest by ozone treatment followed by the mixed culture of *Eichhornia* and *Hydrilla* (Fig. 10.2).

Nitrate

Activated charcoal treatment showed nitrate reduction by 62.949% and ozone treatment by 88.908%; similarly nitrate reduction by monoculture of *Eichhornia* was 70.418%, by monoculture of *Hydrilla* 41.426%, and by the mixed culture of *Eichhornia* and *Hydrilla* to 81.942% (Table 10.2).

Maximum reduction was found by ozone treatment and it was closely followed by the mixed culture of *Eichhornia* and *Hydrilla*.

Phosphate

Charcoal showed phosphate reduction by 76.063% and ozone treatment by 94.129%; similarly phosphate reduction by monoculture of *Eichhornia* was 87.273%, by monoculture of *Hydrilla* 66.521%, and by the mixed culture of *Eichhornia* and *Hydrilla* by 92.680% (Table 10.2).

Maximum reduction was found by ozone treatment and it was closely followed by the mixed culture of *Eichhornia* and *Hydrilla*.

Dissolved Oxygen (DO)

Charcoal treatment showed that DO of the water sample reduced by 18.322%, in ozone treatment the DO increased to about more than 3-fold of the original value and the increase was recorded to be 386.392%. The monoculture *Eichhornia* treatment showed increase of DO by 48.569%, monoculture of *Hydrilla* showed the increase of DO by 189.109%, and the mixed culture of *Eichhornia* and *Hydrilla* showed the increase of DO by 232.719%.

Increase in DO was recorded in all the treatments except in the charcoal treatment. Maximum DO increase was recorded in ozone treatment followed by the mixed culture of *Eichhornia* and *Hydrilla* treatment.

Biological Oxygen Demand (BOD)

Charcoal treatment showed increase in BOD by 23.700% but BOD was decreased by ozone treatment by 95.831%. Monoculture of *Eichhornia* showed reduction in BOD by 17.579%, that of monoculture of *Hydrilla* showed reduction by 36.133%, and mixed culture showed reduction by 59.729% (Table 10.2).

Only the charcoal treatment experiment showed increase in BOD while in all the other experiments reduction was recorded; maximum reduction by ozone treatment followed by the mixed culture of *Eichhornia* and *Hydrilla* treatment.

Chemical Oxygen Demand (COD)

Charcoal treatment showed increase in COD by 20.737% but COD was decreased by ozone treatment by 94.976%. Monoculture of *Eichhornia* showed reduction in COD by 26.690%, that of monoculture of *Hydrilla* showed reduction by 44.146%, and mixed culture showed reduction by 53.469% (Table 10.2).

Only the charcoal treatment experiment showed increase in COD while, in all the other experiments, reduction was recorded; maximum reduction by ozone treatment followed by the mixed culture of *Eichhornia* and *Hydrilla* treatment.

Total Solids

Reduction in total solids was recorded by 55.598% in charcoal treatment while the ozone treatment showed increase in total solids by 41.324%. Reduction of total solids by 36.132% was recorded in monoculture of *Eichhornia*; reduction by 42.512% by monoculture of *Hydrilla*, and 67.601% in mixed culture of *Eichhornia* and *Hydrilla* treatment was recorded (Table 10.2).

All the treatment experiments of the river water samples showed decrease in the value of total solids except in the ozone treatment process were the amount of total solids increased. Maximum reduction in total solids was recorded in the charcoal treatment process closely followed by mixed culture of *Eichhornia* and *Hydrilla* treatment.

Table 10.2: Mean percentage reduction of various parameters

Parameters	Charcoal treatment	Ozone treatment	Monoculture *Eichhornia*	Monoculture *Hydrilla*	Mixed culture *Eichhornia* and *Hydrilla*
Acidity (mg/l $CaCO_3$)	64.647	99.088	51.706	49.636	74.971
Nitrate (mg/l)	62.949	88.908	70.418	41.426	81.942
Phosphate (mg/l)	76.063	94.129	87.273	66.521	92.680
DO (mg/l)	18.322	–386.392	–48.569	–189.109	–232.719
BOD (mg/l)	–23.700	95.831	17.579	36.133	59.729
COD (mg/l)	–20.737	94.976	26.690	44.146	53.469
Total Solids (mg/l)	55.598	-41.324	36.132	42.512	67.601
Total Hardness (mg/l)	69.162	99.870	40.624	45.415	62.184
Oil & Grease (mg/l)	44.617	98.849	32.506	54.146	76.752
Cd (mg/l)	52.579	70.040	26.587	21.627	42.857
Cu (mg/l)	67.072	90.287	49.636	45.051	64.447
Cr (mg/l)	77.276	93.353	47.774	36.477	73.139
Ni (mg/l)	78.271	95.659	57.449	65.082	82.200
Pb (mg/l)	65.796	87.686	54.489	45.343	64.311
Zn (mg/l)	62.801	97.871	41.143	35.200	68.280

Total Hardness

Charcoal treatment of the water sample of site 2 showed reduction of total hardness by 69.162% and, through ozone treatment, reduction by 99.870%. The monoculture *Eichhornia* treatment showed reduction by 40.624%, by monoculture of *Hydrilla* by 45.415% and the mixed culture by 62.184% reduction in total hardness (Table 10.2).

Maximum reduction in total hardness was found by ozone treatment followed by charcoal treatment and the mixed culture of *Eichhornia* and *Hydrilla* treatment.

Oil and Grease

Charcoal treatment showed reduction of oil & grease by 44.617% and, through ozone treatment process, the reduction was recorded by 98.849%. The monoculture *Eichhornia* showed reduction in oil and grease by 32.506%, by monoculture of *Hydrilla* to 54.146%; and by the mixed culture the reduction was recorded by 76.752% (Table 10.2).

Maximum reduction in oil & grease was found by ozone treatment followed by mixed culture of *Eichhornia* and *Hydrilla* treatment and charcoal treatment.

Cadmium

Charcoal treatment showed the reduction of Cd in the water sample by 52.579% and through ozone treatment by 70.040%. Monoculture of *Eichhornia* showed the reduction by 26.587%, and that by monoculture of *Hydrilla* by 21.627%, the mixed culture of *Eichhornia* and *Hydrilla* showed reduction by 42.857% (Table 10.2).

Maximum reduction in Cd was found by ozone treatment followed by charcoal treatment and mixed culture of *Eichhornia* and *Hydrilla* treatment.

Copper

Charcoal treatment showed the reduction of Cu in the water sample by 67.072% and through ozone treatment by 90.287%. Monoculture of *Eichhornia* showed the reduction by 49.636%, and that by monoculture of *Hydrilla* by 45.051%, the mixed culture of *Eichhornia* and *Hydrilla* showed reduction by 64.447% (Table 10.2).

Maximum reduction in Cu was found by ozone treatment followed by charcoal treatment and mixed culture of *Eichhornia* and *Hydrilla* treatment.

Chromium

Charcoal treatment showed the reduction of Cr in the water sample by 77.276% and through ozone treatment by 93.353%. Monoculture of *Eichhornia* showed the reduction by 47.774% and that by monoculture of *Hydrilla* by 36.477%, the mixed culture of *Eichhornia* and *Hydrilla* showed reduction by 73.139% (Table 10.2).

Maximum reduction in Cr was found by ozone treatment followed by charcoal treatment and mixed culture of *Eichhornia* and *Hydrilla* treatment.

Nickel

Charcoal treatment showed the reduction of Ni in the water sample by 78.271% and through ozone treatment by 95.659%. Monoculture of *Eichhornia* showed the reduction by 57.449%, and that by monoculture of *Hydrilla* by 65.082%, the mixed culture of *Eichhornia* and *Hydrilla* showed reduction by 82.200% (Table 10.2).

Maximum reduction in Ni was found by ozone treatment followed by charcoal treatment and mixed culture of *Eichhornia* and *Hydrilla* treatment.

Lead

Reduction in Pb content in the water sample through charcoal treatment was recorded by 65.796%, through ozone treatment by 87.686%, through monoculture of *Eichhornia* by 54.489%, through monoculture of *Hydrilla* by 45.343%, and by the mixed culture the reduction was recorded by 64.311% (Table 10.2).

Maximum reduction in Pb content was recorded by ozone treatment followed by charcoal treatment and the mixed culture of *Eichhornia* and *Hydrilla* treatment.

Zinc

Reduction in Zn content in the water sample through charcoal treatment was recorded by 62.801%, through ozone treatment by 97.871%, through monoculture of *Eichhornia* by 41.143%, through monoculture of *Hydrilla* by 35.200%, and by the mixed culture the reduction was recorded by 68.280% (Table 10.2).

Maximum reduction in Zn content was recorded by ozone treatment followed by charcoal treatment and closely followed by the mixed culture of *Eichhornia* and *Hydrilla* treatment.

11

General Discussion

The advent of the Industrial Revolution since 1760 has irreversibly impacted on the way people across the globe live their daily lives. The process of industrialisation has left none untouched, in some way or the other, though in varying measures. While it has influenced both family and society, its impact on humankind's struggle against its environmental after-effects has been most profound.

The larger environmental repercussions of our Industrial Age have to do with the pollution that accompanies it. Pollution accompanies every outshoot of industrialisation, be it industrial production, generation of electric power or vehicular transport. It has also become a market feature of the lifestyles that have come to mark the beginning of the twentyfirst century. The varied sources and forms of pollution are only matched by the various technologies developed to control pollution, be it pollution generated from industries, vehicles, use of fuel in generation of power steam, liquid and solid wastes generated from municipal/residential areas. Indeed, the scientific community all over the world has been giving an extra thrust to researching and designing pollution control mechanisms.

Present investigation deals with the study of physico-chemical properties and heavy metal content in river Varuna water at four selected sites. The study also covers analysis of the water sediments of the respective sites in addition to the study of monthly variation in macrophytic composition at the selected sites for complete one year. The study also covers the laboratory experiments conducted to control the pollution load. Chemical and biological treatments for the river water were performed. The results obtained are discussed herewith.

❐ Water Pollution

Industries generate a significant quantity of wastewater which ultimately find its way to streams or rivers. Industrial discharges containing toxic and hazardous substances contribute to the severe kind of pollution in the aquatic systems. Industrial development is largely because of the production of chemicals resulting in the generation of toxic and hazardous substances which have been continuously on the increase during the last three decades. The number of pesticide production had reached to 56.20 thousand tonnes during 1986-87 which was only 1.46 thousand tonnes during 1960. Similarly, fertilizer production had reached 700 thousand tonnes during 1986-87 which was only 153 thousand tonnes in 1960. All this contribute to the pollution of water ultimately, either their production or their utilisation.

❒ The Study Sites

For the study of the chemistry of river Varuna, four study sites were located. Site 1 was selected at Rameshwar in Jansa area. This site was free from any prominent source of pollution, thus it was treated as the control site. The other three sites consisted of one of the prominent small scale industrial groups. Site 2 was selected in the Nadesar area, the prominent industrial source was battery industries. Site 3, the site near Chaukaghat, consisted of mushrooming of automobile servicing stations. Site 4, which was in Kazzakpura area, consisted of small scale washing and dyeing industries. The above small scale industries were selected for study because in most of the investigations generally the small scale industries are overlooked, which are low in magnitude individually but collectively affect on large scale.

❒ Meteorology

Studies of meteorological variables are essential because they directly or indirectly affect the concentration of pollutants. During summer season the temperature was recorded much higher, precipitation was also recorded to be low, which, ultimately, causes high rate of evaporation from the surface of water bodies, due to which the water bodies become concentrated.

In rainy season the average temperature was lower, the amount of precipitation increases manifold, also the rate of evaporation decreases. Rate of evaporation from surface of water bodies is inversely proportional to the relative humidity also. This results in flow of large amount of water through the rivers, as a result the water body becomes diluted and pollutant concentration lowers. Due to large water content in river in rainy season the rate of flow of river increases manifold as compared to the other seasons, which lowers the pollutants content also by continuous washing.

❒ Properties of the River Water

Physico-chemical properties of river Varuna were studied throughout the year in reference to the following parameters:

Temperature

Temperature was found highest at site 4 and lowest at site 1. The other two sites were intermediate. The contribution for temperature may be attributed to the pollution load of the different sites. Increase in temperature may be due to the chemical reactions taking place among the pollutants. Site 1, which was poor in pollutant, did not undergo such reaction; therefore, the temperature of this site was recorded to be least throughout the study. Most of the chemical reactions are exothermic. As we move downstream the amount of pollutants increases, thus, the rate of increase of temperature follows a positive trend.

pH, Acidity and Alkalinity

pH and alkalinity of site 1 was higher as compared to the other sites. As we move down to sites 2, 3 and 4 the value of pH and alkalinity gradually falls. Value of acidity shows inverse relationship to alkalinity and pH. The reason for higher pH and alkalinity at the control site may be due to the addition of fertilisers and other organic components from the agricultural runoff. Most of the agrochemicals including the fertilisers are basic in nature due to the presence of phosphatic and nitrogenous compounds. During rainy season, pH of the river water increases at all the sites; this is attributed towards the various street runoffs, nitrogenous waste washing from open fields at the bank of the river, etc. Comparatively, lower pH of sites 4, 3 and 2 throughout the study may be due to the reaction of acidic components with pollutants at these sites which lower the pH; and also during the flow the level of alkaline compounds continuously decreases.

Nitrate and Phosphate

Lowest concentration of phosphate and nitrate was found at site 1; but comparatively higher concentration was recorded during the initial part of rainy season. This was attributed to the run off water reaching the river in concentrated form by the initial shower of rain. Nitrate and phosphate concentration was found gradually increasing from site 2 to site 4. This nitrate and phosphate would have been due to the city sewage, which gradually increases as the river moves downstream. Largest amount of phosphate at site 4 was also due to addition of the effluents from the small scale washing and dyeing industries of Banarasi sarees. In addition, at most of the sites, lower concentrations of phosphate and nitrate were recorded during rainy season due to dilution of the river in this season.

Chloride

Chloride content of an aquatic habitat gives an idea of the organic matter and nitrate present in it. Chloride content in the river gradually decreases from summer to rainy season and increases again in winter at all the sites. This may be due to dilution of the river water in rainy season. Comparatively increasing trend in concentration of chloride were recorded from site 1 to site 4 because chloride is one of the most common anions present in industrial discharges; while moving down the stream accumulation of chloride occurs.

DO, BOD and COD

DO shows inverse relationship with BOD and COD, while BOD and COD are parallel with each other at all the sites. DO, BOD and COD is an important indicator of the oxidisable organic pollutants present in the sample. Value of DO at site 1 was higher throughout the study as compared to the other sites, these show that the other sites are rich in organic compounds. The highest value of BOD and COD were obtained at site 3 which was followed by site 4 and site 2—throughout the study. The above observations may be contributed to the high amount of organic matter present in the water of site 3, which was due to the large number of automobile servicing stations present in the area. Seasonally, increase in DO and reduction in BOD and COD was found due to dilution and addition of water in the river during rainy season.

Total Solids

Higher value of total solids were obtained at site 4 followed by site 3 and site 2. The lowest value of total solids at site 1 shows it to be comparatively pollution free because the pollutants ultimately accumulate and produce colloidal particles which contribute for the total solids. Highest value of total solids at site 4 indicates this site to be the most polluted site. During summer months the value of total solids was higher followed by winter and least during rainy season at all the sites, this value corresponds to the contribution of rain and dilution of the river during rainy season.

Total Hardness and Electrical Conductance

Hardness of water is due to presence of the calcium and magnesium salts in water. Electrical conductance is the conductivity of charges in a solution and this is also directly proportional to the charged molecules present in the solution. As water moves downstream in the river from site 1 to site 4 it shows gradual accumulation of the charged molecules released from battery industries at site 2, from automobile servicing stations at site 3 and from the dyeing industries at site 4. Hence, site 4 shows maximum level of total hardness and electrical conductance.

Oil and Grease

Oil and grease was found in highest proportion at site 3, followed by site 4, and site 2. Site 1 shows least amount of oil and grease throughout the study. The little amount of oil and grease at site 1 may be due to the oil discharged at various levels in agricultural practices, e.g. by tractors and various mechanical acts. The reason for extremely high concentration of oil and grease at site 3 was washing activity and servicing of the automobiles. Large amount of oil and grease are discharged in this act. Any prominent source of oil and grease was not present at site 4, but presence of still higher concentration of the same was due to its high persistence owing to which the oil and grease was carried by water till site 4 with nominal change in concentration.

Heavy Metals

Heavy metal analysis in water shows that the highest concentration of Cd was recorded at site 4 followed by site 2 throughout the study. Cd is a prominent heavy metal required by battery industry; higher concentration was found at site 2, which may be due to its presence in the effluent of such industries. The reason for its higher concentration at site 4 may be due to the fact that Cd is an important component of dye.

Lowest concentration of Cu was recorded at site 1 with gradual increase from site 1 to 4. Similar trend was recorded in the case of Cr and Ni also. Their performation was attributed to the three important industrial sources at the specific sites. The river gradually collects the pollutants and shows its high concentration at site 4. Another similar observation common to the above three heavy metals was reduction in their concentration during rainy season with highest in summer; this was due to the fact that during summer the rivers become concentrated as also reported.

Lead distribution also follows pattern similar to Cd, i.e. highest concentration at site 2 followed by site 4, site 3 and site 1. This variation was also because of lead being used prominently in battery industry and in the dyes. Painting and polishing activities are also performed in the automobile servicing centres to some extents—that was why lead was present in considerable amount at site 3 also.

Zinc content was also found to be highest at site 2 because of its discharge from the battery industries. Gradual decreasing trend was also recorded at the following sites. Heavy metal analysis shows lower concentration at generally all the sites during rainy season. Heavy metals content in the river water was contributed directly to the industrial units.

Properties of Water Sediments

Study of physical and mechanical properties of the water sediments at the research sites show that the colour of water sediment of site 1 was lighter as compared to the other sites throughout the year. As we move downstream, colour of the water sediments gradually darkens and the colour of the water sediment of site 4 was darkest. Similar observation was reported in the case of dry as well as wet sediments. Darkness of the sediment is directly controlled by the level of pollution. Due to very low DO at the polluted sites the condition becomes anaerobic in which the population of anaerobic bacteria (sulphur bacteria) increases. This bacteria converts most of the sulphur into sulphide which is black, and, due to deposition of the sulphides at polluted sites, colour of the water sediments becomes dark. During rainy season the colour of the sediment turns slightly light, it is due to deposition of fresh colluvial soil in the water sediments.

Texture of the water sediment remains more or less same throughout the study, showing slight change in composition of the sediment components. During rainy season the loam component of sediment increases and this increase was recorded initially at site 1, it was due to soil erosion from the banks during rain.

Physico-chemical Properties

pH: Variation in the value of pH of the water sediments was recorded during summer and winter season among the sites. The variation among sites was least during rainy season, this may be due to the fact that during rainy season the variation among different variables of rain water becomes nearly constant due to dilution. Throughout the study, pH was alkaline which indicates nature of the water flowing throughout the year.

Potassium: Potassium in water sediments was found to be highest at site 2 followed by sites 1, 3 and 4. The reason for high potassium content in water sediments at site 1 was due to accumulation of agricultural runoff rich in chemical fertilisers, as potassium is an important component of NPK fertilisers. Water sediment sample at site 2 was rich in K because of accumulation of K in largest amount. K is used in battery industries as KCl and $KMnO_4$, thus its amount must be discharged in the effluents in excess. Further, accumulation of K in water sediments at the following sites was recorded—gradually lesser amount; this may be due to consistency of potassium in the flowing water throughout the following sites.

Sodium: Highest Na was recorded in the water sediments of site 2 but lowest in that at site 3. Reason for high Na content at site 1 and site 2 was similar as that for potassium, i.e. from agricultural runoff and discharged from battery industries. Na was released during washing process of the batteries and also from site 4 during washing and dyeing of the Banarasi sarees. Low Na content in water sediments was recorded at site 3 because of low precipitation reaction at this site due to the presence of high amount of oil and grease in water.

Calcium and Phosphorus: Lowest Ca was recorded in the water sediments of site 1, with continuous increasing trend till site 4. Agricultural washing and decay of plants and their parts are prominent source of Ca at site 1. Therefore, Ca gradually increases as the water flows forward, because Ca is an important component of sewage discharge also which are introduced into the river intermittently. Therefore, Ca increases in the water sediments downstream the river. Ca is also an important component of dye, thus its accumulation in water sediments at site 4 is more pronounced as compared to the other sites.

More or less similar trend was observed in the case of phosphorus accumulation in the water sediments. Considerably higher proportion of phosphorus at site 1 was recorded as compared to Ca because P was an important component of chemical fertiliser and agricultural runoff. P is also used in detergents, so it is discharged in high proportion from site 3 during automobile washing. Similarly, at site 4 also it was released during washing of the Banarasi sarees. Seasonally, slight fluctuation in Ca and P was recorded because water sediment is a comparatively stable component,

Total Nitrogen: Total nitrogen was found to be highest in the water sediments at site 1 with least at site 3. Very high total nitrogen at site 1 was due to nitrogenous component released by urea and other chemical fertilisers. Decomposition of plants in water also adds nitrogen to the water sediments. From site 1 to site 3, gradual reductions in total nitrogen in water sediments was recorded due to regular precipitation down the stream. Slightly higher concentration of total nitrogen was recorded at site 4 because of sewage discharge. Seasonally, slightly lower concentration of nitrogen in water sediments was recorded during rainy season at all the sites because of dissolution of little amount of nitrogenous components due to dilution.

Organic Carbon: Highest organic carbon was recorded in water sediments at site 3 because of accumulation of organic compounds, oil and grease etc. During washing and servicing process of automobiles, large amount of oil is discharged because washing of motor parts is performed in oil. Oil, during its flow, reacts with other components and precipitate; it is for this reason that accumulation of organic carbon is highest in the water sediments at site 3. Due to consistency, high proportion of organic carbon was recorded at site 4 also. Comparatively lower organic carbon was recorded at sites 1 and 2 because of the absence of any prominent source of carbon except plant decomposition.

Macrophytic Study

The study of river Varuna in Varanasi was conducted for macrophytic analysis. To study the exact figure of vegetation in the polluted river the following parameters were considered:

- Macrophytic Composition
- Similarity and Dissimilarity Index; and
- Phytosociological Study

Macrophytic Composition

Macrophytic composition of an area depends upon the prevailing environmental conditions. Six plants at site 1 and site 2 each were recorded during the study. At site 3 five and, at site 4, four plants were recorded. Reduction in biodiversity was recorded from site 1 to site 4, this may be contributed to the increasing pollution load from site 1 to site 4, as biodiversity is inversely proportional to pollution load as also reported. The plants were also found to be present only during summer and winter season, during rainy season they were washed by the running water.

Similarity and Dissimilarity Index

This was a comparative study conducted to establish similarity and dissimilarity between different sites on the basis of macrophytes present at the sties. Maximum similarity index was found between sites 1 and 2 and between sites 3 and 4. This was because of similarity among the above pair of study sites. Site 1 was non-polluted while site 2 was less polluted. Similarly, site 3 was more polluted but site 4 was most polluted. Dissimilarity index between sites 1 and 4 was recorded to be the highest because site 1 was the control site, i.e. the least polluted site, and site 4, which was the most polluted site.

Phytosociological Study

Density: Least density of plants was found during rainy season because all the plants were washed by rain water. At all the sites highest density of plants were recorded during winter season followed by summer season. During summer, decrease in their density started because by increase in temperature the rate of physiological reactions increases, specially respiration; therefore, decline in their population was recorded.

Frequency: Frequency was also found to be higher during winter season because the river was nearly calm and the plants got proper time for growth and development. *Salvenia molesta* showed higher frequency during June 2001 at sites 2, 3 and 4 where the plant was found. *Salvenia molesta* is a pollution loving plant, so its higher frequency was found in summer, when pollutants were in highest concentration in the river water.

The macrophytic compositions of more polluted sites differ from the less polluted sites. For example *Eichhornia crassipes, Lemna minor* and *Salvenia molesta* were found only at the polluted sites, while *Potamogeton pectinatus, Pistia stratiotes* etc. were not found at the polluted sites because they were sensitive to pollutants. The plants preferring polluted area are pollution resistant, thus, they absorb the pollutants from the medium.

Treatment of the River Water

During the study from April 2001 to March 2002, it revealed that April was the most polluted month, because due to high temperature and scanty rain the water flowing through the river decreased. On the other hand, the amount of pollutants flowing into the river remained the same, thus the river turned concentrated in April. Therefore, April 2002 was the month selected for the laboratory experiments for treatment. The samples were subjected to chemical and biological treatments.

Chemical Treatment

Depending on the nature of pollutants, activated charcoal and ozone treatment was supposed to be the most suitable chemical treatment practice. Reduction in all the pollution parameters was recorded in the case of samples of all the sites. Charcoal treatment showed marked reduction in heavy metal, nitrate, phosphate, total hardness, etc. in the water sample. But due to highly absorptive and porous nature, reduction in DO was also recorded by charcoal treatment. Reduction in DO resulted in increase in BOD and COD. These three are very sensitive parameters for the water quality, thus, this was recorded as a prominent drawback of this treatment.

Marvellous response was recorded in the case of ozone treatment where 100% removal of chromium from polluted water was surprising. Most of the heavy metals were nearly washed along with reduction in acidity, nitrate, phosphate, BOD, COD, and total hardness. Similar results were obtained in the treatment of water samples of all the three sites. Ozone treatment also showed increase in the value of DO and total solids. Enormous increase in DO was recorded because ozone gas dissolves in the water and manifold increase in DO was recorded. The reason for increase in total solids may be due to precipitation of all the pollutants in the form of oxides, as a result the amount of total solids by this treatment would have increased. Except only one drawback, i.e. increase in the total solids, the ozone treatment was the most convincing treatment process.

Biological Treatment

On the basis of the nature of pollutants, and keeping in view the resistance and sensitivity of plants, two plants were selected for the water treatment experiments. The two plants were *Eichhornia crassipes* and *Hydrilla verticillata*. *Eichhornia crassipes* is a floating macrophyte while *Hydrilla verticillata* is a submerged plant. In monoculture of *Eichhornia* considerable reduction in pollutants was recorded, specially in the case of nitrate, phosphate and some heavy metals like Cr, Ni, Pb and Zn in case of treatment of samples of all the sites. Slight increase in DO was recorded by this treatment.

Monoculture of *Hydrilla* also showed marked reduction in pollution load, specially in case of BOD, COD, total hardness, phosphate, nitrate, oil & grease, Ni, Pb and Zn. High increase in DO was also recorded in this treatment. This may be due to the fact that since *Hydrilla* is a submerged plant, during photosynthesis it releases high amount of oxygen directly in the water due to which pollutants were oxidised and DO also increased. The value of total solids does not increase as in the case of ozone treatment because the rate of oxygen production was slow and steady in this case.

Mixed culture of *Eichhornia* and *Hydrilla* showed brilliant response. In this treatment extensive reduction in nearly all the parameters were recorded. Reduction in pollutant was recorded because the pollutants are absorbed by the growing resistant plants and they are taken as fertilisers of the plants. DO also increase manifold in this treatment. In this treatment no drawbacks were recorded. Comparatively, mixed culture experiment was also found to be the most feasible and practicable in the rivers as it required least input. During study it was also recorded that the aquatic macrophytes can be harvested and can be used for production of paper. The plants used in waste water treatment can also be used for energy production or as fodder.

12

METHODOLOGIES

The complete methodology involved in the given study is summarised in the following flowchart:

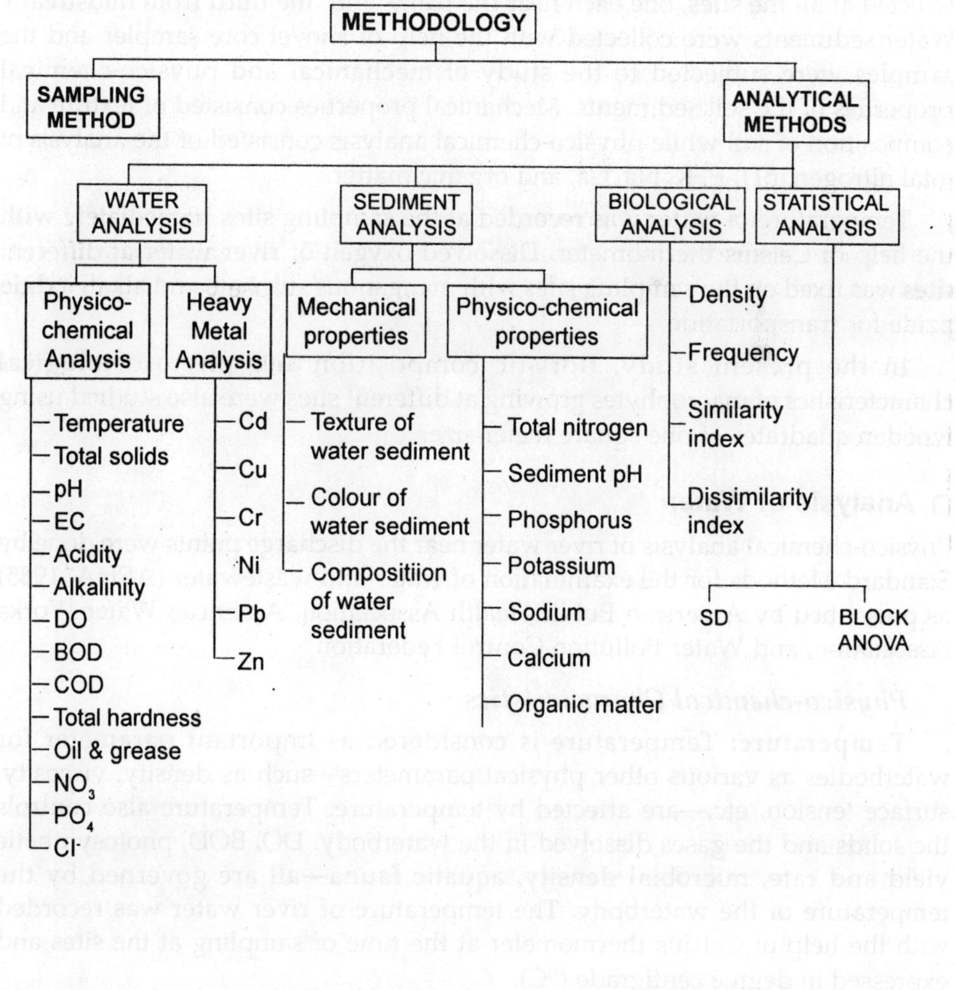

❒ Sampling

Samples were collected from river Varuna, 100 feet (30 meters) downstream from the target nala discharge points, fortnightly, starting from April 2001 to March 2002. Water samples were collected from five points transversely in the river. Two points were near the two banks and remaining three at vertically three points in the midstream. Collection of samples vertically was conducted with the help of a specially designed deep sampler. Samples, each of four litres, were collected at a time in double cap container between 8 to 10 a.m. from each sampling site and brought to the laboratory in ice boxes for the analysis of various physico-chemical characteristics, i.e. total solids, pH, electrical conductance (EC), acidity, total alkalinity, dissolved oxygen (DO), biochemical oxygen demand (BOD), chemical oxygen demand (COD), total hardness, nitrate, phosphate, oil and grease, and for some heavy metals, i.e. Cd, Cu, Cr, Ni, Pb and Zn. The samples were collected up to top without leaving any space for bubbles in the container.

Collection of samples of water sediment was performed from three sub-sites selected at all the sites, one each near the banks and the third from midstream. Water sediments were collected with the help of shovel core sampler and the samples were subjected to the study of mechanical and physico-chemical properties of the soil sediments. Mechanical properties consisted of texture and composition of soil while physico-chemical analysis consisted of the analysis of total nitrogen, pH, P, K, Na, Ca, and organic matter.

Temperature of water was recorded at the sampling sites immediately with the help of Celsius thermometer. Dissolved oxygen of river water at different sites was fixed on the sampling sites with manganous sulphate and alkali iodide azide for transportation.

In the present study, floristic composition and phytosociological characteristics of macrophytes growing at different sites were also studied using wooden quadrates of one square meter size.

❒ Analysis of Water

Physico-chemical analysis of river water near the discharge points were done by Standard Methods for the examination of water and wastewater (APHA, 1985) as prescribed by American Public Health Association, American Water Works Association, and Water Pollution Control Federation.

Physico-chemical Characteristics

Temperature: Temperature is considered as important parameter for waterbodies as various other physical parameters—such as density, viscosity, surface tension, etc.—are affected by temperature. Temperature also controls the solids and the gases dissolved in the waterbody. DO, BOD, photosynthetic yield and rate, microbial density, aquatic fauna—all are governed by the temperature of the waterbody. The temperature of river water was recorded with the help of Celsius thermometer at the time of sampling at the sites and expressed in degree centigrade (°C).

Total Solids: Total solids of the samples were estimated by evaporating a measured volume of the samples in an oven at 105°C in a dry constant weight crucible. The following formula was used to calculate the total solids:

$$\text{Total solids mg } l^{-1} = \frac{\text{(Weight of crucible with residue} - \text{Weight of empty crucible) mg}}{\text{ml sample}} \times 1{,}000$$

pH (Potential Hydrogen): Hydrogen ion concentration, i.e. pH of an aquatic system is regulated as well as affected by the chemical content of the system. The optimum range of pH for aquatic life is 6.8 to 9.0. pH was measured in the laboratory with the help of an electronic glass electrode pH meter (CK-701) with a precision of 0.05. The pH meter was standardised with stock buffers before each reading.

Electrical Conductivity: Electrical conductivity of the samples was measured with the help of an electronic pH-mho meter with conductivity cell and the value of electrical conductivity is expressed in mS cm^{-1} at 25 °C.

EC of the sample is calculated as follows:

Electrical conductivity (μS cm^{-1}) = Reading × cell constant (0.54) × range

Temperature correction was made for adjustment at 25 °C.

Acidity: Potentiometric titration method was used for the determination of acidity of water. Titrant Sodium hydroxide (0.025N) was used to raise the pH of sample water (100 ml) up to 8.3 (Phenolphthalein acidity). Phenolphthalein gives pink colour above pH 8.3, below which it remains colourless.

The acidity was calculated using the following formula:

$$\text{Acidity} = \frac{V \times N \times 50{,}000}{\text{ml of sample}} \text{ mg } l^{-1}\ CaCO_3$$

where V and N are Volume and Normality of the titrant, respectively.

Total Alkalinity: Alkalinity is anionic phenomena; all the anions present in the medium together constitute the alkalinity of the solution. The ideal alkalinity of water for domestic use should be less than 103 as $CaCO_3$ alkalinity. Potentiometric titration method was used for the determination of alkalinity of water. Titrant Sulphuric acid (0.025N) was used to lower down the pH of water (100 ml) at 8.3 (Phenolphthalein alkalinity) and to the pH 3.7 (Methyl orange alkalinity).

The following formula was used to calculate the alkalinity of water

$$\text{Total Alkalinity} = \frac{V \times N \times 5{,}000}{\text{ml sample}} \text{mg}l^{-1}C_aDO_3$$

where

V and N are Volume and Normality of the titrant, respectively.

The pH more than 8.3 showed presence of hydroxide alkalinity (which is rare) and carbonate alkalinity along with bicarbonate alkalinity, when pH of the water sample was below 8.3, the total alkalinity represented the amount of bicarbonate alkalinity only:

Carbonate Alkalinity = 2 × Phenolphthalein alkalinity

Bicarbonate Alkalinity = Total alkalinity – Carbonate alkalinity.

Dissolved Oxygen (DO): The dissolved oxygen is a parameter which reflects the health and ability of the aquatic system to purify itself through the biochemical process. When DO falls below 5, the desirable species of fishes migrate. Further falls in DO promotes anaerobic organisms. Winkler's modified azide method was used for the estimation of Dissolved Oxygen in water. DO was estimated by adding 2 ml of manganese sulphate solution (prepared by dissolving 364 gm $MnSO_4.4H_2O$ in 1 litre distilled water) to the water sample in BOD bottle of 300 ml capacity. The content is mixed by swirling 2 ml of alkaline sodium iodide azide (prepared by dissolving 700 gm of NaOH, 135 gm of NaI and 10 gm of sodium azide in 1 litre of distilled water) solution is then added. The content is mixed thoroughly and the resulting brown precipitate is allowed to settle for 5 minutes. Later on, 2 ml concentrated H_2SO_4 is added, as a result the precipitate dissolves producing yellow coloured solution. 200 ml of the above solution is titrated against 0.025 N sodium thiosulphate solution using starch as indicator.

The amount of titrant consumed directly gives the value of DO in mg/l or it can be calculated by the formula:

Dissolved oxygen =

where, V and N are Volume and Normality of the titrant, respectively.

The chemical reactions involved are:

$$2Mn(OH)_2 + O_2 = 2MnO(OH)_2$$

(Basic Manganese oxide)

$$MnO(OH)_2 + 2H_2SO_4 = Mn(SO_4)_2 + 3H_2O$$

(Manganese sulphate)

$$Mn(SO_4)_2 + 2KI = MnSO_4 + K_2SO_4 + I_2$$

$$2Na_2S_2O_3 + I_2 = Na_2S_4O_6 + 2NaI$$

Biochemical Oxygen Demand (BOD_5): Biochemical oxygen demand (BOD_5) is a test of great value in the analysis of sewage, industrial effluents and polluted water. BOD_5 refers to the quantity of oxygen required by bacteria and other microorganisms in the biochemical degradation and transformation of organic matter under aerobic conditions.

The basic principle underlying the BOD_5 determination is the measurement of the dissolved oxygen content of the sample before and after five days' incubation at 20 °C. Biochemical chemical oxidation is a slow process and therefore, 20-30 days are required for complete degradation of the waste but up to 95-99% oxidation of glucose, 65% oxidation of sewage and about 45% oxidation of other organic compounds take place in 5 days. Therefore, 5 days' incubation period was taken as standard by the British Royal Commission for sewage disposal. Further, this is because none of the rivers in England has a reaching time to the sea of more than 5 days. 20°C incubation temperature is used as an average value, as this is the average temperature of slow moving water bodies in temperate climate. To measure the dissolved oxygen content of the water samples, Winkler's modified azide method was used:

$$BOD_5 = \frac{D.O._{(initial)} - D.O._{5\ days'\ incubation}}{\text{Decimal fraction of dilution}}\ mg l^{-1}$$

where,

$DO_{(initial)}$ = Dissolved oxygen of the sample for the first BOD bottle, which is not incubated.

$DO_{(5\ days'\ incubation)}$ = Disssolved oxygen of the sample after 5 days' incubation in dark.

Chemical Oxygen Demand (COD): The dichromate reflux method was used to analyse the COD of water sample. COD is a measure of oxygen equivalent of those constituents in the sample which are susceptible to dichromate oxidation in acidic condition for two and half hours. The known volume of water sample was refluxed with known volume of potassium dichromate and concentrated sulphuric acid for two hours. The remaining amount of potassium dichromate after completing reflux was titrated with ferrous ammonium sulphate using ferroin indicator. The reaction involved was:

$$K_2Cr_2O_7 + 4H_2SO_4 = K_2SO_4 + Cr_2(SO_4)_3 + 4H_2O + 3O$$

COD was calculated using the following formula:

$$COD = \frac{(a-b) \times N \times 8,000}{\text{ml sample}}\ mg l^{-1}$$

where

a = ml of Ferrous ammonium sulphate used for blanks

b = ml of Ferrous ammonium sulphate used for water sample, and

N = Normality of Ferrous ammonium sulphate.

Generally, the value of COD is higher than BOD. The ratio of value of BOD : COD shows the type of treatment required for the particular waste water sample. When BOD : COD is above 0.6, it shows that the waste is rich in putreascible matter and, therefore, biological treatment would be the best for the such samples. On the other hand, if the value is below 0.3 it shows that chemical treatment is the best for such waste. At the same time, if BOD : COD falls between 0.3 to 0.6 this indicates that the sample requires acclimatisation prior to subjecting it for the biological treatment.

Chloride: Previously, the sudden increase in chloride content of waterbodies was directly correlated to the addition of toilet discharge into the waterbody as, high amount of chloride is released in human excreta. Chloride ions are non-biodegradable and are not removed from waste water even after secondary treatment process.

For chloride estimation 100 ml of water sample was taken in porcelain basin to which 1 ml of 5% potassium dichromate solution is added as indicator and is titrated against standard silver nitrate solution (prepared by dissolving 4.79 gm of silver nitrate in 1 litre distilled water). Multiplying the titrant consumed by 10 directly gives the reading for chloride content of the water sample.

Total Hardness: The estimation of hardness is of vital significance as it affects certain chemical reactions in the waterbody and also affects the physiology of the organisms present in the medium. Total hardness of water was estimated by EDTA titrimetric method. Hardness of water is caused by the presence of bivalent alkaline earth elements. Calcium, strontium and magnesium are the principal alkaline earth elements in natural water and to a lesser extent the anions are bicarbonate, carbonate, sulphate, chloride, nitrate, etc. but the hardness produced by anions is very low. Hardness determination is based on the fact that disodium dihydrogen ethylene diamine tetra-acetic acid (Na_2EDTA) forms a slightly ionised colourless stable complex with alkaline earth ions. The indicator Eriochrome Black-T is bright blue in the absence of alkaline earth ions but with them, forms a deep red complex at a pH of 10.0 ± 1. Thus, using Eriochrome Black-T as an indicator, the Ca and Mg ions can be titrated with Na_2EDTA (0.01 M).

Hardness of sample water was calculated as:

$$\text{Hardness} = \frac{\textbf{ml of EDTA used} \times \textbf{1,000}}{\textbf{ml sample}} \, \text{mg}_1{}^{-1}\text{C}_a\text{CO}_3$$

When the value of total alkalinity is higher than that of total hardness, it indicates the carbonate type of hardness. On the other hand, if total hardness exceeds the total alkalinity, then the value of total alkalinity is for carbonate hardness; and the difference of the two shows the value of non-carbonate hardness.

Oil and Grease: The determination of oil and grease includes all the substances that are extractable by the specified solvent. Solvent extraction method is used to estimate oil and grease. Generally, the extractable substances are, oils, fats and waxes. The results obtained indicate the non-volatile fraction of these materials.

Oil, grease and other extractable matters are dissolved in petroleum ether in the presence of dilute sulphuric acid and separated from the aqueous phase. The solvent layer is then evaporated and the residue is weighed as oil and grease, according to the given equation:

$$\text{Oil and grease (mg l}^{-1}) = \frac{\text{Residue in the distilling flask}}{\text{sample taken for determination}} \times 1{,}000$$

Nitrate: The phenol disulphonic acid method was applied for the analysis for nitrate-nitrogen. The steam dried water samples were dissolved in phenol disulphonic acid (2 ml). The alkaline medium was made by adding ammonium hydroxide (10 ml). The development of yellow colour denoted the presence of NO_3. The intensity of colour is proportional to the amount of NO_3-N present in the water sample, which was measured by colorimeter at 410 nm in terms of optical density.

The final calculation was made with the help of the standard graph:

$$\text{Nitrate} = \frac{\text{reading of standard} \times 1{,}000}{\text{ml sample}} \text{ mgl}^{-1}$$

Phosphate: Stannous chloride method was used for the determination of phosphate concentration in water sample. 4ml ammonium molybdate solution (prepared by dissolving 25 gm ammonium molybdate in 75 ml of distilled water) and 5 drops of freshly prepared stannous chloride solution of 2.5% strength were added to the 50 ml sample water and measured to 100 ml with the distilled water. The development of blue colour indicates the presence of phosphate-P. The colour intensity is proportional to the amount of phosphorus present and is measured in terms of optical density with the help of spectrophotometer at 690 nm. The final calculation was made with the help of standard graph, prepared from known concentration of phosphate in solution.

Analysis of Water Sediments

Water sediments consist of the bed present at bottom of the rivers. The quality of water sediments differ from place to place. It depends upon the quality of water flowing through the river and also upon the macrophytic composition of the waterbody. The water sediment is chemically, physically and biologically complex dynamic system. It also acts as a sink of various nutrients and other components flowing in the water. It also consists of fresh alluvium transported by the river.

The properties of sediment of the river banks remain under constant flux, which are influenced by a number of factors such as erosion, silting, run-off, etc. Properties of water sediment also varies seasonally because of the water flowing through it, water soluble substances leaving the sediments and colloidal substances settling in the water. During summer and winter the amount of water in the river decreases, also the velocity of flow of water decreases. Thus, settlement of colloidal particles over the river bed increases, which affect the property of water sediment. Therefore, it is significant to evaluate certain characteristics of the water sediments at periodic intervals. Water sediments from the three zones of each study sites have been analysed for this purpose.

Water sediments were taken fortnightly from all the zones of study sites. The samples were kept in polythene bags and were brought to the laboratory for analysis. Air dried water sediments were lightly ground in a mortar, passed through 2 mm sieve and stored in polythene bags for further analysis.

Mechanical Properties

Texture of Water Sediments: Texture refers to weight proportion in percentage of different size particles, such as coarse sand, fine sand, silt and clay. The method of separating the sediment particles into groups is known as mechanical analysis, i.e., percentage ratio of different size particles was done by Robinson pipette method (Piper, 1966).

Colour: The colour of dry and wet water sediment was determined by comparing with Munsell's soil colour chart (Munsell, 1905).

Physico-chemical Properties

Total Nitrogen: The total nitrogen was analysed by micro-Kjeldahl method (Misra, 1968) by digesting 10 g powdered and sieved sample of water sediment in 20 ml concentrated H_2SO_4 using catalyst mixture (copper sulphate + mercuric oxide + selenium powder + sodium sulphate) and distilling in a Markhan unit. The results obtained are expressed in terms of N mg g^{-1}.

Sediment pH: The pH is defined as the negative logarithm of hydrogen ion activity or concentration. A suspension of water sediment having soil and water proportion of 1.5 was prepared in distilled water and its pH value was recorded electrometrically (pH-meter Elico make, Model$_{-1}$$^{-12}$, with combined glass electrode.

Phosphorus: 5 g samples of water sediment were used for determination of available phosphorus by chlorostannous reduced molybdophosphoric blue colour in hydrochloric acid system. The intensity of blue colour is directly proportional to phosphorus content which was determined spectro-colourimetrically at 660 nm. The amount of phosphorus in the aliquot was calculated with the help of standard curve. The results obtained are expressed in mg g^{-1} water sediment.

Calcium, Potassium and Sodium: Calcium, potassium and sodium were measured by using Systronic-Type 127 Flame-Photometer with acetylene burner—characteristic light is produced due to excitation of electron when the samples having Ca, K and Na were sprayed into the flame. The intensity of this radiation is directly proportional to the concentration of the element present. For water sediment analysis, sample was digested by adding conc. HNO_3 to make the aliquot. Known concentration of respective element (Ca, K and Na) was prepared from $CaCO_3$, KCl and NaCl for galvanometer adjustment and transmission standardisation. The transmission of unknown solution was recorded and concentrations were calculated using the formula given in systronic-type 127 manual:

$$C = C_2 + \left(\frac{C_1 - C_2}{a_1 - a_2}\right)(a_1 - a_2)$$

where

C = concentration of unknown solution.

C_1= maximum concentration in ppm of $CaCO_3$ solution.

C_2= minimum concentration in ppm of $CaCO_3$ solution.

a = transmission reading of unknown solution.

a_1 = transmission reading at maximum concentration of $CaCO_3$ solution.

a_2 = transmission reading at minimum concentration of $CaCO_3$ solution.

Organic Matter: The method based upon the oxidation of carbon by nascent oxygen liberated from $K_2Cr_2O_7$ in the presence of sulphuric acid was applied for determination of organic matter. Percentage of carbon present was determined by using diphenylamine as indicator and titrating with ferrous ammonium sulphate solution in burette.

$$\text{Percentage of carbon (\%C)} = \frac{V_1 - V_2}{W} \times 0.003 \times 100$$

where

V_1 = ml of 1N $K_2Cr_2O_7$

V_2 = ml of 1N ferrous ammonium sulphate used

W = weight of sediments sample used

% of organic matter = % C x 1.724

Analysis of Biological Parameters

Density: Density gives an expression of the numerical strength of a species in the community. Density of the plants was expressed in number of individuals of species per meter square (Mishra and Puri, 1954).

It was calculated by the following formula:

$$\text{Density} = \frac{\text{Total number of individuals of each species}}{\text{Total number of quadrates studied}}$$

Frequency: Frequency shows the distribution pattern of individuals of a species in an area, and was expressed in terms of percentage occurrence. Percentage frequency was calculated by the following formula (Mishra and Puri, 1954):

$$\text{Frequency \%} = \frac{\text{Number of quadrates in which the species occurred}}{\text{Total number of quadrates studied}}$$

Similarity Index: Similarity index was calculated using the formula given by Sorenson (1988)

$$S = \frac{2C}{A + B}$$

where

S = Similarity index.

A = Number of species at one site.

B = Number of species at the second site.

C = Number of species common at the two sites.

Dissimilarity Index: Dissimilarity index was calculated by the following formula:

$$D = 1 - S$$

where

D = Dissimilarity index.

S = Similarity index.

Analysis of Heavy Metals in the River Water

Heavy metals are usually present in trace amounts in river waters. Several heavy metals can be determined in Varuna river water, but in this investigation only six heavy metals have been taken into account viz. Cd, Cr, Cu, Ni, Pb and Zn. For the analysis of heavy metals 50 ml of samples were acidified with concentrated nitric acid to make the pH of the solution around 2.0 and boiled for 10 minutes, then filtered, when a clear solution was obtained. The filtrate was concentrated and made up to a volume of 100 ml. From this solution analyses of different heavy metals were performed.

The method of choice for the determination of heavy metals in the water sample depends on the capability to detect extremely low concentration. Some of the techniques are:

1. Colourimetry
2. Flame atomic absorption spectrophotometry
3. Polarography
4. Mass spectrometry
5. Atomic absorption spectroscopy
6. Fluorimetry
7. Atomic emission spectroscopy
8. X-ray methods
9. Electrochemicals methods

In present investigation, the heavy metal contents of the sample were analysed by flame atomic absorption spectrophotometer using Perkin-Elmer 50,000 model with automatic burner control. All furnace injections were made with micro-pipetts.

The samples were then analysed by using the corresponding hollow cathode lamp and the signals were measured for each metal at their respective wavelength to get the concentration. Table 2.1 shows the analytical conditions for the determination of six heavy metals by atomic absorption spectroscopy flame method.

Table 12.1: Analytical conditions for the automatic absorption spectroscopic determination of heavy metal in Varuna river water

Metal	Slit width (nm)	Wavelength (nm)	Flame type
Cadmium	0.7	228.8	Air-Acytelene (O)
Chromium	0.2	357.9	Air-Acytelene (R)
Copper	0.7	324.8	Air-Acytelene (O)
Lead	0.7	283.3	Air-Acytelene (O)
Nickel	0.2	232.0	Air-Acytelene (O)
Zinc	0.7	213.9	Air-Acytelene (O)

O = Oxidising, R = Reducing

Statistical Analysis

The data obtained were subjected to different statistical analyses to determine the significance of variation in the data through Standard Deviation and ANOVA.

Analysis of Variance

BLOCKS ANOVA was calculated to test the validity of the data and significance of the variation in the data between the sites and among the months.

13

Summary, Conclusion and Recommendations

In recent age of science and technology the pollution problems are becoming more and more severe due to rapid and unplanned growth of industries. Varuna, an important tributary of Ganga in Varanasi, receives effluents directly from many small scale industrial units. The important industries located during the study were battery industries, automobile servicing stations, and printing and dyeing industries of Banarasi sarees. Their numerical strength was higher, sufficient enough to result in tremendous pollution. From literature survey it was noted that there is a lack of information on the impact of such industries on the quality of river water, water sediments and plants and also in control and management of the river.

Therefore, a project was started to monitor the physico-chemical properties of river water and its sediment, to conduct the heavy metal analysis in water, to study macrophytic composition throughout the year, to develop pollution control technique to minimise the pollutants and suggest management practices for the river to reduce the pollution load.

Present investigation was carried out at Varanasi, the cultural capital of India, and the oldest inhabited city of the world. Site 1 was selected at Rameshwar in Jansa area which was free from any pollution source, site 2 was at Razabazar area which received the effluents from battery industries, site 3 at Chaukaghat area, receiving the effluents from automobile servicing station, and site 4 at Kazzakpura area pouring the discharge from printing and dyeing industries. For water sampling five subsites were located at each site but for water sediment analysis three subsites were located.

Laboratory experiments for pollution control were conducted. Activated charcoal and ozone was used in chemical treatment, monoculture of *Eichhornia crassipes*, monoculture of *Hydrilla verticillata* and mixed culture of *Eichhornia crassipes* and *Hydrilla verticillata* was used as biological treatment.

For charcoal treatment, 50 litre of water sample was maintained in 100 litres of aquarium. 10 small packets of tissue paper containing 1 gm activated charcoal each were sunk with the help of weight. Initial reading of all the variables was recorded and the same was analysed on 24 hour basis for 5 days. Maximum pollutant removal was recorded on the fourth day. Thus, the value of variables on the 4th day is expressed in the record.

For ozone treatment, two tier bubbling chamber of 12 litre capacity of glass was constructed, whose common surface consisted of profuse perforation. The chamber was filled with 10 litres of water sample collected from the polluted study sites. Inlet of the lower tier was connected to ozone generator. Ozonized gas was passed through the bubbler which comes above across the water in the form of minute bubbles. Change in the parameters was recorded hourly and the maximum pollution removal was found after 6 hours' treatment, thus, only this value is expressed in the record.

For monoculture experiment *Eicchornia crassipes* and *Hydrilla verticillata* were cultured separately in 50 litre of water in aquarium of 100 litre capacities. For mixed culture both the above plants were cultured together. Maximum pollution removing capacity in most of the experiments were found on 16th day, thus, the record of that day is expressed.

Results obtained during the investigation revealed the following important facts:

❐ Meteorology

Monthly mean of minimum and maximum temperatures was recorded during the study (April 2001 to March 2002). Lowest minimum temperature (10.03 °C) was recorded during December 2001, but lowest maximum temperature (22.71 °C) was recorded during January 2002, likewise highest minimum temperature (29.65 °C) was recorded during June 2001 and highest maximum temperature (38.16 °C) was found in April 2001.

During April 2001 to March 2002 highest monthly rainfall was recorded during July 2001 (380.5 mm) while minimum during November 2001 (0.6 mm). Winter season was dry with slight precipitation during summer, rainy season was wet with heavy rainfall.

Humidity varies widely in different seasons, maximum being in the rainy and minimum in the summer season. The maximum average relative humidity during the study period was in December 2001 (92.54%) while the minimum was in April 2001 (41.26%).

❐ Properties of River Water

The minimum temperature of water (20.75 ± 0.243 °C) was recorded during October 2001 at site 1 and the maximum temperature (34.35 ± 0.190 °C) during April 2001 at site 4. Seasonally, temperature of water was found to be highest during summer followed by rainy season and it was minimum during winter at all the sites.

The minimum pH of water (7.61 ± 0.05) was recorded during April 2001 at site 4 and the maximum pH (8.66 ± 0.05) during November 2001 at site 1. Seasonally, pH was found to be highest during rainy season followed by winter and summer seasons at all the sites.

Minimum acidity (0.21 ± 0.052 mg/l $CaCO_3$) was recorded during April 2001 at site 1 and the maximum acidity (34.46 ± 0.819 mg/l $CaCO_3$) during April 2001 at site 4. Seasonally, acidity of the river water was found to be highest during summer season followed by rainy and winter seasons at most of the sites.

Minimum alkalinity (126.00 ± 5.85 mg/l $CaCO_3$) was recorded during March 2002 at site 3 and the maximum alkalinity (461.66 ± 3.14 mg/l $CaCO_3$) during November 2001 at site 1. Seasonally, alkalinity of the river water was found to be highest during rainy season followed by winter and summer seasons at all the sites.

Minimum nitrate (0.023 ± 0.005 mg/l) was recorded during May 2001 and January 2002 at site 1 and the maximum nitrate (0.968 ± 0.028 mg/l) during April 2001 at site 4. Seasonally, nitrate of the river water was found to be highest during summer season followed by winter and rainy seasons at all the sites.

Minimum phosphate content (0.015 ± 0.002 mg/l) in water of river Varuna was recorded during August and September 2001 at site 1 and the maximum phosphate (1.565 ± 0.028 mg/l) during April 2001 at the site 4. Seasonally, phosphate content in river water was found to be highest during summer season followed by rainy and winter seasons at all the sites.

Minimum chloride (12.66 ± 1.63 mg/l) was recorded during July 2001 at site 1 and the maximum chloride (79.50 ± 2.58 mg/l) during April 2001 at site 4. Seasonally, chloride in the river water was found to be highest during summer season followed by winter and rainy seasons at all the sites.

Minimum DO (1.93 ± 0.30 mg/l) was recorded during April 2001 at site 4 and the maximum DO (9.16 ± 0.25 mg/l) during November 2001 at site 1. Seasonally, DO in the river water was found to be highest during winter season followed by rainy and summer seasons at all the sites.

Minimum BOD (1.81 ± 0.07 mg/l) was recorded during August 2001 at site 1 and the maximum BOD (84.16 ± 3.40 mg/l) during April 2001 at site 3. Seasonally, BOD of the river water was found to be highest during summer season followed by winter and rainy seasons at all the sites.

Minimum COD (5.10 ± 0.23 mg/l) was recorded during June 2001 at site 1 and the maximum COD (136.66 ± 5.46 mg/l) during April 2001 at site 3. Seasonally, COD of the river water was found to be highest during summer season followed by winter and rainy seasons at all the sites.

Minimum total solids (193.50 ± 1.41 mg/l) was recorded during October 2001 at site 1 and the maximum total solids (1128.50 ± 10.80 mg/l) during May 2001 at site 4. Seasonally, total solids in the river water were found to be highest during rainy season followed by summer and winter seasons at all the sites.

Minimum total hardness (38.83 ± 2.31 mg/l $CaCO_3$) was recorded during August 2001 at site 1 and the maximum total hardness (963.83 ± 5.56 mg/l $CaCO_3$) during April 2001 at site 4. Seasonally, total hardness of the river water was found to be highest during summer season followed by winter and rainy seasons at all the sites.

Minimum electrical conductance (114.66 ± 7.29 μmhos/cm) was recorded during July 2001 at site 1 and the maximum electrical conductance (857.50 ± 9.13 μmhos/cm) during November 2001 at site 4. Seasonally, electrical conductance of the river water was found to be highest during winter season followed by rainy and summer seasons at all the sites.

Minimum oil and grease (0.11 ± 0.030 mg/l) was recorded during August 2001 at site 1 and the maximum oil and grease (6.09 ± 0.09 mgl) during March 2002 at site 3. Seasonally, oil and grease of the river water was found to be highest during summer season followed by winter and rainy seasons at all the sites.

Cd was not found during June, July and August 2001 at site 1 and the maximum Cd (0.049 μg/l) during April 2001 and March 2002 at site 4. Seasonally, Cd in the river water was found to be highest during summer season followed by winter and rainy seasons at all the sites.

Cu was not found during July and September 2001 in the river water at site 1 and the maximum Cu (0.496 μg/l) during May 2001 at site 4. Seasonally, Cu in the river water was found to be highest during summer season followed by winter and rainy seasons at all the sites.

Cr was not found during August 2001 at site 1 and the maximum Cr (0.081 μg/l) during April 2001 at site 4 in the river water. Seasonally, Cr was found to be highest during summer season followed by winter and rainy seasons at all the sites.

Ni was not found during August 2001 at site 1 and the maximum Ni (0.050 μg/l) during April 2001 at site 4. Seasonally, Ni in the river water was found to be highest during summer season followed by winter and rainy seasons at all the sites.

Pb was minimum (0.001 mg/l) during July 2001 at site 1 and the maximum Pb (0.201 μg/l) during April 2001 at site 2. Seasonally, Pb in the river water was found to be highest during summer season followed by winter and rainy seasons at all the sites.

Zn was minimum (0.042 μg/l) during September 2001 at site 1 and the maximum Zn (1.712 μg/l) during April 2001 at site 2 in the river water. Seasonally, Zn in the river water was found to be highest during summer season followed by winter and rainy seasons at all the sites.

❒ Properties of River Water Sediment

Colour of the water sediment was found light at the control site while dark at the polluted sites. The texture of water sediment at nearly all the sites was silty clay throughout the year but silty clay loam during rainy season.

The minimum pH of water sediments (6.8) was recorded during June and August 2001 at site 1 and maximum pH (9.0) during April 2001 at site 4. Seasonally, pH was found to be highest during summer season. The value of pH was nearly uniform during rainy and winter season at sites 1 and 2, however, it was higher at sites 3 and 4 during rainy season as compared to winter.

Minimum potassium (0.440 μg/g) was recorded during April 2001 at site 4 and the maximum potassium value (0.926 μg/g) during August 2001 at site 2. Seasonally, potassium of the water sediments of the river was found to be higher during rainy season followed by summer and winter seasons at most of the sites.

Minimum sodium (0.170 μg/g) was recorded during September 2001 at site 3 and the maximum sodium value (0.669 μg/g) during May 2001 at the site 2. Seasonally, sodium of the water sediments of the river was found to be higher during summer season followed by winter and rainy seasons at most of the sites.

Minimum calcium (1.764 μg/g) was recorded during August 2001 at site 1 and the maximum calcium value (7.022 μg/g) during April 2001 at site 4. Seasonally, calcium of the water sediments of the river was found to be higher during summer season followed by winter and rainy seasons at most of the sites.

Minimum phosphorus content (0.053 mg/g) in water sediments of river Varuna was recorded during September 2001 at site 1 and the maximum phosphorus (0.119 mg/g) during May 2001 at site 4. Seasonally, phosphorus content in water sediments of the river was found to be highest during summer season followed by winter and rainy seasons at all the sites.

Minimum total nitrogen (0.046 mg/g) was recorded during September and October 2001 at site 3 and the maximum total nitrogen (0.169 mg/g) during May 2001 at site 1. Seasonally, total nitrogen in the water sediments of the river was found to be highest during summer season followed by winter and rainy seasons at all the sites.

Organic carbon was found to be minimum (0.411%) during August 2001 at site 2 and the maximum organic carbon (0.715%) during May 2001 at the site 3. Seasonally, organic carbon in the water sediments of the river was found to be highest during summer season followed by winter and rainy seasons at all the sites showing slight fluctuation.

❒ Macrophytic Study of River Varuna

Apomogeton natans was found to be present at site 1 only. Likewise, *Azolla pinnata* was present only at site 2 and *Potamogeton pectinatus* and *Wolffia* only at site 1.

Hydrilla verticillata was present at sites 1, 2 and 3 but was not found at site 4. *Ipomoea aquatica* was present only at site 3, however, it was not reported at sites 1, 3 and 4. *Eichhornia crassipes* was present only at sites 3 and 4, however, it was absent at sites 1 and 2. Contrary to it, *Salvenia natans* was present only at sites 1 and 2 but not at sites 3 and 4. *Salvenia molesta* was present at sites 2, 3 and 4 but was not recorded at site 1. *Pistia stratiotes* were present only at sites 1 and 2, however, it was not found at sites 3 and 4. *Lemna minor* was not present at site 1 but it was recorded at sites 2, 3 and 4.

By the study of similarity and dissimilarity index, different habitat condition, quality and quantity of pollutants at the respective sites and response of the plants growing in the area can be interpreted. The same values with respect to the aquatic plants were calculated. The results indicate that maximum dissimilarity was found between site 1 and site 4 (0.9). Similarity index between site 1 and site 2 and also between site 3 and site 4 were highest and the value was 0.33. Likewise least value of similarity index (0.1) was recorded between site 1 and site 4.

Least density of plants was found during rainy season because all the plants were washed by rain water. At all the sites highest density of plants were recorded during winter followed by summer season. During summer decrease in their density started because by increase in temperature the rate of physiological reactions increases—specially, respiration, therefore, decline in their population was recorded.

Frequency was also found to be higher during winter season because the river was nearly calm and the plants got proper time for growth and development. *Salvenia molesta* showed higher frequency during June 2001 at sites 2, 3 and 4.

The macrophytic composition of more polluted sites differ from the less polluted sites. For example *Eichhornia crassipes, Lemna minor* and *Salvenia molesta* were found only at the polluted sites, while *Potamogeton pectinatus, Pistia stratiotes*, etc. were not found at the polluted sites. The plants preferring polluted area are pollution resistant, thus, they absorb the pollutants from the medium.

❐ Result of Water Treatment

Charcoal treatment showed marked reduction in heavy metal, nitrate, phosphate, total hardness, etc. in the water sample. But, due to highly absorptive and porous nature, reduction in DO was also recorded by charcoal treatment. Reduction in DO resulted in increase in BOD and COD. These three are very sensitive parameters for the water quality, thus, this was recorded as a prominent drawback of this treatment.

Marvellous response was recorded in the case of ozone treatment where 100% removal of chromium from polluted water was surprising. Most of the heavy metals were nearly washed along with reduction in acidity, nitrate, phosphate,

BOD, COD and total hardness. Similar results were obtained in the treatment of water samples of all the three sites. Ozone treatment showed significant increase in the value of DO and total solids.

In monoculture of *Eichhornia* considerable reduction in pollutants was recorded, especially in the case of nitrate, phosphate and some heavy metals like Cr, Ni, Pb and Zn in case of treatment of samples of all the sites. Slight increase in DO was recorded by this treatment. Monoculture of *Hydrilla* also showed marked reduction in pollution load, especially in case of BOD, COD, total hardness, phosphate, nitrate, oil and grease, Ni, Pb and Zn. High increase in DO was also recorded in this treatment. Mixed culture of *Eichhornia* and *Hydrilla* showed brilliant response. In this treatment, extensive reduction in nearly all the parametres were recorded. DO also increases manifold in this treatment.

The macrophytes cultivated for pollution control must be harvested from time to time regularly. The failure of which may lead to death and decay of the plants in the system. This would ultimately lead to secondary problems. The plants may deposit on water bed causing siltation, further, it may increase the value of BOD—reducing the DO.

❐ Important Findings

- 5,277 industrial units were located to be operating in Varanasi.
- The important small scale industries pouring directly into river Varuna were:
    - Battery and allied industries.
    - Automobile servicing stations.
    - Banarasi sarees printing and dyeing industries.
- The number of battery and allied industries pouring effluents directly in river Varuna were 596 in Razabazar area.
- The number of automobile servicing stations pouring effluents directly in river Varuna was 117 in Chaukaghat area.
- The number of Banarasi sarees printing, dyeing and allied industries pouring effluents directly in river Varuna was 164 in Kazzakpura area.
- Temperature of river water was found highest in Kazzakpura area.
- High pH, alkalinity, and DO were found in the water at Rameshwar.
- High nitrate, phosphate, acidity, chloride, total solids, total hardness, etc. in water was found in Kazzakpura area.
- BOD, COD and oil & grease were found highest in the river water at Chaukaghat area.
- High concentration of Cd, Cu, Cr and Ni in the river water was found in Kazzakpura area.

- Concentration of Cd, Pb and Zn was found high in Razabazar area.
- Considerable amount of Cu, Cr, Ni, Pb and Zn in the river water was found in Chaukaghat area.
- Colour of water sediment of river water is light in Rameshwar area.
- In polluted sites, colour of water sediments appears dark.
- Concentration of K, Na, Cd, Zn and Pb in the water sediment of river water at Razabazar area was higher.
- Concentration of K, Na, P, Total nitrogen, organic carbon was higher in the water sediments of the river at Rameshwar.
- Water sediment of the river at Kazzakpura area shows high concentration of Ca, P, Cd, Cu, Ni, Cr, Pb, and pH.
- Macrophytic investigation shows highest similarity index value between sites 1 and 2 and also between sites 3 and 4.
- Macropytically, site 1 and site 4 show maximum dissimilarity index.
- River contains 6 aquatic macrophytes at Rameshwar and at Razabazar.
- 5 plants were present in the water at Chaukaghat while only 4 plants in Kazzakpura area.
- Out of the five treatments of river water, ozone treatment was found most effective in the control of water pollution.
- Charcoal treatment was also highly effective in the control of water pollution but it decreased the DO of water.
- Mixed culture of *Eichhornia crassipes* and *Hydrilla verticillata* was found to be the best and most feasible practice of water pollution control because it increased DO in addition to absorption of nutrients and heavy metals from the waterbody.

❒ Recommendations

- The industrial units directly pouring their effluents into the river Varuna should discharge their effluents after treatment.
- Selected macrophytes must be cultivated in the river to check the pollution load of the river.
- Combination of *Eichhornia crassipes* and *Hydrilla verticillata* which gave brilliant performance in pollution abatement must be cultured in the river.
- Mix culture for river pollution control was also recommended because this process involves the least input.
- Macrophytes harvested as a result of this treatment practice can be used for production of bio-gas, paper and also be used as fodder.
- Charcoal bags must be suspended in highly polluted area in the river for pollutant adsorption.

Most of the fresh water is present in river, ponds and under-ground reservoirs. The surface water bodies get polluted easily whereas ground water reservoirs become polluted only after prolonged exposure. Natural water, in contact with foreign matters during either industrial process or domestic use, becomes polluted. Such polluted water is termed as Waste water. The used-up community water is called domestic waste water, whereas the effluent discharged from the industry is called industrial waste water.

In order to control the pollution in any system, it is important to know about:

- Sources of emission of pollutants.
- Nature and concentration of pollutants.
- Physicochemical and biological properties of the receiving aquatic body.

The study of the aforesaid helps in the development of some control devices and ecomanagement of the aquatic eco-systems. Different health agencies have prescribed standards of different category of water. Standards are essential because the quality of water directly affects the human health. The standards are periodically revised to take advantage of the new treatment techniques and to make use of the new test methods. The tests are carried out to determine whether or not the water meets the established bacteriological, physical, chemical and radioactivity standards.

The use of water for drinking and other domestic purposes by human beings is generally considered to be its highest and most essential use. As a result the water quality criteria that permit this use are those most attentively implemented. Except for sanitary considerations, other uses may have more specific requirements, but on balance, drinking water represents and is accorded a quality superior to all others.

About 1,500 substances have been listed as pollutants in fresh water ecosystems and a generalised list of pollutants includes acids and alkalies, detergents, domestic sewage and farm manure, nutrients (phosphates and nitrates), oil and oil dispersants, organic toxic wastes (formaldehydes, phenols) pathogens, pesticides; domestic sewage contains detergents, nutrients, metals, pathogens and a variety of other compounds.

Wastes from municipalities, sanitories, tanneries, slaughtering houses, sugar mills, dairies, agricultural farms, etc. discharged into different water bodies are the potential sources of different infective and pathogenic agents like bacteria, viruses, protozoans, fungi, platihelminths which cause several fatal and infectious diseases such as typhoid, cholera, hepatitis, scabies, trachoma, sleeping sickness, dysentery, yellow fever, amoebiosis, diarrhea, ascariosis distomatosis, etc. in human beings.

Traditional waste water treatment is directed towards the treatment processes which include specially the reduction of suspended matters' biochemical oxygen demand and bacterial concentration. Conventional treatment plants use chlorination as the final treatment process to reduce the concentration of bacteria. Prechlorination—performed on the plant influent, used in the incoming sewage which is septic or—if the flows are low and the holdup time in the plant is such that the waste will become septic.

The advanced waste water treatment process can further be designated as modified traditional or conventional waste water treatment processes. Chemicals may be added to improve the separation of oils, the density of which is very close to that of water or to oils that are slightly soluble. As a general rule, oils are rendered less soluble under both extreme acid and extreme basic conditions. Most commonly sulphuric acid (H_2SO_4) is used; however, lime at a pH of 8.4 has also been shown to be effective. In the interest of recycling, a system is there that recovers both the chemicals added and the oil separated. In this system, Ferric chloride ($FeCl_3$), lime, ferrice sulphate ($Fe_2(SO_4)_3$)and a polymer are added to the oily liquid waste. The precipitated sludge containing the oils is treated with sulphuric acid at 90 ^oF (32.2 ^oC) which releases the oil from the sludge. This oil is then separated and reused, whereas the ferric sulphate is also reclaimed from the sludge.

Disinfection ideally should kill not only all pathogenic bacteria but also the viruses in the water. Sterilisation is not always necessary. The removal of contaminants that impart colour and objectionable taste and odour to the water improves the water's palatability. These contaminants are usually present in such low concentration that their detection and identification is often difficult. Few disinfection treatment techniques are successful in accomplishing the objectives of disinfection coupled with colour, taste, and odour removal. Ozonation is the most effective technique in this regard. The irradiation of water by ultraviolet light kills bacteria and viruses in the water. This bactericidal action of ultraviolet light is most effective in the wavelength range of 250 to 260 mμ.

❐ Relevance of the Study

In light of the above study we are in a position to state that almost no surface water on the earth is fit for direct consumption without any prior treatment. The above study—which consisted of discussion of water quality standards, its need according to different purposes and its importance; water pollutants and their effects; traditional and advanced waste water treatments—has been done. We have tried to summarise all the waste water treatment processes—whether advanced or traditional. As an outcome of this study, one can select any of the described methods for waste water treatment according to choice.

Relevance of the study also lies in the literature as the methods described can be applied in small scale as well as large scale units. The methods also deal with water treatment processes starting from domestic level to the large treatment plants. The literature also deals with methods of removal of all sorts of general pollutants, viz. nitrates, phosphates, total hardness, oxygen demand, as well as oil and grease.

❐ Future Prospects

The study has not reached the final destination; instead, it has opened a new path for further studies. On the basis of this study several new aspects of pollution treatment can be studied.

We have discussed all the treatment methods in isolation, i.e. consideration of different pollutants and also different treatment processes separately. If two or more than two pollutants are considered together or more than two treatment methods are applied simultaneously the result may be still better. However, much further study in this respect needs to be done.

Furthermore, series of experiments need to be conducted to screen out the specific plant for specific pollutant. Mostly combination of plants, i.e. mixed culture, are to be preferred, and the right combination is to be explored to get the best performance. Chemical and physical methods of pollution control should also be applied wherever necessary, in addition to the biological treatment.

Appendix I

BLOCK ANOVA with Respect to Site and Month

Variables of river water	Site		Month	
	df	F-ratio	df	F-ratio
Temperature	3	17.13***	11	469.84***
Total Solids	3	85.05***	11	4.90***
pH	3	67.98***	11	4.71***
EC	3	38.86***	11	20.64***
Acidity	3	42.34***	11	0.82*
Alkalinity	3	44.90***	11	9.23***
DO	3	66.40***	11	4.74***
BOD	3	73.20***	11	4.69***
COD	3	60.44***	11	4.57***
Total Hardness	3	191.33***	11	4.89***
Oil and Grease	3	67.96***	11	6.16***
NO_3	3	184.62***	11	2.196**
PO_4	3	71.61***	11	3.64***
Cl^-	3	44.64***	11	47.10***
Cd	3	72.53***	11	6.97***
Cu	3	66.40***	11	4.74***
Cr	3	27.37***	11	4.20***
Ni	3	67.56***	11	8.28***
Pb	3	33.33***	11	10.06***
Zn	3	71.90***	11	5.58***

* — Non-significant (N.S.)

** — $p < 0.05$

*** — $p < 0.001$

APPENDIX II

Result of treatment of water samples of Site 2 by chemical methods

Parameters	Initial reading	Charcoal treatment		Ozone treatment	
		Final reading	% reduction	Final reading	% reduction
Acidity (mg/l $CaCO_3$)	0.48	0.21	56.250	0.012	97.500
Nitrate (mg/l)	0.211	0.097	54.028	0.032	84.834
Phosphate (mg/l)	0.896	0.252	71.875	0.067	92.522
DO (mg/l)	4.13	3.85	6.780	13.81	–234.383
BOD (mg/l)	54.28	64.96	–19.676	2.76	94.915
COD (mg/l)	76.32	93.53	–22.550	5.31	93.042
Total Solids (mg/l)	336.21	128.13	61.890	576.26	–71.399
Total Hardness (mg/l)	686.25	231.11	66.323	0.93	99.864
Oil and Grease (mg/l)	1.58	0.64	59.494	0.027	98.291
Cd (mg/l)	0.042	0.016	61.905	0.011	73.810
Cu (mg/l)	0.138	0.053	61.594	0.017	87.681
Cr (mg/l)	0.012	0.003	75.000	0	100.000
Ni (mg/l)	0.018	0.003	83.333	0.001	94.444
Pb (mg/l)	0.253	0.076	69.960	0.023	90.909
Zn (mg/l)	1.857	0.651	64.943	0.036	98.061

Result of treatment of water samples of Site 2 by biological process

Parameters	Initial reading	Monoculture of *Eichhornia*		Monoculture of *Hydrilla*		Mixed culture of *Eichhornia* and *Hydrilla*	
		Final reading	% reduction	Final reading	% reduction	Final reading	% reduction
Acidity (mg/l $CaCO_3$)	0.48	0.31	35.417	0.26	45.833	0.16	66.667
Nitrate (mg/l)	0.211	0.068	67.773	0.126	40.284	0.041	80.569
Phosphate (mg/l)	0.896	0.136	84.821	0.385	57.031	0.087	90.290
DO (mg/l)	4.13	4.87	–17.918	6.91	-67.312	8.61	–108.475
BOD (mg/l)	54.28	43.11	20.578	38.15	29.716	21.51	60.372
COD (mg/l)	76.32	58.2	23.742	47.12	38.260	34.13	55.280
Total Solids (mg/l)	336.21	261.26	22.293	223.11	33.640	135.11	59.814
Total Hardness (mg/l)	686.25	411.07	40.099	397.29	42.107	316.71	53.849
Oil and Grease (mg/l)	1.58	1.03	34.810	0.79	50.000	0.47	70.253
Cd (mg/l)	0.042	0.029	30.952	0.031	26.190	0.019	54.762
Cu (mg/l)	0.138	0.081	41.304	0.092	33.333	0.067	51.449
Cr (mg/l)	0.012	0.006	50.000	0.007	41.667	0.005	58.333
Ni (mg/l)	0.018	0.008	55.556	0.007	61.111	0.004	77.778
Pb (mg/l)	0.253	0.107	57.708	0.119	52.964	0.084	66.798
Zn (mg/l)	1.857	0.873	52.989	0.905	51.265	0.684	63.166

Result of treatment of water samples of Site 3 by chemical methods

Parameters	Initial reading	Charcoal treatment		Ozone treatment	
		Final reading	% reduction	Final reading	% reduction
Acidity (mg/l $CaCO_3$)	7.98	1.92	75.940	0.015	99.812
Nitrate (mg/l)	0.246	0.091	63.008	0.029	88.211
Phosphate (mg/l)	1.261	0.305	75.813	0.071	94.370
DO (mg/l)	2.96	2.46	16.892	10.52	–255.405
BOD (mg/l)	98.67	113.16	–14.685	3.51	96.443
COD (mg/l)	167.31	193.41	–15.600	6.17	96.312
Total Solids (mg/l)	821	276.11	66.369	1057.66	–28.826
Total Hardness (mg/l)	976.33	285.05	70.804	0.859	99.912
Oil and Grease (mg/l)	7.54	4.19	44.430	0.093	98.767
Cd (mg/l)	0.021	0.014	33.333	0.01	52.381
Cu (mg/l)	0.165	0.071	56.970	0.021	87.273
Cr (mg/l)	0.047	0.011	76.596	0.005	89.362
Ni (mg/l)	0.035	0.009	74.286	0.002	94.286
Pb (mg/l)	0.121	0.049	59.504	0.02	83.471
Zn (mg/l)	1.3	0.494	62.000	0.031	97.615

Result of treatment of water samples of Site 3 by biological process

Parameters	Initial reading	Monoculture of *Eichhornia*		Monoculture of *Hydrilla*		Mixed culture of *Eichhornia* and *Hydrilla*	
		Final reading	% reduction	Final reading	% reduction	Final reading	% reduction
Acidity (mg/l $CaCO_3$)	7.98	3.11	61.028	3.96	50.376	1.69	78.822
Nitrate (mg/l)	0.246	0.071	71.138	0.137	44.309	0.044	82.114
Phosphate (mg/l)	1.261	0.181	85.646	0.462	63.362	0.088	93.021
DO (mg/l)	2.96	3.4	–14.865	5.86	–97.973	7.89	–166.554
BOD (mg/l)	98.67	72.66	26.361	57.31	41.918	34.17	65.369
COD (mg/l)	167.31	119.35	28.665	72.51	56.661	67.65	59.566
Total Solids (mg/l)	821	520.01	36.661	484.15	41.029	253.18	69.162
Total Hardness (mg/l)	976.33	589.32	39.639	513.07	47.449	331.06	66.091
Oil and Grease (mg/l)	7.54	5.16	31.565	3.19	57.692	1.55	79.443
Cd (mg/l)	0.021	0.016	23.810	0.017	19.048	0.013	38.095
Cu (mg/l)	0.365	0.217	40.548	0.231	36.712	0.126	65.479
Cr (mg/l)	0.047	0.025	46.809	0.031	34.043	0.009	80.851
Ni (mg/l)	0.035	0.015	57.143	0.012	65.714	0.006	82.857
Pb (mg/l)	0.121	0.06	50.413	0.073	39.669	0.046	61.983
Zn (mg/l)	1.3	0.909	30.077	1.006	22.615	0.684	47.385

Result of treatment of water samples of Site 4 by chemical methods

Parameters	Initial reading	Charcoal treatment		Ozone treatment	
		Final reading	% reduction	Final reading	% reduction
Acidity (mg/l $CaCO_3$)	39.66	15.17	61.750	0.019	99.952
Nitrate (mg/l)	1.139	0.321	71.81	0.072	93.679
Phosphate (mg/l)	1.954	0.381	80.502	0.088	95.496
DO (mg/l)	1.47	1.01	31.293	11.31	–669.388
BOD (mg/l)	81.22	111.06	–36.740	3.14	96.134
COD (mg/l)	139.86	173.51	–24.060	6.19	95.574
Total Solids (mg/l)	1067.5	656.15	38.534	1321	–23.747
Total Hardness (mg/l)	1056.21	313.07	70.359	1.743	99.835
Oil and Grease (mg/l)	4.11	2.88	29.927	0.021	99.489
Cd (mg/l)	0.056	0.021	62.500	0.009	83.930
Cu (mg/l)	0.513	0.089	82.651	0.021	95.906
Cr (mg/l)	0.086	0.017	80.233	0.008	90.698
Ni (mg/l)	0.057	0.013	77.193	0.001	98.246
Pb (mg/l)	0.159	0.051	67.925	0.018	88.679
Zn (mg/l)	1.261	0.486	61.459	0.026	97.938

Result of treatment of water samples of Site 4 by biological process

Parameters	Initial reading	Monoculture of *Eichhornia*		Monoculture of *Hydrilla*		Mixed culture of *Eichhornia* and *Hydrilla*	
		Final reading	% reduction	Final reading	% reduction	Final reading	% reduction
Acidity (mg/l $CaCO_3$)	39.66	16.39	58.674	18.76	52.698	8.16	79.425
Nitrate (mg/l)	1.139	0.315	72.344	0.687	39.684	0.192	83.143
Phosphate (mg/l)	1.954	0.169	91.351	0.407	79.171	0.103	94.729
DO (mg/l)	1.47	3.13	–112.925	7.38	–402.041	7.69	–423.129
BOD (mg/l)	81.22	76.51	5.799	51.36	36.764	37.81	53.447
COD (mg/l)	139.86	101.17	27.663	87.39	37.516	76.14	45.560
Total Solids (mg/l)	1067.5	539.71	49.442	503.15	52.867	279.39	73.828
Total Hardness (mg/l)	1056.21	611.2	42.133	563.09	46.688	352.66	66.611
Oil and Grease (mg/l)	4.11	2.83	31.144	1.86	54.745	0.799	80.560
Cd (mg/l)	0.056	0.042	25.000	0.045	19.643	0.036	35.714
Cu (mg/l)	0.513	0.169	67.057	0.179	65.107	0.121	76.413
Cr (mg/l)	0.086	0.046	46.512	0.057	33.721	0.017	80.233
Ni (mg/l)	0.057	0.023	59.649	0.018	68.421	0.008	85.965
Pb (mg/l)	0.159	0.071	55.346	0.09	43.396	0.057	64.151
Zn (mg/l)	1.261	0.752	40.364	0.861	31.720	0.072	94.290

SELECT BIBLIOGRAPHY

Abaychi, J.K. 1987. Concentrations of trace elements in aquatic vascular plants from shatt al. Arab river, Iraq. *Journal of Biological Sciences Research.* 18(2): 123–129.

Abdullah, M.I. and Royle, L.G. 1972. Heavy metal content of some rivers and Lake in Wales. *Nature.* 238: 329–330.

Abo-Rady, M.K. 1980. Makrophytische Wasserpflanzenals Bioindika-toren fur die Schwermetallbelastung der oberen leine. [Aquatic macrophytes as indicator for heavy metal pollution in the River Leine (West Germany).] *Arch. Hydrobiol.* 89: 387–404.

Adarkatti , I.B., and Rao, G.S.C.1980 Treatment and disposal of distillery effluent —an integrated approach *Proc. Disposal of sugar mill and distillery effluents.* 1–10.

Agami, M., Litav, M. and Waisel, Y. 1976. The effects of various components of water pollution on the behaviour of some aquatic macrophytes of the coastal rivers of Israel. *Aquat. Bot.* (2) 203–213.

Agrawal, D.K., Gaur, S.D., Sen, P.C. and Marwah, S.M. 1976. Bacteriological study of Ganges Water at Varanasi. Indian. *J. Med. Res.* 64(3): 373–383.

Agrawal, I.C., and Srivastava, H.C. 1984. Pollution Survey of major drains discharged into river Ganga and Yamuna at Allahabad. *Instn. Pub. Lic. Hlth. Engrs. TS III–39. TS III–48.*

Agrawal, S.K. 1983. Water quality of sewage drains entering in to Chambal river at Kota. *Acta. Ecol.* 5:2.

Ainozaily, F., Alaerts, G., and Veenstra, S. 2000. Performance of duckweed Covered Sewage lagoons—II. Nitrogen and phosphorus balance and Plant productivity. *Water Res.* 34(10): 2734–2741.

Ajmal, M. 1980. Detrimental effects of pharmaceutical Industrial waste on microorganisms. *J. Water, Air and Soil Pollution.* 13(4): 447–452.

Alich, J. and Inman, R. 1976. Energy from agriculture. *Proceedings of clean fuels from biomass, sewage, urban refuse, and agriculture wastes*. 150: 172.

Allen, S.E. 1974. Chemical analysis of Ecological materials. Blackwell Scientific Publications. Oxford.

Allenby, K.G. 1981. Some analysis of aquatic plant and their waters. *Hydrobiologia*. 77: 177–189.

Anderson, Y., and Stentrom, T.A.1987. Waterborne outbreak in Sweden – causes and etiology. *Wat. Sci. Tech*. 19: 375–380.

Antonic, R.L., The bio-disc process: new technology for the treatment of biodegradable industrial waste water. CEP symposium series 67: 585, 1971.

APHA (1998) Standard Methods for the Examination of Water and Wastewater, American Public Health Association. 1015 Fifteen Street NW, Washington DC 20005-2605 (19th Edn.)

Arceivala, S.J. 1986. Waste water treatment for pollution control. Tata McGraw Hill, New Delhi.

Archer, A.J. 1985. Disinfection: sunlight Photo-Oxidation of organic pollutants in wastewater. *J. Water Science and Technology*. 17(4–5): 623.

Arora, B.R., Azad, A.S., Singh. B. and Sekhar, G.S. 1985. Pollution potential of municipal waste water of Ludhiana, Punjab. *Indian Jnl. of Ecology*. 12(i): 1–7.

Arora, H.C., Routh, T., Chattopadhya, S.N., and Sharma, V.P. 1974. Survey of sugar mill effluent disposal, part II A comparative study of sugar mill effluent characterstics. *Indian J. Environ. Hlth*. 16(3): 233–246.

Arvin, E. 1985. Biological removal of phosphorus from wastewater. *J. Crc. Critical Review in Environ. Control*. 15(1): 25.

Atkins, R., Rose, T. Brown, R. S. and Robb, M. 2001. The Microcystis cyanobacteria bloom in the swam River—February 2000. *Wat. Sci and tech*. 43 (9): 107–114.

Attionu, R.H. 1976. Some effects of water lettuce (*Pistia stratiotes. L*) on its habitat. *Hydrobiologia*. 50(3): 245–254.

Ault, T., Velzeboer, R., Zammit, R. 2000. Influence of nutrient availability on phytoplankton growth and community structure in the Port Adelaide River, Australia : Bioassay assessment of potential nutrient limitation. *Hydrobiologia*. 429 (1–3): 89.

Austin, R.J., and Vause, E.H., Chemical Coagulation of Refinery Wastewater Proceedings of the 6th Industrial Waste Conference, Purdue University, 1951.

Ayoma, I., Hisao, N. and Ma, S.Y. 1986. Uptake of nitrogen and phosphate, and water purification capacity of water hyacinth. Ber. Ohara Inst. Landw. *Biol., Okayama University*. (19) 77–89.

Ayoma, I., Nishizaki, H., Yogi, M. 1987. Uptake of Nitrogen and phosphate and Water purification capacity by water hyacinth (*Eichhornica crassipes* (Mart.) Solms.). *J. Soils and Fertilizers*.50 (3): 345–349.

Azad, A.S., Arora, B.R. and Sekhar, G.S. 1982. Nature and extent of heavy metal pollution from industrial units in Ludhiana. Indian Jl. of Ecology. 11(1): 1–5.

Bachmann, V. ánd Ussieglio P.P. 1999. Contribution of the macrobenthic compartment to the oxygen budget of a large regulated river: the *Mosel. Hydrobiol.* 410: 39–46.

Badola, S.P. and Singh, H.R. 1981. Hydrobiology of the river Alaknanda at the Garhwal, Himalaya. *Ind. J. Ecol.* 8(2): 269–276.

Bagde, U.S. and Verma, A.K. 1982. Distribution and periodicity of total, fecal Colifrom bacteria in an aquatic ecosystem. *Int. J. Env. Studies.* 91: 215–220.

Bagnall, L.O., Boldwin, J.A. and Hentges, J.F. 1974. Processing and storage of water hyacinth silage. *Hyacinth Control J.*, 12: 73–79.

Balchand, A.N., and Nambisan, P.N.K. 1986. Effect of pulp paper effluent on the water quality of Muvattupuzha river emptying into Cochin backwaters. *Indian J. Marine Sciences*. 15: 253–259.

Balmer, M., Krebs, R., Lothembach, B., Gieger, G., and Schulin, R. 1999.The influence of Nitriloacetate on heavy metal uptake of Lettuce and ryegrass. *J. Environ. Qual.* 28 (6): 1699–1704.

Balmforth, D.J. 1990. The pollution aspects of storm sewage overflows. Water and Environmental management. 4(3): 219–226.

Bandy, J.T. 1984. Water characteristics. *J. Wat. Poll. Cont. Fed.* 56(6): 544–548.

Bansho, K. and Miyazaki, A. 1983. Analysis of waste water and effluents. *Bunsek.* 11: 862–868.

Barko, J.N. and Smart, R.M. 1981. Comparative Influence of light and temperature on the growth and metabolism of selected Submerged freshwater macrophytes. *Ecol. Monogr.*, 51 (2): 219–225.

Bartell, S.M., Campbell, K.R., Lovelock, C.M., Nair, S.K. and Shaw, J.L. 2000. Characterising aquatic ecological risk from pesticides using diquate-di-bromide, a case study, *Environmental Toxicology and Chemistry*. 19(15): 1441.

Basu A.K. 1966. Studies in effluents from pulp paper mill and its role in bringing the physico-chemical changes around several discharge points in the Hooghly Estuary. *Indian J. Int. Eng.* 46: 108–116.

Bates, G.R. and Phipps 1958. Water hyacinth and its control in Southern Rhodesia. *First Afr. Weed Control Conf.* 1958. p.6.

Bates, R.P. and Hentges, J.F. 1976. Aquatic weeds eradicate or cultivate? *Econ. Bot.* (30) 39–50.

Behrendt, H. and Opitz, D. 1999. Retention of nutrients in river systems: dependence on specific runoff and hydraulic load. *Hydrobiol.* 410: 111–122.

Behura, B.K. 1981. Pollution everywhere. *Science Reporter, New Delhi*. 18: 170–172.

Bell, B.A. 1984. Treatment of high strength industrial waste in continuously fed intermittently operated activated sludge system. *J. Wat. Poll. Cont. Fed.* 55(11): 1160–1164.

Bell, G.R., Design criteria for diatomic filters. J. AWWA 54: 1241, 1962.

Berber, A., and Winter. 1984. The influence of extended anaerobic retention time on the performance of Phoredox nutrient removal plant. *Water, Science Technology*. 17(81).

Berner, L.M. 1951. Limnology of the lower Missouri river. *Ecol.* 3(1):1.

Bewtra, J.K. and Charan, R. 1965. Effect of temperature on biochemical oxygen demand. *Environ. Hlth.* 7(3): 143–164.

Bhargava, D.S. 1977. Water quality in three typical rivers in U.P. – Ganga, Yamuna and Kali. Ph.D. Thesis, IIT Kanpur.

Bhargava, D.S. 1985. Variation in quality in the Ganges. *Jnl. of Effluent Water Treatment*. 25(2).

Bhaskaran, T.R., Chakraborty, R.N. and Trivedi, R.C. 1963. Studies on the river pollution: 1. Pollution on purification of Gomati river near Lucknow. *J. Inst. Engrs. India*. 45(6): 39–50.

Bhatt, S.D., Bisht, Y. and Negi, U. 1985. Hydrology and phytoplankton populations in river Koshi of Western Himalaya (U.P.). *Ind. J. Ecol.* 12(1): 141–146.

Bhuyan, B.R. 1970. Physico-chemical qualities of the water of some ancient tanks in Sibsapur. *Environ. Hlth.*, 12: 129–134.

Bishai, H.M. 1960. Effect of *Eichhornia crassipes* on the hydrobiology of Nile water. *Rep. Hydrobiol. Res.* Unit. Univ. Khartoum. 7: 2–3.

Bishop, P. and De Waters, J. 1986. Heavy metal removal by aquatic macrophytes in a temperate climate aquatic treatment system. *Proc. Intl. Conf. Innnovative Biological Treatment of Toxic Waste Waters*, Arlington, Va, 100–107.

Blanchard, P.E. and Lerch, R.N. 2000. Watershed vulnerability to losses of agricultural chemicals : Interactions of chemistry, hydrology, and land-use. *Environmental Science and Technology*. 34(16): 3315.

Bloesch, J. 1999. Large river ecosystems : Concepts and biodiversity, with special emphasis on the Danube and the International Association for Danube Research (IAD)—*Edutorial. Arch. Hydrobiol.* (3), 115s: 235–238.

Bode, H. and Klopp, R. 2001. Nutrient in the river basin of the Rhur—A German case study. *Wat. Sci. and Tech.* 44(1): 15–24.

Bode, H., Seyfried, C.F. and Kraft, A. 1987. High rate denitrification of concentrated nitrate waste water. Activated sludge waste water treatment. J. 13th Biennial Conf. of the International Water Pollution. *Water Sci. Technol.* 19(1-2): 163–174.

Bollinger, J.E., Steinberge, L.J., Harrison, M.J., Crews, J.P., Englande, A.J., VelascoGonzales, C., White, L.E., and George, W.J. 1999. Comparative analysis of nutrient data in the lower Mississippi River. *Water Res.* 33 (11): 2627–2632.

Bose, P.K. 1945. The problem of water hyacinth in Bengal. *Sci. Cult.* 11: 167–171.

Boyd, C.E. 1968a. Evaluation of some common aquatic weeds as possible feed stuffs. *Hyacinth Control Jour*. 7: 26–27.

Boyd, C.E. 1968b. Freshwater plants: A potential source of protein. *Econ. Bot*. 22: 359–368.

Boyd, C.E. 1969. The nutritive value of three species of water weeds. *Economic Botany*. 23: 123–127.

Boyd, C.E. 1969. Vascular aquatic plants for mineral nutrient removal from polluted water. *Econ. Bot.*, 24: 95–103.

Boyd, C.E. 1970. Vascular aquatic plants for mineral nutrient removal form polluted water. *Econ . Botany*. 24: 51–56.

Boyd, C.E. 1976. Accumulation of dry matter, nitrogen and phosphorus by cultivated water hyacinths. *Econ. Botany* (30) 51–56.

Boyd, C.E. and Vickers, D.H. 1971. Variation in the elemental content of *Eichhornia crassipes*. *Hydrobiol.* (38) 409–414.

Brenzonik, L.P. 1972. Nitrogen : Sources and transformation in natural waters. Nutrients in natural waters. A Willay-Int. Publ. New York (8).

Brion, N., and Billen, G. 2000. Wastewater as a source of nitrifying bacteria in river systems: the case of the River Scine downstream from Paris. *Water Res.* 34(12): 3213–3221.

Brix, H. 1993. Wastewater treatment in constructed wetlands: System design, removal processes, and treatment performance. In: constructed wetlands for Water. quality improvement, G.A. Moshiri, ed. Lewis Publishers, Boka Raton, pp.9–22.

Brix, H. 1998. Denmerk. In: Vymazal, J., Brix, H., cooper, P.F., Green, M.B., Haberl, R. (Eds): Constructed Wetlands for Wastewater treatment in Europe. Backuys Publishers, Leiden, The Netherlands.

Brix, H. and Johansen, N.H. 1999. Treatment of domestic sewage in a two-stage Constructed wetland-design principles. In: Vymazl, J. (Ed.), Nutrient cycling and retention in natural and retention in natural and constructed wetlands. Backays Publishers, Leidew, The Netherlands, pp.155–163.

Brix, H. and Schierup, H.H. 1989a. Danish experience with Sewage treatment in constructed wetlands. In: Constructed Wetlands for Wastewater treatment. Municipal, industrial and agricultural, D.A. Hammer, ed. Lewis Publisher lnc. Chelsea, MI, pp. 565–573.

Brix, H. and Schierup, H.H. 1989b. The use of aquatic macrophytes in water pollution control. *Ambio*. 18: 100–107.

Brooker, M.P. 1984. The behaviour of phosphate, nitrate, chloride and hardness in 12 Welsh rivers (U.K.). *J. Water Res.* 18(9): 1152–1164.

Brower, G.R. 1985. Industrial wastes and water quality. *J. Wat. Poll. Cont. Fed.* 57 (6):625.

Brown, D.H. and Beckett, R.P. 1985. Intracellular and extracellular uptake of cadmium by the moss *Rhytidiadelphus squarrosus*. *Ann. Bot*. 55: 179–185.

Brown, R.D. 1971. The use of biological analysis as indicators of water quality. *J. Environ. Hlth.* 34: 62–66.

Bruijin, J. and Tuinzaad, H., The relationship between depth of U-tubes and aeration process. Amer. Water Works Assoc. J. 50: 879, 1958.

Budd, K. and Kerson, G.W. 1987. Uptake of phosphate by two cyanophytes: Cation effects and energetics. *Canadian Journal of Botany*. 65(9): 1901–1907.

Burgoon, P.S., Reddy, K.R., De Busk, T.A. and Koopmen, B. 1991. Vegetated submerged beds with artificial substrates II: N and P removal. *J. of Enginr. Mech. (ASCE)*, 117(8): 408–424.

Cain, J.R., Paschal, D.C. and Hayden, C.M. 1980. Toxicity and bioaccumulation of cadmium in colonial green algae. *Scenedesmus obliquus Arch. Env. Contam. Toxicol.* 9: 9–16.

Cairns, J. Jr. 1968. Suspended solids standards for the protection of aquatic organisms. *Purde Univ. Engineer Bull*. 129: 16–27.

Cairns, John. Jr. and Niederlhner, B.R. 1987. Problems associated with selecting the most sensitive species for toxicity testing. *Hydrobiol*. 153: 87–94.

Canton, L. and Grimalt., J.O. 1991. Distributions of River-Transported Halogenated Biphenyls and Terphenyls in Coastal Environments. *Chemosphere* (G.B.). 23: 327.

Carty, W. 1991. Toward an Urban world. *Earthwatch* 43: 2–4.

Carvalieri, B. 1986. Some effects of Hexavalent Chromium in *L. minor L. Giornale Botanic Italiano*. 120(1–6): 80–81.

Center, T.D. and Spencer, N.R. 1981. The phenology and growth of water hyacinth (*Eichhornia crassipes* [Mart] Solms) in a eutrophic North Central Florida lake. *Aquatic Bot*. 10: 1–32.

Chadwick, M.J. and Obeid, M. 1963. The response to variations in nitrogen level of some weed species of the Sudan. *Weed Res*. 3: 230–241.

Chadwick, M.J. and Obeid, M. 1966. A comparative study of the growth of *Eichhornia crassipes* Solms and *Pistia stratiotes* L. in water culture. *J. of Ecol*. 54: 563–575.

Chakraborty, D. and Mukherjee, J. 2001. Watershed management. *Emp. News*. XXV(51): 1–2.

Chandra, P. and Sinha, S. 1992. Assessment of heavy metal (Cu, Cd, Pb, Cr, Mn) uptake by wetland plant *Bacopa monnieri* from artificially contaminated sediments. Proc. IV INTECOL. Int. Wetland Conf., Columbus, Ohio, USA. p. 118.

Chatterjee, A., Khan, I.A., Ali, M. and Mumtaz. 1981. A study on the ecology of river Kali in Aligarh. *Indian J. Animal Res*. 15: 63.

Chen, G.H., Leong, T.M., Liu, J. and Huang, J.C. 1999. Study of oxygen uptake by tidal river sediment. *Water Res*. 33(13): 2905–2912.

Chen, R.H., Twillery, R.R. 1999. Pattern of Mangrove forest structure on soil nutrients dynamics along the Shark river estuary, Florida. *Estuaries*. 22(4): 995.

Cheng, K.N. and Bray, R.H. 1951. Determination of calcium and magnesium in soil and plant material. Soil Sci. 72: 449–458.

Choung, Y.K., Jean, S.J. 2000. Phosphorus removal in domestic waste water using anaerobic fixed beds packed with iron contactors. *Water Science and Technology*. 41(1): 241.

Ciaccia, L.1972. Water and water Pollution Handbook. Mercel Dekker. Inc. New York, 3: 801–808.

Ciba, J., Korolewicz, T., and Turek, M. 1999. The occurrence of metals in composted municipal waste and their removal. *Water Air Soil Pollut*. 111(1–4): 159–170.

Cloern, J.E. 1991. Tidal Stirring and Phytoplankton Bloom Dynamics in an Estuary. *J. Mar. Res*. 49:203.

Cooke, J.G. 1994. Nutrient transformations in a natural wetland receiving sewage effluent and the implications for waste treatment. *Water Sci. Technol.* 29: 209–217.

Cooley, T.N., Martin, D.F., Durden, W.C. Jr. and Perkins, B.D. 1979. A preliminary study, metal distribution in 3 water hyacinth biotypes. *J. Wat. Res.* 13: 343–348.

Cornwell, D.A. Jr., Zottek., Patrinely, C.O., Des Furman, T. and Kim, J.I. 1977. Nutrient removal by water hyacinth. *J. Water Pollution Control Fed*. 49: 57–65.

Cossa, C.B. and Noel, J. 1987. Concentration of mercury in near shore surface waters of the Bay of Biscay and in the Gironde Estuary France. *Mar. Chem.* 20(4): 389–396.

Crabtree, B., Hickman, M., and Martian, D. 1999. Integrated Water quality and environmental Cost-benefit modelling for the management of River Tame. *Wat. Sci. Technol*. 39(4): 213–220.

Crowder, A. 1991. Acidification, metals and macrophytes. *Env. Pollut*. 71: 171–203.

Crowder, A.A., Bristow, J.M., King, M.R. and Vanderkloet, S. 1977. The aquatic macrophytes of some lakes in South eastern Ontario. *Naturaliste Can*., 104: 457–464.

Culley, D.C. Jr. and. Epps, A.E. 1973. Use of duckweed for waste treatment and animal feed. *J. Water Poll. Control Fed*. 45: 337–347.

Cully D.D. Jr., Rejmankova J., Kvet J. and Frye J.B. 1981. Production, chemical quality and use of duckweeds (Lemnaceae) in aquaculture. Waste Mgmt. Animal Feed. *World Mariculture Soc*. 12: 27–49.

Curtis, E.J.C. and Harrington, D.W. 1970. Effect of organic wastes on rivers. *Process Biochemistry*. 5: 44–46.

Curtis, E.J.S. and Curds. C.R. 1971. Sewage fungus in rivers in the United Kingdom: The slime community and its constituent organisms. *Wat. Res.* 5: 1147–1159.

Dahmanimuller, H., VanOort, F., Gelie, B., and Balabane, M. 2000. Strategies of heavy metal uptake by three plant species growing near a metal smelter. *Environ. Pollut*. 109(2): 231–238.

Dakshini, K.M.M. and Soni, J.K. 1979. Water quality of sewage drains entering Yamuna In Delhi. *Indian J. Environ. Hlth*. 21: 354–360.

Dale, H.M. 1986. Temperature and light: the determining factors in maximum depth distribution of aquatic macrophytes in Ontario. Canada. *Hydrobiol.* 133: 73–77.

Dale, H.M. and Gilliespie, T.J. 1976. The influence of floating vascular plants on the diurnal fluctuations of temperature near the water surface in early spring. *Hydrobiol.* 49: 245–256.

David, A. 1956. Studies on the pollution of Bhadra river fisheries at Bhadravathi, Mysore state, with industries effluents. *Proc. Nat. Inst. Sci. India.* 22B(3): 132–160.

Davis, J.A., and Jacknow, J. 1975. Heavy metals in wastewater in urban areas. *J. Wat. Poll. Cont. Fed.* 47: 2293–2298.

Davis, L.S., Hoffmann, J.P. and Cook, P.W. 1990. Production and nutrient accumulation by periphyton in a waste water treatment facility. *J. Phycol.* 26: 617–623.

Dawson, R.N. and Murphy, K.L. 1972. The temperature dependency of biological denitrification. *Water Res.* 6: 71–83.

De Busk, T.A. and Dierberg, F.E.1989. Effect of nutrient availability on water hyacinth standing Crop and detritus deposition. *Hydrobiol.* 174: 151–159.

De Busk, T.A., Reddy, K.R., Hages, T.D. and Schwegler Jr., B.R. 1989. Performance of a pilot-scale water hyacinth based secondary system. *J. Water Poll. Cont. fed.* 61(7): 1217–1224.

De Busk, T.A., Ryther, J.H., Hanisak, M.D. and Williams, L.D. 1981. Effects of seasonality and plant density on the productivity of some freshwater macrophytes. *J. Environ. Qual.* 10: 133–142.

De Bussy, R.P., and Whitmore, H.B., Reverse Osmosis for Industrial Water Treatment. *Proceedings for Liberty Bell corrosion* course. Phila. Section of National of Association corrosion Engineers, Phila, 1970.

De Wet, L.P.D., Schoonbee, H.J. and Pretorius, J.1990. Bioaccumulation of selected heavy metals by the water fern, *Azolla filiculoides* Lam, in a wetland ecosystem affected by sewage mine and industrial pollution. *Water SA WASADV.* 16(14): 281–286.

Deshmukh, S.B., Phadke, N.S. and Kothandaraman, V. 1984. Physico–chemical characteristics of Kanhan river water, Nagpur City. *Environ. Hlth.* 6(3): 181–183.

Diaper, E.W.J., Tertiary treatment by micro straining. Water and sewage works: 116, 1969.

Dinges, R. 1978. Upgrading stabilization pond effluent by water hyacinth culture. *J. Water Poll, Cont. Fed.* 50: 833–845.

Duarte, C.M. and Kalff, J. 1990. Biomass density and the relationship between submerged macrophytes, biomass and plant growth. *Hydrobiol.* 196(1): 17–24.

Dugan, R. 1972. Biochemical Ecology of Water Pollution. Plenum Publishing Co. Ltd. New York.

Duncan, Annie. 1990. A review: Limnological management and Bio-manipulation in the London reservoirs. *Hydrobiol*. 200–201.

Dwivedi, A. K., Hasan, H. and Shashi. 2009. Anthropecology of Water Bodies, In Plant Physiology in Agriculture and Forestry (Ed. P.C. Trivedi), Aavishkar Publishers and Distributors, Jaipur, India: 248–254.

Dwivedi, A. K., Pandey, S. and Shashi. 2009. Hospital Waste: At a Glance, In Microbes Applications and Effect (Ed. P.C. Trivedi), Aavishkar Publishers and Distributors, Jaipur, India: 114–119.

Dwivedi, A.K. and Shashi. 2006. Dawn to the darkness of misconception in science scholars. *Indian Science Cruisier*, 20(2): 9–12.

Dwivedi, A.K., Shashi, J. Singh. 2006. Water pollution and groundwater recharging. *Current Science*, 91(4): 407–408.

Dwivedi, A.K. and Shashi. 2007. Species erosion, the shrinking biodiversity—An approach, *Indian Science Cruiser*, 20(5): 8–14.

Dwivedi, A.K., U.B. Prajapati and Shashi. 2007. Waste Water and its Management, *Indian Science Cruiser*, 21(4): 36–40.

Dwivedi A.K. 2008. An Express Issue, *Down to Earth*, 16(22): 4–6.

Dwivedi, A.K., B.D. Tripathi and Shashi. 2008. Effect of ambient air sulphur dioxide on Sulphate accumulation in plants. *Journal of Environmental Biology*, 29(3): 377–379.

Dwivedi, A.K., Sweta Pandey and Shashi. 2008. Hospital Waste, *Indian Science Cruiser*, 22(2): 10–14.

Dwivedi, A.K., Shashi and Singh, J. 2006. Water pollution and ground water recharging. *Current Science*. 91(4): 407–408.

Dwivedi, A.K. and Shashi. 2007. Species erosion, the shrinking biodiversity—An approach. *Indian Science Cruiser*. 20(5): 8–14.

Dwivedi, U.P. 2000. Impact of different pollutants on physico-chemical and biological characteristics of selected ponds. Ph.D. Thesis, Banaras Hindu University, Varanasi, India.

Dwivedi, A.K. 1999. Effect of sulphur dioxide on growth behaviour of *Abelmoscus esculentus*. L. Proc. Nat. Conf. for Better Environ. in 21st Century, Oct. 8-10, 1999: 19–23.

Dwivedi, A.K. 2005. Merit must be promoted. *Current Science*, 89(8): 1305.

Dwivedi, A.K. 2009. Ecological Backlashes of Ganga Expressway Proc. 1st Rastriya Yuva Vaigyanik Sammelan, Nov. 28-30, 2008: 207–209.

Dwivedi, A.K. and M.P. Singh. 2003. Effect of coal fired industry on higher plant diversity and phytosociological behaviour. *Journal of Ecobiology*, 15(5): 345–353.

Dwivedi, A.K. and Shashi (2006). Dawn to the darkness of misconception in science scholars. *Indian Science Cruisier*, 20(2): 9–12.

Dwivedi, A.K. and Shashi (2007) Biodiversity in Danger http://www.shvoong.com/exact-sciences/biology/ecology-evolutinary-biology/conservation-biology/1684208-biodiversity-danger/

Dwivedi, A.K., A.R. Upadhyay, T. Pandey, A.K. Pandey and U.P. Dwivedi (2000). Variation in roadside vegetation with reference to vehicular pollution. *Bangladesh Journal of Forest Sciences*, 29(1): 53–60.

Dwivedi, A.K., Hadi Hasan and Shashi (2007) Monetary Value of Lake and Wetlands http://www.shvoong.com/exact-sciences/earth-sciences/water-science/1688267-monetary-value-lake-wetlands/

Dwivedi, A.K., Pandey, S. and Shashi. (2009) Fate of Hospital Waste in India, *Biology and Medicine*, 1(3): 25–32.

Dwivedi, A.K., Prajapati, U.B., Hasan, H., Singh, R., Shashi and Singh, J. (2008) Study of pre and post monsoon water quality in a tropical river ami, *Modern Journal of Life Sciences*, ¾ (1): 161-166.

Dwivedi, A.K., Rahul Singh and Shashi (2007) Lakes, rivers and ground water interactions http://www.shvoong.com/exact-sciences/earth-sciences/water-science/1698637-lakes-rivers-ground-water-interactions/

Dwivedi, A.K., Rahul Singh and Shashi. (2008) Groundwater Pollution: Causes and Impact, *Indian Science Cruiser*, 22(4): 29–33.

Dwivedi, A.K., Shashi, J. Singh (2006), Vermicomposting biotechnology – Demand of the date. *Proc. Nat. Sem. on Global Pollution: A Serious Threat to Indian Biodiversity*, 31st Jan. and 1st Feb. 2006.

Dwivedi, A.K., Sweta Pandey and Shashi (2007) Need in Practices of Hospital Waste Management http://www.shvoong.com/medicine-and-health/epidemiology-public-health/health-policy-administration/1687828-need-practices-hospital-waste-management.

Dwivedi, A.K., U.B. Prajapati and Shashi (2007) Pollution of River Aami in India http://www.shvoong.com/exact-sciences/earth-sciences/water-science/1687304-pollution-river-aami-india.

Dwivedi, A.K.and Shashi (2007) Air Pollution and Plants Sensitivity http://www.shvoong.com/exact-sciences/biology/ecology-evolutionary-biology/developmental-evolution/1684183-air-pollution-plants-sensitivity/

Dymond, G.C. 1949. The water hyacinth : a Cinderella of the plant world. In: Van Vuran, J.P.J. (ed.). Soil fertility and sewage. Dover Publications, New York.

Ebise, S., and Inoue, T. 1991. Change in the C: N: P Ratios During Passage of water Areas from River to Lake. *Water Res.* (G.B.), 25: 95.

Edawards. R.W. and Owens, M. 1962. The effect of plants on river conditions. IV. The oxygen balance of chalk stream. *J. Ecol.*, 50: 207–220.

Edmondson, W.J. 1974. Freshwater biology. John Wiley and Sons, Inc., New York, London.

Edwards, C.J., Hudson, P.L., Duffy, W.G. Nepszy, S.J., McNabb, C.D. Haas, R.C., Liston, C.R., Manny, B.A. and Busch, W.D.N. 1989. Hydrobiological, morphometrical, and biological characteristics of the connecting rivers of the International Great Lakes: A review. In: D.P. Dodge Ced (.) Proc. International. Large Rivers Symp., *Can. J. Fish. Aquat. Sci.* 106: 240–264.

Edwards, R.W. and Owens, M. 1960. The effects of plants on river conditions. I. Summer crops and estimates of net production of macrophytes in a chalk stream. *J. Ecol.*, 48: 151–160.

Eighmy, T.T. and Bishop. P.L. 1989. Distribution and role of bacterial nitrifying populations in nitrogen removal in aquatic treatment systems. *Wat. Res.* 23(8): 947.

Ellis, M.M. 1937. Detection and measurement of stream pollution. *Bull. Bur. Fish. Washington*, 48(2): 365–437.

Elmore, H.L. and Wast, W.F. 1961. Effect of water temperature on stream reaeration. *J.A.S.C.F.*, 87: 546–551.

Engler, R.M., and Patrick Jr., W.H. 1974. Nitrate removal from floodwater overlying flooded soils and sediments. *J. Environ. Qual.* 3:409–413.

Everbecq, E., Gosselain, V., Viroux, L., and Descy, J.P. 2001. Potamon: A dynamic model for predicting phytoplankton composition and Biomass in lowland rivers. *Wat. Res.* 35(4): 901–912.

Falbo M.B. and Weaks, T.E. 1990. A Comparison of *Eichhornia crassipes* (Pontedariaceae) and *Sphagnum guinguefarium* (Sphagnaceae) in treatment of acid mine water. *Econ. Bot.* 44:40–49.

Falkenmark, M. 1993 Water Scarcity: Time for realism. *Populi.* 20(6): 11–12

Fauris, C. 1985. Toxicological evaluation of water treatment. *J. Environmental Technology Letters.* 6(7): 279.

Fauvet, G., Claret, C. and Marmonier, P. 2001. Influence of benthic and interstitial processes on nutrient changes along regulated reach of a large river (Rhone River, France). *Hydrobiol.* 445(1-3): 121–132.

Findlay, D.L. 1984. Effects on phytoplankton Biomass, succession and composition in Lake 223 as a result of lowering pH levels from 5.6 to 5.2. Data from 1980–1982, *Can.* M/s *Report of Fish. Aquat. Sci.* No. 1761. p.10.

Forstner, U. and Wittman, G.T.W. 1983. Metal pollution in Aquatic Environment. Springer Verlag, Berlin, Heidelberg, New York, Tokyo.

Frith, C.F., Jr, Membrane Filters. Proceedings of Liberty Bell corrosion course, sponsored by Phila. section of National Association of Corrosion Engineers. Phila, Pa. 1971.

Gabrielson, J.O. 1984. The uptake translocation and release of phosphorus by *Elodea densa*. *Hydrobiol.* 111: 43–48.

Gajghate, D.G. and Reddy P.J. 1989. COD-BOD relationships for Industrial Wastes. *Indian J. Env. Prot.* 9(11): 805–807.

Galiulin, R.V., Bashkin, V.N., and Galiulina, R.R. 2001. Behaviour of 2, 4-D herbicide in coastal area of Oka river, Russia. *Wat. Air, and Soil Poll*. 129(1-4): 1–12.

Galtsoff, P.S. 1924. Limnological observations in the upper Mississippi, 1981. U.S. Dep. Commerce, *Bull. Bur. Fish*. 39: 347–438.

Ganf, G.G. 1974. Diurnal mixing and the vertical distribution of phytoplankton in a shallow equatorial lake (Lake Georg). *J. Ecol*. 62: 611–629.

Ganpati S.V. 1972. Organic production in several types of aquatic system in India. In: Tropical Ecology, with Emphasis on Organic Production, Ed. by. P.M. Golley and F.B. Golley, 313–350.

Ganpati, S.N. and Chacko, P.I. 1951. An investigation of the river Godavari and the effects of the paper mill pollution at Rajahmundry. *Proc. Indo-Pac. Fish Counc. Madras Meeting, Sec*: II and III. 70.

Ganpati, S.V. 1962. A five year investigation of Almati reservoir Part 1–4. *Environ. Hlth.*, 6: 1–39.

Ganpati, S.V. and Alikunhi, K.H. 1950. Factory effluent from the Mettur Chemical and Industrial Corporation Ltd., Mettur Dam, Madras and their pollutional effects on the fishes of the River Cauvery. *Proc. Nat. Inst. Sci. India* 16: 104–124.

Ganter, M., Gajin, S. and Dalacija, B. 1985. The possibility of phosphate elimination by the use of algae in the process of wastewater purification *Microbiologia*. 21: 63–73.

Gao Bin, Wang Xiaorong, Zhang Mirg, Huang Hua and Yang Linyan. 2000. Sorption of oil in simulated oil polluted water by modified soil. *Huanjing Kexue*. 21(3) 30 May 2000: 89–92.

Garg, P. and Chandra, P. 1990. Toxicity and accumulation of Chromium in *Ceratophyllum demersum* L. *Bull. Env. Contam. Toxicol*. 44: 473–478.

Garlaschi, G., Schalcha, E.B., Vergara, I. and Chang, A.C. 1985. Trace metals in sediments of Mapocha river, Chile. *Tech. Letters*. 6: 405–414.

Gaudet, J. 1977. Uptake, accumulation and loss of nutrient by *Papyrus* in tropical swamps. *Ecology*. 58: 415–422.

Gay, P.A. 1958. *Eichhornia crassipes* in the Nile of the Sudan. *Nature*, Lond. 182: 538–9.

Gay, P.A. and Berry, L. 1959. The water hyacinth : A new problem on the Nile. *Geogrl. J.* 125: 89.

Geldreich, E.E. 1970. Applying bacteriological parameters to recreational water quality. *J. Am. Wat. Work Ass.* 62:113–120.

George, K. 1976. Studies on the chemical control of some important aquatic weeds of Kerala, *Salvinia* and *Cyprus*. In: C.K. Varshney and J. Rzoska (eds.), Aquatic Weeds in South East Asia. Junk, the Hague.

Gerber, A., Mostert, E.S., Winter, C.T. and Devilliers, P.H. 1987. Interactions between phosphate and organic substrate in biological nutrient removal processes. Activated sludge waste water treatment. *Water Sci. Tech*. 19(1-2): 183–194.

Gersberg, R.M., Elkins, B.V. and Goldman, C.R. 1983. Nitrogen removal in artificial wetlands. *Water Res*. 17: 1009–1014.

Gersberg, R.M., Elkins, B.V. and Goldmanm, C.R. 1984a. Use of artificial wetlands to remove nitrogen from wastewater. *J. Wat. Poll. Cont. Fed.* 56(2): 152–156.

Gersberg, R.M., Elkins, B.V., Lyon, S.R. and Goldman, C.R. 1986. Role of aquatic plants in waste water treatment by artificial wetlands. *Water Res.* 20: 363–368.

Gersberg, R.M., Lyon, S.R., Elkins, B.V and Goldman, C.R. 1984b. Removal of heavy metals by artificial wetlands. *Future of Water Reuse*. 2: 639–648.

Gibbs, R.J. 1972. Water chemistry of the Amazon river. *Geochim. Cosmochin Acta.* 36: 106–1068.

Giblin, A.E. 1985. Comparisons of the processing of elements by ecosystems II: Metals. Ecological Considerations in Wetlands Treatment of Municipal Wastewaters. 158–179.

Giblin, A.E., Bourg, A., Valiela, I. and Teal, J.M. 1980. Uptake and losses of heavy metals in sewage sludge by a New England Salt Marsh. *Am. J. Bot.* 67: 1059–1068.

Gleick, P. An introduction to global freshwater issues: Gleick, P. ed. Water in crisis. New York, Oxford University Press, 1993, pp.3–12.

Gobeil, C. 1999. Silver in sediments from St. Lawrence River and Estuary and the Seguenay Fjord. *Environ. Sci. Technol.* 33(17): 2953–2957.

Goel, P.K. and Trivedi, R.K. 1984. Some considerations on sewage disposal to freshwater and resultant effects. *Poll. Res.* 3: 7–12.

Goldman, J.C. 1972. The effect of inorganic carbon on eutrophication, pp.3–53. In: R.L. Brown and M.G. Tunzi (eds.) Proceedings of a seminar on Eutrophication and Biostimulation. California Department of Water Resources, San Francisco.

Gonzalez, A.E., Rodriguez, M.T., Sanchez, J.C.J., Espinosa, A.J.F. and dela Rosa, F.J.B. 2000. Assessment of metals in sediments in a tributary of Gudalquiver River (Spain). Heavymetal partitioning and relation between the Water and Sediment system. *Water, Air, Soil Pollut.* 121(1-4): 11–30.

Gonzalves, E. and Joshi, D.B. 1946. Freshwater algae near Bombay: The Seasonal succession of the algae in a tank at Bandra. *J. Bomb. Nat. Hist. Soc.*, 46(1): 29–31.

Goodwin, P. and Denton, R.A. 1991. Seasonal influences on sediment transport of Sacramento River, California. *Proc. Inst. Civ. Eng.* (G.B.). Part 2, 91: 163.

Grover, S.P., Bisht, S. and Bhatt, A.M. 1988. Effect of distillery wastes on physico-chemical characteristics of the Sone river in the Doon valley. *Indian J. Phy. Sci.* 8: 38–41.

Guilizzoni, P. 1991. The role of heavy metals and toxic materials in physiological ecology of submerged macrophytes. *Aquatic Bot.* 87: 109.

Gunnerson, C.G. and Bailey, T.E. 1963. Oxygen relationship in Sacramento river. *J. Sanit. Eng. Am. Soc. Civ. Engrs.* 89: 95–124.

Guntenspergen, G.R., Stearns, F. and Kadlec, J.A. 1989. Wetland vegetation, Constructed Wetlands for Wastewater Treatment: Municipal, Industrial and Agricultural. Chelsea, MI: Lewis Publish., Inc. 73–88.

Gupta, V.S. 2001. Environmental protection – The battle for survival. *Emp. News.* XXVI(9): 1–3.

Gupta, A.K. and A.K. Dwivedi. (2002). Impact of air pollutants on biochemical characteristics of *Parthenium hysterophorus*. *Plant Archieves*, 2(1): 19–22.

Gupta, A.K., B.D. Tripathi and A.K. Dwivedi (2001). Productive behaviour of a tropical deciduous plant in response to air pollution by brick industry. *International Journal Mendel*, 18(3): 91–92.

Gyeduababio, T.K., Furstenberg, J.P., Baird, D., and Vanreusel, A. 1999. Nematodes as indicators of pollution: a case study from the Swartkops River system, South Africa. *Hydrobiol.* 397: 155–170.

Hades, O., Shteinman, B. and Pinkas, R. 2000. Distribution of fecal coliforms in the Jordan river mouth originating from anthropogenic activities in the Watershed. *Water Sci. Technol.* 42(1-2): 129–134.

Haider, S.Z. 1984. Mechanism of adsorption of chemical species from aqueous medium by water hyacinth and prospects of its utilization. *International Symposium on Water Hyacinth, Hyderabad. Proceedings*. p.41–57.

Haigh, J.C. 1940. The propagation of water hyacinth (*Eichhornia crassipes* Solms.) by seed. *Trop. Agric. Mag. Ceylon Agric. Soc.* 94: 296–7.

Hakim, M.Y.H. 1984. Impact of pollution on the ecosystem of Burhi Gandak river near Samastipur town, North Bihar. pp.83–88. In: B.D. Tripathi (eds.), *River Ecology and Human Health. NECA*, Varanasi.

Hamdy, Y. and Post, L. 1985. Distribution of Mercury, trace organics, and other heavy metals in Detroit River sediments. *J. Great Lakes Res.* 11: 353–365.

Hammer, D.A. (ed.) 1989. Constructed wetlands for waste water treatment: Municipal, industrial and agricultural. Lewis Publ., Boca Raton, FL.

Hammer, D.A. and Knight, R.L. 1993. Designing constructed wetlands for nitrogen removal. *Water Sci. Technol*. 29(4): 15–27.

Hancock, F.D. 1973. The ecology of the diatoms of the Klip river, Southern Transvaal. *Hydrobiol*. 42: 243–284.

Haque, A. and Sharma, S. 1986. Water hyacinth to fight water pollution. *Science Reporter*. Dec. 757–762.

Harding, J.P.C. and Whitton, B.A. 1981. Accumulation of Zinc, Cadmium, and lead by field populations of *Lemanea. Wat. Res.* 15: 301–319.

Hardy, James K. 1985. Zinc uptake by the water hyacinth. Effects of solution factors. *J. Chemosphere*, 14(9):1155–1162.

Harrison, W.G., Eppley, R.W., and Renger, E.H. 1977. Phytopankton nitrogen metabolism, nitrogen budget and observation on copper toxicity: Controlled Ecosystem Pollution Experiment. *Bulletin of Marine Science*. 27: 44–57.

Harvey, R.M. and Fox, J.L. 1973. Nutrient removal using *Lemna minor. J. Wat. Pollut. Contr. Fed.* 45:1928-1938.

Hasan, A., Satyakala, S.B. and Kaiser, J. 1986. Effect of aquatic pollution on the mineral accumulation in water hyacinth. *Proc. Indian Acad. Sci. Plant Science.* 1(76): 37–40.

Hasan, H. (2009) Remedy of water pollution of Ramgarh lake through Macrophytes, DDU Gorakhpur University, Gorakhpur (Ph.D. Thesis).

Hashimoto, H., Kawakami, H., Murata, M., Ushijima, H., Nakao, N., Yanagi, M. and Koni, K. 1976. On the contamination of sea water with *Salmonalla* and fecal indicator organisms, II. Occurrence and distribution of Salmonella and fecal indicator organisms in coastal sea water of Fukcuyama. *J. Fac. Fish Arum. Husb.* Hiroshima. Univ. 15(2): 207–218.

Haslam, S. M. 1978. River Plants. The Macrophytic vegetation of Water Courses. Cambridge Univ. Press, New York. pp.396. ISBN 0-521-29172-0.

Hauser, R. 1984. Use of water hyacinth aquatic treatment Systems for ammonia control and effluent polishing. *J. Water Poll. Control Fed.* 56: 219–223.

Herut, B., Kress, N. and Hornuyng, H. 2000. Nutrient pollution at the lower reaches of Mediterranean coastal rivers in Israel. *Water Sci. Technol.* 42(1-2): 147–152.

Hibbs, D.E., and Gulliver, J.S. 1999. Dissolution rate coefficients for surface slicks on rivers. *Wat. Res.* 33(8): 181–1816.

Hicket, B.1937. Limnological investigation in lakes of the Pokhara Valley, Nepal. *Int. Rev. Gen. Hydrobiol.* 58: 659–672.

Higashi, Y., and Seki, H. 2000. Ecological adaptation and acclimatization of natural freshwater phytoplanktons with a nutrient gradient. *Environ.Pollut.* 109(2): 311–320.

Hill, B.H., and Webster, J.R. 1983. Aquatic macrophyte contribution to the New River organic matter budget. In: T.D. Fontaine III and S.M. Bartell (eds.) Dynamics of Lotic Ecosystems. Ann Arbor science, Ann Arbor, Mich, 273–282.

Hill, D.E., and Sawhney, B.L.1981. Removal of phosphorus from wastewater by soil under aerobic and anaerobic conditions. *J. Environ. Qual.* 10: 401–405.

Hilton, B.L. 1985. Industrial Wastes Agricultural wastes. *J. Wat. Poll. Cont. Fed.* 57(6): 578.

Hiraishi, A., Saheki, K. and Horie, S. 1987. Relationship of total coliform, fecal coliform and organic pollution levels in Tamagawa river. *Bull. Japanese Soc. Fish.* 50(6): 991–997.

Ho, G. E., Mathew, K. and Newman, P.W.G. 1983. Water quality improvement of treated wastewater by soil percolation. In Proc. of Seminar, 'Water Quality, Its Significance in Western Australia'. Water Research Foundation of Australia, Perth.

Ho, G.E., Gibbs, R.A. and Mathew, K. 1991. Bacteria and virus removal from secondary effluent in sand and red mud columns. *Wat. Sci. Technol.* 23: 261–270.

Ho, G.E., Mathew K. and Gibbs, R.A. 1992. Nitrogen and phosphorus removal from sewage effluent in amended sand columns. *Wat. Res.* 26 (3): 295–300.

Ho, G.E., Mathew, K. and Newman, P.W.G. 1983. Water quality improvement of treated wastewater by soil percolation. In Proc. of Seminar, 'Water Quality. Its Significance in Western Australia'. Water Research Foundation of Australia. Perth.

Hornberger, G.M. and Kelly, M.G. 1975. Atmospheric reaeration in a river using productivity analysis. *J. Environ. Div.* 101: 729–739.

Hosetti, B.B. and Patil, H.S. 1986. Impact of *Lemna minor* on the effluent quality of sewage stabilization pond. *Geobios.* 13(6): 244–247.

Hoskin, C.M. 1959. Studies of oxygen metabolism of streams in North Carbina. Publ. Inst. Mar. Sci. Univ. Texas, 6: 186–192.

House. W.A., Leach, D.V. and Armitage, P.D. 2001. Study of dissolved silicon and nitrate dynamics in a freshwater stream. *Wat. Res.* 35 (11): 2749–2757.

Howard, C.W. 1981. Studies on the ability of *Potamogeton pectinatus* community to remove dissolved nitrogen and phosphorus compounds from lake water. *J. Appl. Ecol.* 18: 619–637.

Howard, C.W. 1985. Cycling and retention of nitrogen and phosphorus in wetlands: A theoretical and applied perspective. *Freshwater Biol.* 15: 391–431.

Huang, J., Reneau, R.B. and Hagedorn, C. 2000. Nitrogen removal in constructed wetlands employed to treat domestic waste water. *Wat. Res.* 34(9): 2582.

Hubbell, J.W., New wastewater treatment plant reuses its oil sludge. Civil Eng. 40(9): 81, 1970.

Hynes, H.B.N. 1966. The Biology of Polluted Water. Liverpool University Press, Liverpool, 2.

Ice, J. and Couch, R. 1987. Nutrient absorption by duckweed. *J. Aquat. Plant Manag.* 25: 30–31.

Imaoka, T. and Terashima, S. 1985. Improvement of water quality by water hyacinth *Eichhornia crassipes* (Mart.) Solms. for the removal of nutrient salts, I. Effect of environmental conditions on growth rate and phosphate uptake rate of water hyacinth. *J. Wat. Poll. Res.* 8: 314–322.

Imevbore, A.M.A. 1978. The chemistry of river Niger in the Kainj reservoir area. *Arch. Hydrobiol.* 67: 412–431.

Indian Council of Medical Research. 1962. Ministry of Health Committee on Public Health Engineering Manual and Code of Practice. Manual of Water Supply, New Delhi.

Jackson, M.L. 1962. Soil chemical analysis. Prentice-Hall. Inc. Englewood Cliffs. N.J. U.S.A.: 183–190.

Jackson, M.L. 1967. Soil chemical analysis. Prentice-Hall of India Private Limited, New Delhi, India.

Jain, S.K., Vasudevan, P. and Jha, N.K. 1990. *Azolla pinnata* and *Lemna minor* for removal of lead and zinc from polluted water. *Wat. Res.* 24(2): 177–183.

Jana, S. 1988. Accumulation of Hg and Cr by three aquatic species and subsequent changes in several Physiological and Biochemical parameters. *Wat., Air, Soil Pollut.* 38: 105–109.

Janauer, G.A. 1999. Marcrophytes of the River Danube: A diversity study of the Austrian stretch. *Arch. Hydrobiol.* (3),115s: 399–412.

Jannalagadda, S.B. and Mhere, G. 2001. Water quality of the Odzi River in the Eastern Highlands of Zimbabwe .*Wat Res.* 35(10): 2371–2376.

Janssen., M.A. and Walker, K.F. 1999. Processing of riparian and wetland plant litter in the River Murray, South Australia. *Hydrobiol.* 411: 53–64.

Jepson, F.P. 1933. The water hyacinth problem in Ceylon. *Trop. Agric. Mag. Ceylon Agric. Soc.* 81: 339–55.

Juanico, M. and Friedler, E. 1999. Wastewater reuse for river recovery in semi-arid Israel. *Wat. Sci. Technol.* 40(4–5): 43–50.

Jubermann O., and Krause. G, The central treatment plant of Erdolchemic Gmbh. Chem- Ing.- Techn. 40:288, 1968.

Jude, D.J., Winnell, M., Evans, M.S., Tesar, F.J. and Futyma, R. 1986. Drift of zooplankton, benthos, and larval fish and distribution of macrophytes during winter and summer, 1985, U.S. Army Corps, Engin., Detroit, Mich. Rep. DACW-35-85-C-0005, 174, pp—appendices.

Kadono, Y. 1982. Occurrence of aquatic macrophytes in relation to pH, alkalinity, Ca, Cl and Conductivity. *Jap. J. Ecol.* 32: 39–44.

Katyal, T. and Satake, M. 2001. Environmental pollution, Anmol Publication, New Delhi, pp.65–121.

Kaul, V. 1981. Role of macrophytes in aquatic ecosystems of Kashmir. *J. of I.B.S.* 3(60): 16–20.

Kaushik, N.K. and Hynes, H.B.N. 1987. The fate of dead leaves that fall into streams. *Arch. Hydrobiol.* 68: 463–515.

Kaushik, N.K. and Prasad, D. 1964. Coliform periodicity in water of river Jamuna at Wazirabad, Delhi. *Environ. Hlth.* 5(2): 118–124.

Kemp, W.M. and Murray, L. 1986. Oxygen from roots of the submerged macrophytes *Potamogeton perfoliatus* L. regulating factors and ecological implcations. *Aquat. Bot.*, 271–283.

Khamar, M., Bouya, D. and Ronneau, C. 2000. Metallic and organic pollutants associated with urban waste water in the waters and sediments of Moraccan river. *Water Quality and Research Jnl. of Canada*. 35(1): 147.

Khitoliya, R.K. and Khitoliya, J. 1996. Environmental protection and legislation. *Emp. News*. XXI(12): 1–2.

Kim, Y. and Kim, W.J. 2000. Roles of water hyacinths and their roots for reducing algal concentration in the effluent from Waste stabilization ponds, *Wat. Res*. 34(13): 3285–3294.

King, D.L. 1970. The role of carbon in eutrophication. *J. Wat. Poll. Cont. Fed*. 42: 2035–2051.

King, J.E. and Smith Jr., A.L. 1947. Investigations of the effect of water hyacinth on the fish and fish habitat of Louisiana waters. *USDI, Fish Wildlife Spec. Sci. Rep*. 39: 1–29.

Klaus, R, Kopp, P. and Dietz., F. 1980. Heavy metals in Ruler river and their budget in catchment area . *Prog. Wat. Tech*. 12: 735–749.

Knipling, E.B., West, S.H. and Haller, W.T. 1970. Growth characteristics, yield potential, and nutritive content of water hyacinths. *Soil Crop Sci. Soc. Florida*. 30: 51–63.

Kothandaraman, V., Thergaonkar, V.P., Koskij, T. and Ganapati, S.V. 1963. Physico-chemical and biological aspects of Ahmedabad Sewage. *Environ. Hlth*. 5: 356–363.

Kronvang, B., Svendsen, L.M., Jensen, J.P., and Dorge, J. 1999. Scenario analysis of nutrient management at the river basin scale. *Hydrobiol*. 410: 207–212.

Kudesia, V.P. and Verma, S.P. 1986. Physico-chemical studies on industrial pollution of Kali Nadi due to combined effluent of sugarcane, chemical industry and distillery and rubber industries in Meerut region. *Indian J. Environ. Agri*. 1(1): 11.

Kugelman, I.J., Schwartz, W.A., and Cohen, J.M., Advance Waste Treatment Plants for Treatment of Small Waste Flows. Advance Waste Treatment and Reuse Symposium, Dallas, Texas, 1971.

Kullberg, R.G. 1974. Distribution of Aquatic macrophytes related to paper mill effluents in a Southern Michigan Stream. *Am. Midl. Nat*. 91(2): 271–281.

Kumar, R.J. 1985. Categorisation of some important weeds based on nutrient concentration. *Maltras Agri. J*. 72(11): 646–649.

Kunishi, H.M. 1988. Sources of nitrogen and phosphorus in an estuary of Chesapeake Bay. *Environ. J. Qual*. 17(2): 185–188.

L'vovitch, M.J. 1979. World water resources and their future (English tr.) Ed. Nace, pp.415

Lakshminarayana, J.S.S. 1965. Studies on the phytoplankton of the river Ganga, Varanasi, India, Part I. Physico-chemical characteristics of river Ganga. *Hydrobiol*. 25: 138, pp.165.

Lange, N.A., Langes Handbook of Chemistry (10th ed.), New York: Mc Graw-Hill, 1967.

Lau, Y.L., Oliver, B.G. and Krishnappan, B.G. 1989. Transport of some chlorinated contaminants by the water, suspended sediments, and bed sediments in the St. Clair and Detroit. *Env. Tocicol. Chem.* 8: 293-301.

Law, C.S., Rees, A.P., and Owens, N.J.P. 1993. Nitrous oxide production by estuarine epiphyton. *Limnol. Oceanogr.* 38: 435–441.

Lazaridou Dimitriadou M., Artemicedou, V., Yfantis, G., Mourelatos, and Mylopoulos, Y. 1999. Contribution to the ecological quality of Aliakman river (Macedoninia, Greece): a Multivariate approach. *Hydrobiol.* 410: 47–58.

Lee, J.H., and Bang, K.W. 2000. Characterization of urban stormwater runoff. *Wat. Res.* 34(6): 1773–1780.

Lee, K.W. and Keeney, D.R. 1975. Spectrophotometric determination of Cadmium and Zinc in soil and commercial fertilizer. *Water, Air and Soil Pollution*. 5: 109–112.

Leonard, A.W. Hyne, R.V., Lin, R.P., Leigh, K.A., Le., J. and Beckett, R. 2001. Fate and toxicity of Endosulphan in Namoi River water and bottom sediment. *J. Environ. Qual.* 30(3): 750–759.

Lester, W.F. 1969. Standard based on the quality of receiving water. *J. Wat. Poll. Cont. Fed.* 68(3): 324–332.

Letswaart, T., Brebaart, L., van Zanten, B. and Brijkerk, R. 1999. Plankton dynamics in the river Rhine downsteream transport as influenced by biotic interactions and hydrological conditions. *Hydrobiol.* 410: 1–10.

Li, S.Y. and Morioka, T. 1999. Optional allocation of waste loads in a river with probabilistic tributary flow under transverse mixing. *Wat. Environ. Res*. 71(2): 156–162.

Linstedt, K.D., Houck, C.P. and O'Connor, J.T., Trace element removals in advanced wastewater treatment processes. J. WPCF 3: 1507, 1971.

Lock, M.A. 1993. Attached microbial communities in rivers. In T.E. Ford (ed.) Aquatic microbiology. Blackwell Scientific, Oxford. pp.113–138.

Longowaska, I. 1982. Utilization of organic phosphate by selected bacteria and algae. *J. Wat. Res.* 16: 161–167.

Ma, H.Z., Allen, H.E. and Yin, Y.J. 2001. Characterization of isolated fractions of dissolved organic matter from natural waters and a waste water effluent. *Wat. Res.* 35(4): 985–996.

Madsen, J.D. and Adams, M.S. 1988. The nutrient dynamics of a submerged macrophyte community in a stream ecosystem dominated by *Potamogeton pectinatus*. L. *J. Fresh Water Ecol.* 4: 541–550.

Maine. M.A. and Duarte, M.V. 2001. Cadmium uptake by floating macrophytes *Wat. Res.* 35 (11): 2629–2634.

Manawar, M. 1972. Ecological studies on Euglenieae in certain polluted and unpolluted environments. *Hydrobiol.* 39: 307–320.

Mangi J., Schmidt K., Pankow J., Gaines L. and Turner, P. 1978. Effect of chromium on some aquatic plants. *Environ. Pollut.* 16:285–291.

Manja, K.S. 1986. Detection of fungal pollution in drinking water in developing countries, a simple and low cost method, *Ecology* 1(3): 23–27.

Mann, R.A., 1990. Phosphorus removal efficiency of a constructed wetland treatment system. M. App. Sci. (Thesis).

Manny, B.A and Kenaga, D. 1991. The Detroit River. Effect of contaminants and human activities on aquatic plants and animals and their habitats. *Hydrobiol.* 219: 261–279.

Manny, B.A., Edsall, T.A. and Jaworski, E. 1988. The Detroit River, Michigan: An ecological profile. *U.S. Fish Wildl. Ser. Biol. Rep.* 85(7.17), pp.86.

Manny, B.A., Nichols, S.J. and Schloesser, D.W. 1991. Heavy metals in aquatic macrophytes drifting in a large river. *Hydrobiol.* 219: 333–344.

Manoharachry, C. 1978. Physico-chemical factors in relation to fungal and bacterial numbers in two ponds. *Geobios.* 5: 15–17.

Manzano, M.A., Perales, J.A., Sales, J. and Quiroga, J.M. 1999. The effect of temperature on the biodegradation of a nonylphenol polyethoxylate in river water. *Wat. Res.* 33(11): 2593–2600.

Marshall, B.E. and Falconer, A.C. 1973. Physico-chemical aspect of lake Mellwaine (Rhodesia) and eutrophic tropical impoundment. *Hydrobiol.*, 42(1): 45–62.

Martin, P. 1998. River pollution in India: An overview. *Emp. News.* XXII(52): 1–2.

Martin, P., Haniffa, M.A., and Arunachalam, M. 2000. Abundance and diversity of microinvertebrates and fish in the Tamiraparani river, South India. *Hydrobiol.* 430(1-3): 59–76.

Mathew, P.M. 1969. Limnological investigation on the plankton of Govindgarh lake and correlation with physico-chemical factors. *Proc. Symp. on Ecol. and Freshwater Res.* CIFRI Barrackpore, pp.46–65.

Mathis, B.J. and Kavern, W.R. 1975. Distribution of mercury, cadmium, lead and thallium in a eutrophic lake. *Hydrobiol.* 46(2-3): 207–222.

Mathur, A., Sharma, V.C., Rupainwar, D.C., Murthy, B.C. and Chandra, S. 1987. A study of river Ganga at Varanasi with special emphasis on heavy metal pollution. *Poll. Res.* 6:37–44.

Matulewich, V.A. and Finstein, M.S. 1978. Distribution of autotrophic nitrifying bacteria in a polluted river (the Passaic.). *Appl. and Envir. Microbiol.* 35(1).

Mayes, R.A., McIntosh, A.W. and Anderson, V.L. 1977. Uptake of cadmium and lead by a rooted aquatic macrophyte (*Elodea canadensis*). *Ecology*. 58: 1176–1180.

McDonald, R.C., and Wolyerton, B.C.1980. Comparative study of wastewater lagoon with and without water hyacinth. *Econ. Bot*, 34: 101–110.

McVea, C. and Boyd, C.E. 1975. Effects of Water Hyacinth Cover on Water Chemistry Plant Phytoplankton and Fish in Ponds. *J. Environ. Qual.*, 4(3): 375–378.

Mehta, I. and Sharma, R.K. 1972. Control of aquatic weeds by the white amur in Rajasthan. *India. Hyacinth Control J.* 10:16–19.

Mer, G.S., Sati S.C. and Khulbe, R.D. 1981. Occurrence, distribution and seasonal periodicity of some aquatic fungi of Satjal. *Hydrobiol.* 76: 201–205.

Michaels, Eng. Progr., 64: 31, 1968.

Miner, J., Wooten, J.W. and Dodd, J.D. 1971. Water hyacinths to further treat anaerobic lagoon effluent. *Proceedings of International Symposium on Livestock Wastes*. 170–172.

Mishra, K. 1993. Ecology and Management of Freshwater Pond of Varanasi, Ph.D. Thesis, Banaras Hindu University, Varanasi, India.

Mishra, R. 1968. Ecology workbook. Oxford and IBH Publ. Calcutta. 29.

Mishra, R. and G.S. Puri 1954. Indian Manual of Plant Ecology. Oxford Book Co. Calcutta and N. Delhi.

Mitchell, A.W. and Furnas, M.J. 2001. River logger—A new tool to monitor riverine suspended particle fluxes. *Wat. Sci. Tech.* 43(9): 115–120.

Mitchell, A.W. Reghenzani, J.R. and Furnas, M.J. 2001. Nitrogen levels in the Tully river—A long-term view. *Sci and Tech.* 43(9): 99–106.

Mitra, A.K. 1982. Chemical Characteristics of surface water at a selected ganging station in the rivers Godavari, Krishna and Tungbhadra. *Indian J. Environ. Hlth.* 24(2): 165–179.

Mitrovic, S.M., Bowling, L.C. and Buckney, R.T. 2001. Response of phytoplankton to in situ nutrient enrichment, potential influences on species dominance in a river. *Int. Rev. of Hydrobiol.* 86(3): 285–298.

Mittak, S.K. and Ratra, R.K. 2000. Toxic effect of metal ions on Biochemical Oxygen Demand. *Wat. Res.* 34(1): 147–152.

Mohan, C., Balani and Sarkar, H.L. 1965. Some observations on the pollution of Yamuna river at Okhla Waterworks, Intake, Delhi. *Environ. Hlth.* 7(2): 84–86.

Mohanta, K.C. 1984. Microbiology of water supply in the dairy plants. In Dairy microbiology. Osmos Publications, Rajouri Garden, New Delhi.

Montigomery, J.M. and Associatex, Pasadena, C.A, U.S.A. 1991. Biological nitrification/denitrification of high sodium nitrite (Navy Shipyard) waste water. *Enr. Pollution.* 69: 25–36.

Moore, J.W. 1979. Diversity and indicator species as measure of water pollution in Sub Arctic Lakes. *Hydrobiol.* 65(3): 73–80.

Moorhead, K.K., Reddy, K.R. and Graetz, D.A. 1988. Nitrogen transformations in a water hyacinth based water treatment system. *J. Environ. Qual.* 17(1): 71–75.

Mortimer, D.C.1985. Freshwater aquatic macrophytes as heavy metal monitor. The Ottawa river experience. *Environmental Monitoring and Assessment*, 5: 311–323.

Munsell, A.H. 1905. Systematic classification of soil colours. Cited in revised colour charts. M. Cyama and H. Takehara (1967). Research Council of Agriculture Forestry and Fisheries, Ministry of Agriculture and Forestry, Japan.

Murdoch., A. 1985. Geochemistry of the Detroit River sediments. *J. Great Lakes Res.* 11: 1193–200.

Murugesan, A.G. and Sukumaran, N. 1999. Potential utilisation of aquatic weeds for testing industrial effluents. In : Limnological Research in India, S.R. Misra (Ed.), pp. 247-259.

Naiman, R.J., Elliott, S.R., Helfield, J.M. and Okeefe, T.C. 1999. Biophysical interactions and the structure and dynamics of riverine ecosytems: The importance of biotic feedback. *Hydrobiol.* 410: 79–86.

Nair, N.B., Arunachalam, M., Madhusoodan Nair, K.C. and Suryanarayanan, H. 1989. A Spatial study of the Neyyar river in the light of the river continuum-concept. *Trop. Ecol.* 30(1): 101–110.

Nalewajko, C. and Lean, D.R.S. 1980. Phosphorus. In the physiological ecology of phytoplankton. Ed. I. Morris. Blackwell Scientific Publications. pp.235–258.

Nandan, S.N. 1983. Study of algal communities in river Vishwamitri, Baroda (India) as indicators of organic pollution. *Ind. J. Ecol.* 10(1): 11-15.

Netter, R. 1992. Purification efficiency of planted soil filters for wastewater treatment. *Wat. Sci. Tech.* 26(9-11): 2317–2320.

Newman, P.W.G. and Marks, P. 1981. The removal of heavy metals by Perth sands. In *Proc. of the Groundwater Pollution Conference*, Australian Water Resources Council, Conference Series. No.1, pp. 267–289.

Nolan, W.J. and Kirmse, D.W. 1974. The paper making properties of water hyacinth. *Hyacinth Control J.* 12:90–97.

O'Brien W.J. 1981. Use of aquatic macrophytes for Wastewater treatment. *J. Envir. Engg. Div. American Civ. Engrs.* 107: 681–697.

Oake, R.J. 1985. Sludge: Fractionation of heavy metals in sewage sludge. *J. Wat. Sci. Tech.*

Obeid, M and Chadwick, M.J. 1964. Some factors affecting the growth of two aquatic weed species of Nile-water hyacinth (*Eichhornia crassipes* Mart. Solms.) and water lettuce (*Pistia stratiotes* L.) *Proc. 7th Br. Weed Control Conf.* 548–52.

Ofarrell, I., Vinocur, A., and Lonebardo, R.J. 1998. Cross-channel and vertical variation in diversity and abundance of phytoplankton in the lower Parana River, Argentina. Arch. *Hydrobiol.* (2), S 115: 103–124.

Olaniya, M.S., Saxena, K.L. and Sharma, H.C. 1976. Pollution studies of Chambal river and its tributaries at Kota. *Indian J. Environ. Hlth.* 18(3): 219–226.

Oron, G., Porath, D. and Wildschut, I.R. 1986. Waste water treatment and renovation by different duckweed species. *J. Environ. Engineers*. 112: 247–63.

Oron, G., Vegtt, A. DE and Porath 1988. Nitrogen removal and conversion by duckweed grown on waste-water. *Wat. Res.* 2(22): 179–184.

Pacakova, V., Pockeviciute, D., Armalis, S., Stulik, K., Li, J.H. and Vesley, J. 2000. A study of the distribution of Pd, Cd and Cu between water and Kaolin, Bentonite and a river sediment. *Jnl. of Environ. Monitoring*. 2(2): 187.

Pagioro, T.A. and Thomaz, S.M. 1999. Decoposition of *Eichhornia azurea* from limnologically different environments of the Upper Parana River floodplain. *Hydrobiol.* 411: 45–52.

Pamela, M. Stokes. 1986. Ecological effects of acidification on primary producers in aquatic systems. *Wat. Air and Soil Poll.* 30: 421–438.

Panesar, R.S., Singh, J.S. and Kansal, B.D. 1985. Chemical composition of waste waters of Amritsar city. *Ind. J. Ecol.* 12(1): 12–16.

Parija, P. 1934a. Physiological investigations on water hyacinth (*Eichhornia crassipes*) in Orissa with notes on some other aquatic weeds. *Indian J. Agric. Sci.* 4: 399–429.

Parija, P. 1934b. A note on the reappearance of water hyacinth seedlings in cleared tanks. *Indian J. Agric. Sci.* 4: 1049.

Parra, J.V. and Hortenstein, C.C. 1974. Plant nutritional component of some Florida water hyacinth in three soil types. *Hyacinth Control. J.* 12: 85–90.

Parson, W.A., Chemical Treatment of Sewage and Industrial Wastes. National Lime Association Washington D.C., 1965.

Paterniti, M.B. and Mantai, K.E. 1986. Shoot/leaf uptake of phosphate by *Myriophyllum spicatum* and *Ceratophyllum demersum*. *Proc. 7th International Symposium on Aquatic Weeds.* 239–244.

Pathak, H. 1996. Fertilizer and environmental pollution. *Emp. News*. XXI(3): 1–2.

Pathak, V. 1979. Evaluation of productivity in Nagarjuna Sagar Reservoir (Andhra Pradesh) as a function of hydrological and Limno-chemical parameters. *Journal of Inland Fisheries Society of India*. 11(2): 49–68.

Patra, A.K., Nayak, L. and Patnaik, E. 1984. Seasonal primary production of river Mahanadi at Sambalpur in Orissa. *Trop. Ecol.* 25(2): 153–157.

Paul, A.C. and Pillai, K.C. 1983 Trace elements in a tropical river environment distribution. *Water, Air and Soil Pollution*. 19: 63-73.

Paul, L.B. and Taylor, E.T. 1989. Aquatic wastewater treatment using *Elodea nutalli J. Wat. Poll. Cont. Fed.* 61(5): 641-648.

Paulson, W.L., and West, R.W., Jet aeration in activated sludge systems. J. WPCF 41: 1726, 1969.

Pavoni, S., Sfrios, R., Domazzolo, R. and Drios, A.A. 1990. Influence of waste water from the city of Veina, Italy and the Hinterland on the Eutrophication of the lagoons. *Sci. of Total Environ.* 96(3): 235–252.

Peach, K. and Tracey, M.V. 1956. Modern methods of plant analysis. Vol. I. Springer-Verleg, Berlin.

Peder, G.E. and Weisner Stefan, E.B. 1997. Nitrogen Removal in a Waste Water Reservoir : The importance of denitrification by Epiphytic Biofilms on Submersed Vegetation. *J. Environ. Qual*. 26: 905–910.

Penfound, W.T. and Earle, T.T. 1948. The biology of the water hyacinth. *Ecol. Monogr*. 18: 447–472.

Piirsoo, K. 2001. Phytoplankton of Estonian rivers in midsummer. *Hydrobiol.* 444(1-3): 135–146.

Pinoy,G., and Decamps, H.1999. The spiralling concept and nitrogen cycling in large river floodplain, *Arch. Hydrobiol.*(3),115s:281-292.

Pinto, C.R.M. and Greco, M.K.B. 1999. The Contribution of Water hyacinth (*Eichhornia crassipes*) and Zooplankton to the internal cycling of phosphorus in the Entrophic Pampulha Reservoir, Brazil. *Hydrobiol.* 411: 115–128.

Pip, E. 1979. Survey of the ecology of submerged aquatic macrophytes in central Canada. *Aquat. Bot.*, 7: 339–357.

Piper, C.S. 1966. Soil and plant analysis, Hans Publisher, Bombay, India.

Pitchard, P.H. 1985. Fate and effect of pollutants: Fate of environmental pollutants. *Jnl. of Water Pollution Control Federation*. 57(6): 658.

Pocklington, R. and Tan, F.C. 1987. Seasonal and annual variations in the organic matter contributed by the St. Lawrence River to the Gulf of St. Lawrence. *Geochin. Cosmochin. Acta*. 51: 2579–2586.

Postel, S. 1997. Facing Water Scarcity. *New York, Norton,* pp.17–191.

Prakash, M.M. 1994. Seasonal variation in the physico-chemical characteristics of a perennial pond of Jhabua, M.P., *J. Aqu. Biol. Fish*, 1(1): 43-47.

Prakasham, R.S., Reddy L. Poorna Chandra, Amita, Manisha and Ramakrishna S.V. 1998. Defluoridation of drinking water using *Eichhornia* sp.

Prasad, B.N. and Saxena, M. 1980. Ecological study of blue-green alage in river Gomati. *Ind. J. Environ. Hlth*. 22(2): 151–168.

Pritchard, P.H. 1985. Fate and effect of pollutants: Fate of environmental pollutants. *J. Wat. Poll. Cont. Fed*. 57(6): 658.

Ragas, A.M.J. and Leuven, R.S.E.W. 1999. Modelling of Water quality – based emission limits for industrial discharges in rivers. *Wat. Sci. Technol*. 39(4): 185–192.

Rai, D.N. and Datta Munshi, J. 1979. The influence of thick floating vegetation (Water hyacinth: *Eichhornia crassipes*) on the physico-chemical environment of a fresh water wetland. *Hydrobiol*. 62: 65–69.

Rai, H. and Hill, G. 1984. Microbiology of Amazonian waters. In: H. Sioli (ed.), the Amazon. pp.413–441.

Rai, L.C. and Kumar, H.D. 1979. Nutrient uptake of *Chlorella vulgaris* and *Anacystis nidulans* isolated from the effluent of a fertilizer factory. *Ind. J. Ecol*. 4: 127–133.

Rai, S. 1990. Removal and exchange of toxic metals relevant in water pollution. Ph.D. Thesis, BHU, Varanasi.

Rai, U.N. and Chandra, P. 1992. Accumulation of Cu, Pb, Mn and Fe by field population of *Hydrodictyon reticulatum* (Linn.) *Lagerheim. Sci. Total Env*. 116: 203–211.

Rao, D.S. and Govind, B.V. 1964. Hydrology of Tungabhadra Reservoir, *Indian Journal of Fisheries*. 11(1): 321–344.

Raven, J.A. 1970. Exogenous inorganic carbon sources in plant photosynthesis. *Biological Reviews*. 45:16–121.

Rawn, D.F.K., Halldroson, T.H.J. and Muir, D.C.G. 1999. Pesticides in the Red River and its tributaries in Southern Manitoba: 1993-95. *Water Qual. Res. J. Can*. 34(2): 183–220.

Ray. P. and David, A. 1966. Effect of industrial wastes and sewage upon the chemical and biological composition and Fisheries of river Ganga at Kanpur, U.P. *Environ. Hlth*. 8: 307–339.

Reddy, K.R. 1983. Fate of nitrogen and phosphorus in a waste water retention reservoir containing aquatic macrophytes. *J. Environ. Qual*. 12: 137–141.

Reddy, K.R. 1984. Nutrient removal potential by aquatic plants. *Aquatics* 6: 15–16.

Reddy, K.R. and De Busk, W.F. 1985. Nutrient removal Potential of selected aquatic macrophytes. *J. Environ. Qual*.14: 459–462.

Reddy, K.R. and De Busk. 1987. State of the art utilization of aquatic plants in water pollution control. *Water Sci. Technol*. 19: 61–79.

Reddy, K.R. and Tucker, J.C.1983. Productivity and nutrient uptake of water hyacinth, *Eichhornia Crassipes*. I. Effect of nitrogen resource. *Econ.Bot*. 37: 237–247.

Reddy, K.R., Campbell, K.L., Graetz, D.A. and Portier, K.M. 1982. Use of biological filters for agricultural drainage waste treatment. *J. Environ. Qual*. 11: 591–595.

Reddy, M.M. 1979. Variation in bottom sediment nutrients and metal concentration in Genese river, Watershed. *Environ. International*. 2: 9–12.

Reichert, P. 2001. River Water quality model no. 1 (ROM 1): Case study II. Oxygen and Nitrogen conversion processes in the River Glatt (Switzerland). *Wat. Sci. Technol*. 43 (3): 51–60.

Reid, G.K. 1961. Ecology of inland water and estuaries, Reinhold Publishing Co., New Delhi.

Reitemeier, R.F. 1943. Semimicroanalysis of saline soil solution. Indus and Engin. Chem. Analyst. Ed. 15: 393–402.

Risgard, H.U. and Hansen, S. 1990. Biomagnification of Hg in a marine grazing foodchain. *Mar. Ecol. Ser*. 62: 259–270.

Rivas, Z., de Medina, H.L., Gutierrez, J. and Gutierrez, E. 2000. Nitrogen and phosphorus levels in sediments – from tropical Catatumbo river (Venezuela). *Water, Air and Soil Pollut*. 117(1-4): 27–38.

Rodgers, J.H., Jr., Mekevitt, M.E., Hammerlund, D.O., Dickson, K.L. and Cairns, Jr., J. 1983. Primary production and decomposition of submergent and emergent aquatic plants of two Appalachian rivers. In: T.D., Fontaine III and S.M., Bartels (eds.), Dynamics of Lotic Ecosystems. *Ann. Arbor-Science, Ann. Arbor. Mich*.: 283–301.

Rodrignes, A.M. and Oliveira. J.F.S. 1987. Treatment of wastewater from the tomato concentrate industry in high rate algal ponds *Wat. Sci. Technol*. 19: 43–49.

Rogers, H.H. and Davis D.E. 1972. Nutrient removal by water hyacinth. *Weed Sci*. 20: 423–428.

Rosen, A.A., Skeel, R.T. and Effinger, M.B. 1963. Relationship of river water odour to specific organic contaminants. *J. Wat. Poll. Cont. Fed*. 35: 777.

Roush, T.H.1985. Fate and effects of pollutants: Effects of pollution on freshwater organisms. *J. Wat. Poll. Cont. Fed*. 57(6): 667.

Rovedatti, M.G., Castane, Topalian, M.L. and Salibian, A. 2001. Monitoring of organochlorine and orthophosphorus pesticides in the water of the Reconquista river (Buenos Aires, Argentina). *Wat. Res*. 35(14): 3457–3461.

Ruschel, A.P. 1987. N uptake by *Azolla-Anabaena*. *Plant and Soil*. 97(1): 79–83.

Rusincovitch, F. 1985. Use of wetlands for wastewater treatment and effluent disposal: Institutional constraints. *Ecological Considera-tions in Wetland Treatment of Municipal Wastewaters*. 427–432.

Saha, S.K. and Duttamunshi, J.S.1982. Primary productivity, standing crop and efficiency of net production in a thermal stream. *Trop. Ecol.* 23: 300.

Sakai, H., Kujima, Y. and Saito, K. 1986. Distribution of heavy metals in water and sieved sediments in the Toyohira river. *Wat. Res.* 20: 559–567.

Salim, R. 1988. Removal of Ni(II) from water using decaying leaves – Effect of pH and type of leaves. *Jnl. of Env. Science and Health*. A 23(3): 183–197.

Sand-Jenson, K. and Prahl, C. 1982. Oxygen release from roots of submerged aquatic macrophytes. *Oikos*. 38: 349–354.

Sangu, R.P.S., Pathak, P.D. and Sharma, K.D. 1984. River water at Agra Monitoring of Jamuna river, pp.39–45. In: B.D. Tripathi (ed.), Pollution and Human Health. N.E.C.A., Varanasi.

Sauer, T.J., Daniel, T.C., Moore, P.A. Coffey, K.P., Nichols, D.J. and West, C.P. 1999. Poultry litter and grazing animal waste effects on runoff water quality. *J. Environ. Qual.* 28(3): 860–865.

Saunders, D.L. and Kalff, J. 2001. Nitrogen retention in wetland, lakes and rivers. *Hydroboil.* 443(1-3): 205–212.

Sawyer, C.H. 1960. Chemistry for Sanitary Engineers. McGraw Hill Book Co., New York.

Say, P.J. and Witton, B.A. 1983. Accumulation of heavy metals by aquatic mosses. I. *Fontinalis antipyretica* Hedw. *Hydrobiol*. 100: 245-260.

Schiemer, F. 1999. Conservation of biodiversity in flood plain river. *Arch. Hydrobiol.* (3),115s: 423–438.

Schindler, H., Chemical Treating Plant for Refinery Wastewater from White Oil and Petroleum Sulfonates. Proceeding of the 6th Industrial Waste Conference, Purdue University, 1951.

Schloesser, D.W. and Manny, B.A. 1986. Distribution of submerged aquatic macrophytes in the St. Clair-Detroit River System. *J. Freshwater. Ecol*. 3: 537–544.

Schloesser, D.W., Edsall, T.A. and Manny, B.A. 1985. Growth of submerged macrophyte communities in the St. Clair- Detroit River System between Lake Huron and Lake Erie. *Can. J. Bot*. 63.

Scott, W.E., Seaman, M.T., Connell, A.D., Kohlmeyer, S.I. and Toerien, D.F. 1977. The Limnology of some South African impoundments. I. The physico-chemical Limnology of Hartbeespoort Dam. *Journal of Limnological Society of South Africa*. 3(2): 43–58.

Sedlacek, M. 1985. Sludge treatment technology and ionizing radiation. *J. Wat. Sci. Technol.* 17(4–5): 551.

Sekar, I. 2001. Water at risk in the 21st century. *Emp. News*. XXVI(3): 1–3.

Selka, L.D., Williamson, C., Greensmith, G., Balacko, D., Brown and Stackiw. 1987. Bacteriological characteristics of 15 freshwater beaches in Manitoba. *Can. J. Public Health*. 78(3): 181–184.

Selmeczi, J.G., Capture mechanism in deep-bed filtration Ind. Water Engineer, 1971.

Selvapathy P.C. and Sreedhar, P. 1991. Heavy metal removal by water hyacinth. *J. Instr. Publ. Hlth. Eng., India*. 3: 11–17.

Semi, E.F. and Hussaini, A.S. 1985. Accumulation of Cu, Zn, Cd and Pb by aquatic macrophytes. *Environment International*. 11: 77–87.

Shane, M.S., De Michele, E. and Cannon, R. 1971. Water quality and plankton ecology. The Christina River, Delaware, *Environ. Pollut*. 2: 81–95.

Shardendu. 1986. Physico-chemical characteristics, primary production and nutrient dynamics of two ponds of Varanasi. Ph.D. Thesis, Banaras Hindu University, India.

Sharma, B.K. and Sharma, S. 2001. Biodiversity of *Rotifera* in some tropical flood plain lakes of Brahmaputra river basin, Assam (N.E. India). *Hydrobiol.* 446: 305–314.

Sharma, G.R. 1999. Oil pollution at sea and its control. *Emp. News*. XXIV(24): 1-2.

Sharma, K.D., Lal, N. and Pathak, R.D. 1981. Water quality of sewage drains entering Yamuna at Agra. *Indian J. Environ. Hlth.* 23(2): 118–122.

Sharma, K.P., Goel, P.K. and Gopal, B. 1987. Limnological studies of polluted freshwaters. I. physico-chemical characteristics. *Secod Int. Cong. Ecol.*, Israel.

Shashi. 2003. Studies on the chemistry of river Varuna water in response to the discharge of small scale industries, specially automobile servicing, battery and dyeing industries. Ph.D. Thesis. Udai Pratap Auton, P.G. College. Varanasi.

Shashi and A.K. Dwivedi (2008) Ganga Expressway—A path of wetland destruction, *Current Science*, 94(7): 840–841.

Shashi and A.K. Dwivedi (2004). Study of variation in pH of a river water as affected by industrial effluents. Proc. Nat. Sem. on Strategies for Environment Quality Management in Urban Area, 28th Oct. 2004: 76–82.

Shashi and Dwivedi, A.K. (2007) DO, BOD and COD as Water Pollution Indicator http://www.shvoong.com/exact-sciences/earth-sciences/water-science/1684228-do-bod-cod-water-pollution.

Shashi, Dwivedi, A.K. and Dubey, K. (2007) Plants as Vehicular Pollution Indicator http://www.shvoong.com/exact-sciences/earth-sciences/urban-planning/environmental-policy-group/1684233-plants-vehicular-pollution-indicator.

Singh, J., (Mrs.) Shashi and A.K. Dwivedi (2003). Thermal behaviour of a lotic ecosystem in response to pollution load. Proc. Nat. Conf. on Global Air Pollution and Water as Sustainer of Life, 9th–10th Feb. 2003: 15–21.

Singh, J., Chaubey, C.M., Dwivedi, A.K. and Shashi (2007) Water Quality and Pollution Status of Sarang Pond in Varanasi, During Summer http://www.shvoong.com/exact-sciences/earth-sciences/water-science/1691221-water-quality-pollution-status-sarang/

Shashi, J. Singh and Dwivedi, A.K. (2007) Ozone and Charcoal Treatment Method for Effluents of Automobile Servicing Stations http://www.shvoong.com/exact-sciences/earth-sciences/water-science/1684239-ozone-charcoal-treatment-method-effluents/

Shashi, Singh, J. and A.K. Dwivedi. (2009) Numerical analysis of DO, BOD and COD in a polluted tropical river, *Columbian Journal of Life Sciences*, (Accepted).

Shashi, Singh, J. and Dwivedi, A.K. (2007) Variation in Acidity of a Polluted Tropical River http://www.shvoong.com/exact-sciences/chemistry/1684308-variation-acidity-polluted-tropical-river/

Shashi, Singh, J. and Dwivedi, A.K. (2009) Numerical interdependence of pH, acidity and alkalinity in a polluted tropical river, *Journal of Environmental Biology*, 30(5): 773–775.

Sheath R.G. 1986. Characteristics of softwater streams. I. Rhode Island. III. Distribution of macrophytic vegetation in a small drainage basin. *Hydrobiol.* 140: 183–191.

Shialipour, A. and Smith, P.H. 1984. Conversion of biomass into methane gas. *Biomass*. 6: 85–94.

Shieh, S.H., Kondratieff, B.C., Ward, J.V. and Rice, D.A. 1999. The relationship of macroinvertebrate assemblages to water chemistry in a polluted Colorado plains stream. *Arch. Hydrobiol.* 145(4): 405–432.

Shukla, S.C. 1989. Ecological investigation on pollution and management of river Ganga in Mirzapur. Ph.D. Thesis, Banaras Hindu University, Varanasi.

Shukla, S.C., Kant, R. and Tripathi, B.D. 1989. Ecological investigation on Physico-chemical characterstics and phytoplankton productivity of river Ganga at Varanasi. *Geobios*. 16: 20–27.

Shukla, S.C., Tripathi, B.D. and Nagendra, P. 1988. Physico-chemical and bacteriological characteristics of river Varuna at Varanasi. *J. Scientific Res.* 38: 133–141.

Shukla, S.C., Tripathi, B.D., Mishra, B.P. and Chaturvedi, S.S. 1992. Physico-chemical and Bacteriological Properties of the Water of River Ganga at Ghazipur. *Comp. Physiol. Ecol.* 17(3): 92–96.

Shulze, K.L. 1966. Biological recovery of wastewater. *J. Wat. Poll. Cont. Fed*. 38: 1944–1958.

Sikandar, M. 1987. Ecology of river Ganga with special reference to pollution. Ph.D. Thesis. B.H.U., Varanasi.

Silssman, W. 1983. Comparison of water quality in drainage basins under agricultural and forest land use. In Dissolved Loads of Rivers and Surface Water Quality/Quality Relationships. IAHS Publ. No. 141: 431–441.

Sinclair, P., Backett, R., and Hart, B.T. 1989. Trace elements in suspended particulate matter from the Yarra river, Australia. *Hydrobiol.* 176(3): 239.

Singh, A.K. and Bhowmick, B.N. 1985. Effect of sewage on physico- chemical characteristics and bacterial papulation of river Ganga at Patna. *Indian J. Ecol.* 12(1): 17–19.

Singh, B.K. 1998. Ecological indicator plants. *Emp. News.* XXII (48): 1–3.

Singh, J., Kansan, B.D. and Ranesar, R.S. 1985. Chemical composition of waste water of Amritsar city. *Indian Jnl. of Ecology*. 12(1): 12–16.

Singh, N.K.1981. Phytoplankton productivity impact of some ecological factors. *Nat. Acad. Sci. Lett.*, 4: 227–230.

Singh, S.N. and Bhargava, A.K. 1985. Plant distribution as effected by the confluence of a polluted stream with a clean stream. *Ind. J. Ecol.* 1: 15–19.

Sinha, M.P. 1986. Limnobiotic study on trophic status of a polluted freshwater reservoir of a coalfield area. *Poll. Res.*, 5(1): 13–17.

Sinha, S., Rai, U.N., Tripathi, R.D. and Chandra, P. 1993. Chromium and manganese uptake by *Hydrilla verticillata* (I.f.) Royle: amelioration of chromium toxicity by manganese. *J. Env. Sci. Health.* (A 28): 1545–1552.

Sivasubramani, R. 1999. Water quality of river Periyar (River Suruliyar) in Tamil Nadu. In : Limnological Research in India, S.R. Misra (ed.), pp.1–15.

Slayden, R.L. and Schwartz, L.N. 1989. States' actvities, attitudes and policies concerning constructed wetlands for wastewater treatment. *Constructed Wetland for Wastewater Treatment: Municipal, Industrial and Agricultural*. pp. 279–256.

Smith, E. 2001. Pollutant concentrations of storm-water and captured sediment in flood control sumps draining urban wateshed. *Wat. Res.* 35(13): 3117–3126.

Smith, M.D. and Moelyowati, I. 2001. Duckweed based wastewater treatment (DWWT): design guidelines for hot climates. *Wat. Sci. Technol*. 43(11): 291–300.

Smith, R.V., Stevens, R.J., Foy, R.H. and Gibson, C.E. 1982. Upward trend in nitrate concentration in rivers discharging into Lough Neagh for the period 1969–1979. *Wat. Res.* 16: 183–188.

Sorensen, J., Jorgensen, T. and Brandt, S. 1988. Denitrification in stream eplition : Seasonal variation in Gelbaek and Rabis beak, Denmark, FEMS. Microbiol. Ecol. 53: 345–354.

Sorensen, J. and Revesbech, N.P. 1990. Denitrification in stream biofilm and sediment: In Situ Variation and control factors. In Revsbech, N.P. and Sorensen, J. (eds.) Denitrification in soil and sediment. Plenum Press, New York.

Soulsby, P.G. 1985. Eutrophication: The role of phyloplankton in the DO budget of a stratified estuary. *J. Wat. Sci. Technol. Net.* 17(4–5): 745.

Sreenivasan, A. 1965. Limnology of tropical impoundment. III. Limnology and productivity of Amaravathy Reservoir (Madras State) India, *Hydrobiol*. 26: 501–516.

Sreenivasan, A. 1974. Limnological features of a tropical impoundment. Bhavanisagar Reservoir (Tamilnadu) India, Internationale Revue der Gasamten. *Hydrobiol.* 59(3): 327–342.

Sreenivasan, A. and Sunder Raj, R. 1967. Effects of certain wastes on the water quality and fisheries of river Cauvery and Bhavani. *Environ. Hlth*, 9: 13–21.

Sridar, M.K.C. 1986. The elemental composition of *Pistia stratiotes* L. in a polluted lake, Nigeria. *Hydrobiol.* 131(3): 273–276.

Sridar, M.K.C. and Adefunke, O. 1987. Potential health risks at sewage treatment plants in Ibadan, Nigeria. *J. Wat. Environ. Manag.* 1(1): 129–134.

Sridar, M.K.C. and Ademoroti, C.M.A. 1984. Effluent discharge standard needed in Nigeria. *African Asian Wat. and Sewage*. 3: 32–36.

Srinivasu, N. 1992. Removal of Barium and Strontium ions from aqueous solutions by some titanate powders and radio tracer studies. Ph.D. Thesis, BHU, Varanasi.

Srivastava, D. 1996. Studies on Lanthanide-azo dye complexes in aqueous solution. Ph.D. Thesis, BHU, Varanasi.

Srivastava, O.N. 1970. Studies on Limnology and phytoplankton production of some tropical freshwater ecosystems. Ph.D. Thesis, Banaras Hindu University, Varanasi, India.

Starkey, J.E. and Karr, P.K. 1984. Effect of low dissolved oxygen concentration of different turbidity. *J. Wat. Poll. Cont. Fed*. 56(7): 837–843.

Statnake, P., Vagstad, N., Tamminen, T., Wassmaun, P., Jansons, V. and Loigu, E. 1999. Nutrient runoff and transfer from land and rivers to the Gulf of Riga. *Hydrobiol.* 410: 103–110.

Staves, R.P. and Knaus R.M. 1985. Chromium removal by three species of duckweeds. *Aquat. Bot.* 23: 261–263.

Steele, J.G. 1989. High resolution profiles of temperature and dissolved oxygen in water. *Hydrobiol*. 179(1): 17–24.

Stevenson, A.W. 1953. Studies on bathing water quality and health. *Am. J. Pub. Hlth*. 43: 529.

Stoyneva, M.P. 1998. Spring Phytoplankton of the River Danube in the year 1990. *Arch. Hydrobiol.* (2), S115: 167–194.

Stratful, I., and Brelt, S., Scrimshaw, M.B., and Lester, J.N. 1999. Biological phosphorus removal, its role in phosphorus recycling. *Environ. Technol*. 20(7): 681–696.

Stuart, R., Crane and Morre, J.A. 1984. Bacterial pollution of ground water. *J. Water, Air and Soil Pollut*. 22: 67–83.

Sundaravadivel, M. and Vigneswaran, S. 2001. Wastewater collection and treatment technology for semi-urban areas of India : A case study. *Wat. Sci. Technol*. 43(11): 329–336.

Sutton, D.L. and Ornes, W.H. 1977. Growth of *Spirodela polyrrhiza* in static sewage effluent. *Aquatic Bot*.: 231–237.

Suzuki, T., Nissanka, W.G.A. and Kurihara, Y. 1989. Amplification of total dry matter, nitrogen, and phosphorus removal from stands of *Phragmites australis* by harvesting and reharvesting regenerated shoots. *Constructed Wetland for Wastewater Treatment Municipal, Industrial and Arigricultural* 530–535.

Swindle, O.N. and Curtis, T.T. 1957. Phytosociology of the larger submerged plants in Wisconsin Lakes. *Ecology*. 38: 397–407.

Sworobuk, J.E., Law, C.B. and Bissonnette, G.K. 1987. Assessment of bacteriological quality of rural ground Water supplies in North West Virginia. *Water, Air Soil Poll*. 36: 163–170.

Talbot James William D.R., House, A. and Alan D. Pethy Bridge. 1990. Prediction of the temperature dependence of electrical conductance for river water. *Water Research*. 24(10): 1295–1304.

Tam, N.F.Y. and Wang, Y.S. 1989. Wastewater nutrient removal by *Chlorella pyrenoidosa* and *Scenedesmus* sp. *Environ. Pollut*. 58: 19–34.

Thanas, K.V. Hurst, Mathiessen, P. and Sheahan, D. 2001. Toxicity characterization of organic contaminants in storm waters from an agricultural head water stream in south East England. *Wat. Res.* 35(10): 2411–2416.

Thresh, J.C., Suckling, E.V. and Beale, J.F. 1944. The Examination of Waters and Water Supplies, edited by Joylor, E.W.

Tiedje, J.M. 1988. Ecology of denitrification and dissimilatory nitrate reduction to ammonium. In: A.J.B. Zehnder (ed.) Biology of Anaerobic Microorganism John Wiley and Sons, New York.

Timms, B.V. and Midgley, S.H. 1970. The Limnology of Borumba Dam, Queensland. *Proceedings of Royal Society of Queensland.* 81: 27–42.

Tiwari, D. 1983. Pollution phycology of the Varanasi frontage of river Ganga. Ph.D. Thesis, Banaras Hindu University, Varanasi, India.

Tiwari, D. 1993. Studies on Metal (II) dye complexes in solution. Ph.D. Thesis, BHU, Varanasi.

Tiwari, T.N., Das, S.C. and Bose, R.K. 1986. A relation between COD and BOD for the Ganga at Kanpur. *Indian J. Env. Prot.* 6(3): 183–184.

Tokner, K. and Ward, J.V. 1999. Biodiversity along riparian Corridors. *Arch. Hydrobiol.* (3), 115s: 293–310.

Tripathi, B.D. 1986. Recent advances in pollution research in India. In: Recent Advances in Environmental Biology. R.S. Ambasht (ed.) Professor D.N. Rao Commemoration Volume. 72–79.

Tripathi, B.D. and A.K. Dwivedi (2007). Pollution tolerance and distribution pattern of plants in surrounding areas of coal fired industries. *Journal of Environmental Biology*, 28(1): 257–263.

Tripathi, B.D. and Shukla, S.C. 1991. Biological treatment of waste water by selected aquatic plants. *Environ Poll.* 69: 69–78.

Tripathi, B.D. and Srivastava, J. and Mishra K. 1991. Nitrogen and Phosphorus removal capacity of four chosen aquatic macrophytes in tropical freshwater ponds. *Environmental Conservation,* 18(2):143–147.

Tripathi, B.D. Misra, K., Pandey, V.S. and Srivastva, J. 1990. Effect of tissue-N content on decomposition of water hyacinth (*Eichhornia Crassipes*) (Mart.) Solms. *Geobios*. 17(2-3): 67–69.

Tripathi, B.D., Ambasht, R.S. and Sikandar, M. 1984. Ecological investigation of energy consumption for burning of dead bodies at Varanasi Ganga ghats. p. 1 In: R.S. Ambasht and B.D. Tripathi (eds.) River Ecology and Human Health. NECA, Varanasi.

Tripathi, B.D., Srivastava J. and Misra., K. 1990. Impact of Pollution on the elemental composition of water hyacinth (*Eichhornia crassipes*) (Mart.) Solms. and Lemna (*Lemna Minor*) in various ponds of Varanasi. *Science and Culture.* 56: 227–230.

Tripathi, B.D., Upadhyay A.R., Dwivedi, U.P., Singh, M.K., Dwivedi, A.K., Pandey, T. and Pandey, A.K. 1998. Nitrogen and phosphorus contents of water, sediment and some aquatic macrophytes of Ratoi Taal; Distt. Mau, U.P., *India. Adv. Biol. Res.* 16(2): 1–7.

Tripathi, C.K.M. 1982. Investigation on Ganga River to determine biological indicators of water quality. Ph. D. Thesis, B.H.U. Varanasi, India.

Tripathi, G. 1983. Environmental problems of Indian rivers and their ill-effects. River pollution and Human Health. R.S. Ambasht and B.D. Tripathi (ed.), NECA, Varanasi, pp.23–33.

Tripathi, R.D. and Chandra, P. 1991. Chromium uptake by *Spirodela polyrrhiza* (L.) Schleiden in relation to metal chelators and pH. *Bull. Environ. Contam. Toxicol*. 47: 764–769.

Tripathi, B.D. and A.K. Dwivedi (2002). Atmospheric pollution and its outcome —An analysis. *The Botanica*, 52: 88–92.

Tripathi, B.D. and A.K. Dwivedi (2003). Pollution control in brick industries and recent environmental legislation. In: Environmental Management in Mines (Eds. B.K. Srivastva, R. Kumar and A. Jamal), Tara Book Agency, Varanasi, India, 509–514.

Tripathi, B.D., A.K. Dwivedi, T. Pandey, M.K. Singh, A.R. Upadhyay, A.K. Pandey and U.P. Dwivedi (1999). Air, Foliage and Soil sulphur, as a measure of coal generated pollution. *Advances in Biological Research* 17(1): 1–5.

Tripathi, B.D., T. Pandey, A.K. Dwivedi, M.K. Singh, A.R. Upadhyay, A.K. Pandey and U.P. Dwivedi (1999). Responses of *Mangifera indica* and *Ocimum sanctum* with respect to automobile exhaust. *Advances in Biological Research*, 17(2): 14–17.

Tukunga, T., Furstas, N. and Morimoto, M. 1976. Accumulation of Cd in *E. crassipes*. *Eiseikaguka*. 22: 234–239.

Tully, T.J., Sewage and Ind. Wastes 30: 1379, 1958.

U.S. Public Health Service Drinking Water Standards. 1962. P.H.S. Pub. 956. U.S. Department of Health, Education and Welfare, Washington D.C.

Ultsch, G.R. and Anthony, D.S. 1973. The role of the aquatic exchange of carbon dioxide in the ecology of the water hyacinth (*Eichhornia crassipes*). *Florida Sci*. 36(1): 16–22.

Umar, A. 2000. Effect of water on health. *Emp. News*. XXV(22): 1–2.

Unni, K.S. 1972. An ecological study of the macrophytic vegetation of the Doodhadhari Lake, Raipur, M.P., India. 3. Chemical factors, *Hydrobiol*. 38: 25–36.

Unni, K.S., and Pawar, S. 2000. The phytoplankton along a pollution gradient in the river Mahanadi (M.P.State) India—a multivariate approach. *Hydrobiol*. 430 (1–3): 76

VandenBerg, G.A., Loch, J.P.G., VanderHeijdt, L.M. and Zwolsman, J.J.G. 1999. Mobilisation of heavy metals in Contaminated sediments in the river Meuse, The Netherlands. *Water, Air and Soil Pollut*. 116(3-4): 567–586.

Vashisht, H.S. and Sra, G.S. 1979. The biological characteristics of Chandigarh wastewater in relation to physicochemical factors. *Proc. Symp.Environ. Biol.*, pp.429–440.

Venkateswarlu, V. 1986. Ecological studies on the rivers of Andhra Pradesh with special reference to water quality and pollution. *Proc. Indian Acad. Sci.* (Plant Sci.). 96(6): 495–508.

Verma, K.R.1979. Phytosociology, productivity and energetics of macrophytes of Gujar Lake (Khetasarai) Jaunpur. Ph. D. Thesis, Banaras Hindu University, Varanasi, India.

Verma, S.R., Bahel, D.K., Pal, N. and Dalela, R.C. 1978. Studies on the sugar factories and their wastes in western U.P. *Indian J. Environ. Hlth.* 20(3): 204–218.

Verma, S.R., Tyagi, A.K. and Dalela, R.C. 1977. Studies on the characteristics and disposal problem of industrial effluents with reference to Indian Standard Institute. Standard Part II. *Indian J. Env. Hlth.* 19: 93.

Vetter, R. 1972. Preliminary tests on the feeding value for cattle of fresh and processed water hyacinths. Iowa Agriculture and Home Economics Experiment Station Animal Science Leaflet R. 169:1-3.

Villar, C., Stripeikis, J., Tudino, M.D., Huicque, L., Troccoli, O. and Bonetto, C. 1999. Trace metal concentrations in coastal marshes of the lower Parana River and the Rivo de la Plata Estuary. *Hydrobiol.* 397: 187–196.

Villar, I.A., de Cabo, L., Vaithiyanathan, P. and Bonetto, C. 2001. Litter decomposition of emergent macrophytes in a floodplain marsh of the lower Parana River. *Aquat. Bot.* 70(2): 105–116.

Vink, R., Behrendt, H., and Salomons, W. 1999. Development of heavy metal Pollution trends in several European rivers: An analysis of Point and diffuse sources. *Water Sci. Technol.* 39(12): 215–224.

Vishwakarma, P.P. 1992. Some studies on removal of Ni(II) and Mo(VI) from water by adsorption. Ph.D. Thesis, BHU, Varanasi.

Vivian, C.M.G. and Massie, K.S. 1977. Trace metal in waters and sediments of the river Tawe, South Wales, in relation to local sources. *Environ. Pollut.* 14: 47–61.

Vollertsen, J., Almeid, M.D. and Hvitved Jacobson, T. 1999. Effect of temperature and dissolved oxygen on hydrolysis of sewer solids. *Wat. Res.* 33(14): 1319–3126.

Volterra, L., Tosti, E., Verma, A. and Izzo, G. 1985. Microbiological pollution of marine sediments in the southern stretch of the Gulf of Naples. *J. Water, Air and Soil Pollution.* 26: 175–184.

Vymazal, J., Brix, H., Cooper, P.F., Haberl, R., Perfler, R. and Laber, R. 1998. Removal mechanism and types of constructed wetlands. in. Vymazal, J., Brix, H., Cooper, P., Green, M.B., Haberl, R. (eds.), Constructed Wetlands for Wastwater Treatment in Europe. Backhuys Publisher, Leiden, The Netherlands, pp.17–66.

Walker, C.1975. Environmental pollution by chemicals. Hutchinson and Co. Pub. Ltd.,

Wang, J.M., Huang, C.P., Allen, H.E., Poesponegoro, I., Poesponegoro, H. and Takiyama, L.B. 1999. Effects of dissolved organic matter and pH on heavy metal uptake by sludge particulates exemplified by copper (11): Three variable model. *Wat. Environ. Res.* 71(2): 139–147.

Warren, C.E. 1971. Biology and Water Pollution Control. W.B. Saunders, Philadephia, p.434.

Watelet, A. and Johnson, P.G. 1999. Hydrology and water quality of the Raisin River: Overview of impacts of recent land and channel changes in eastern Ontario. *Water Qual. Res. J. Can.* 34(3): 361–390.

Weisner, S.E.B., Eriksson, P.G. and Leonardson, L. 1994. Influence of Macrophytes on nitrate removal in wetlands. *Ambio*. 23: 363–366.

Welker, M. and Walz, N. 1999. Plankton dynamics in a river-lake system-on continuity and discontinuity. *Hydrobiol.* 409: 223–240.

Wendland, F., Kunkel, R., Grimvall, A., Kronvang B. and Muller Wohlfeil, D.I. 2001. Model system for the management of nitrogen leaching at the scale of river basins and regions. *Wat. Sci. Technol.* 43(7): 215–222.

Wesley, W.E. Jr. 1966. Industrial Water Pollution Control. McGraw-Hill Book Company.

Westlake, D.F. 1973. Aquatic macrophytes in rivers. *Pol. Arch. Hydrobiol.* 20(1): 31–40.

Whittion, B.A. and Say, P.J. 1975. Heavy metals, pp.286-311. In: B.A.Whitton (Ed.), River Ecology. Blackwell Scientific Publication, Oxford.

Wiewiorka, Z. and Sarsosiek, J. 1986. Effect of aluminium lithium and strontium on the ecological populations of *Lemna minor* and *Spirodela polyrrhiza*. *Proc. 7th Int. Symp. Aquat. Weeds*. 401-406.

Wild, H.E., Jr., Sawyer, C.N. and MC Mahon, T.C., Factors affecting nitrification kinetics. J. Water Poll. Contr. Fed., 43: 1845, 1971.

Williams, A.T. and Simmons, S.L. 1999. Sources of riverine Litter: The River Taff, South Wales, U.K. *Water, Air, Soil Pollut.* 112(1–2): 197–216.

Williams, W.O. 1941. Rapid determination of potassium with Dipicrylamine. Amer. Soc. Hort. Sci. Proc. 39: 47–50.

Wolverton B.C. and McDonald, R.C. 1979. Water hyacinth (*Eichhornia Crassipes*) (Mart.) Solms. Studies. *Econ. Bot.* 33: 1–10.

Wolverton, B.C. 1981. Water hyacinth for controlling water pollution. In : Varshney C.K. (ed.) Water Pollution and Management Reviews. South Asian Publisher, New Delhi, India. 47: 49.

Wolverton, B.C. and McDonald, R.C. 1981. Energy of vascular plants used in wastewater treatment systems. *Econ. Bot.* 35: 224–232.

Wolverton, B.C. and McDonald, R.C., 1976. Water hyacinths for upgrading Sewage lagoons to meet advanced wastewater treatment standards: *Part II NASA Technical Memorandum TM-X-72730.*

Wolverton, B.C., Barlow, R.M., and McDonald, R.C. 1976. Application of vascular aquatic plants for pollution removal, energy and food production. In: Tourbier. J. and R.W. Pierson. Jr. (eds.). Biological Control of Water Pollution. University of Pennsylvania Press.

Wooten, J.W. and Dodd, J.D. 1976. Growth of water hyacinths in treated sewage effluent. *Econ. Bot*. 30 :29–37.

World Health Organization (WH.O).1992 Our planet, our health—Report of the WHO Commission on Health and Environment, Geneva, WHO. pp.106–144.

Yeoh, B.G. 1983. Use of water hyacinth in waste water treatment. Technical report. Standards of Industrial Research Institute (SIRIM) Res. Div. Malaysia. 67.

Yoshizaki, S. and Tomida, T. 2000. Principle and process of heavy metal removal from sewage sludge. *Environ. Sci. Technol*. 34(8): 1572.

Young, W.C., Hannan, H.H. and Tatum, J.W. 1972. The physico-chemical limnology of a stretch of the Gaudalupe river, Texas, with 5 main stream impoundments. *Hydrobiol.* 40: 297–319.

Zeikus, G. and Brock, T.D. 1972. Effects of thermal additions from the Yellowstone geyser basins on the bacteriology of the firehole. *River Ecology*. 53: 283–290.

Zereen, F., Islam, I., Habib, M.A., Begum, D.A. and Zaman, M.S. 2000. Inorganic pollutants in the Padma river, Bangladesh. *Environmental Geology (Berlin)*. 39(9) July: 1059–1062.

Some exciting gifts are up for grabs with this book!!

RIVER POLLUTION AND SOLUTION

Shashi Dwivedi & Anil K Dwivedi

FREE Gifts Rs. 1000/-

DEAR READERS

By now you must have gone through this book in the entirety. So we invite your assessment on this title with absolute impartiality and candid observations. After all, we publishers blindly depend on your benchmarking. Friends, please fill up the open spaces below with CAPITAL LETTERS. You may add some extra sheets of paper if the space provided is not sufficient for you.

i. What are the important topics of your syllabus which are not adequately covered in this book?

ii. In which chapters and on what topics the treatment of the subject-matter by the author is not satisfactory and why?

iii. Have you come across the typos, factual inaccuracies, inconsistencies, and other forms of mistakes in the book? If yes, then please specify the mistakes and page numbers.

iv. Name top three books on the same subject, which, in your consideration, are better than this book. Could you provide some reasons?

Your 1st Preference: ....

Your 2nd Preference: ....

Your 3rd Preference: ....

v. Any suggestion to improve the quality of illustrations, diagrams etc.?

vi. How did you like the cover design? Any suggestions on colours?

vii. Suggestions for further improvement of production standard:

viii. Who recommended you this book:

☐ Teacher ☐ Friend ☐ Parents ☐ Bookseller ☐ Librarian

ix. Name of the person who has recommended:

Designation: ....

Address: ....

Phone No.: ....

e-mail: ....

x. Name and address of the bookseller from whom you have purchased this book:

....

....

....

xi. Name and address of the library where you would like to find the book:

....

....

xii. Name and address of your institution (Please mention the University or Board):

....

....

xiii. Your name, e-mail, and complete postal address:

....

....

....

xiv. A few other titles published by us that you would like to read:

....

....

The best assessment will be rewarded half-yearly. The award will be in the form of our publications, as decided by the Editorial and Marketing Operations Division, amounting to Rs. 1000/- (Rupees one thousand) only.

....

Please mail the filled up coupon at your earliest to :

Editorial & Marketing Operations Division

NEW CENTRAL BOOK AGENCY (P) LTD

8/1 Chintamoni Das Lane, Kolkata 700 009

West Bengal, INDIA

Ph. No.: 033 + 22418411, 22418573, 22419094

Fax: 033 + 22419573, 22413852

e-mail: ncbapvtltd@eth.net, ncba@cal2.vsnl.net.in

Website: www.centralgroup.com